Praise for

'Daring, smart, unforgettable . . . A rich exploration of our times and the way forward'
Elif Shafak, author of *10 Minutes 38 Seconds in This Strange World*

'Scintillating . . . In a political climate where the oldest human impulse – to move for a better life for ourselves and our kids – is demonised by nationalists across the world, Khanna offers a clear-eyed, unapologetic defence of the right to migrate'
Suketu Mehta, author of *Maximum City* and *This Land Is Our Land*

'Thought-provoking . . . As this book demonstrates, the climate crisis is just one of many forces that will have humans more on the move this century'
Bill McKibben, author *Falter*

'Impressive . . . Parag Khanna proves again why he is one of the world's most incisive thinkers . . . The book's great accomplishment is that it not only reveals what will soon be upon us, but what lies ahead for our children and grandchildren'
Alec Ross, author of *The Industries of the Future*

'Without fundamentally rethinking our economic models, the colliding demographic, environmental and political crises many countries face will snowball into economic disasters. In *Move*, Parag Khanna cuts through the clutter like no one else, providing a roadmap to a more sustainable future'
Nouriel Roubini, author of *Crisis Economics*

'Illuminates a host of new realities. *Move* outlines the forces creating a new geography of opportunity'    Richard Florida, author of *The Rise of the Creative Class*

'A provocative vision. Khanna's nuanced and insightful portrait of a world on the move challenges us to rethink how, where, and with whom we'll inhabit the planet'
Rahul Mehrotra, Professor of Urban Design and
Planning at the Harvard Graduate School of Design

'Parag Khanna's brilliant new book describes a world shaped not just by democracy or capitalism, but, increasingly, by migration'    Balaji Srinivasan, entrepreneur and
former CTO of Coinbase and General Partner at Andreessen Horowitz

'A nuanced discussion of the increasing importance of free movement across the planet. Khanna makes an urgent, powerful argument for more open international borders'    *Kirkus*

## ALSO BY PARAG KHANNA

*The Second World: Empires and Influence in the New Global Order*

*How to Run the World: Charting a Course to the Next Renaissance*

*Hybrid Reality: Thriving in the Emerging Human-Technology Civilization*

*Connectography: Mapping the Future of Global Civilization*

*Technocracy in America: Rise of the Info-State*

*The Future Is Asian: Commerce, Conflict, and Culture in the 21st Century*

# MOVE

How Mass Migration Will Reshape the World
– and What It Means for You

## PARAG KHANNA

WEIDENFELD & NICOLSON

First published in the United States in 2021 by Scribner,
an imprint of Simon & Schuster, Inc
First published in Great Britain in 2021 by Weidenfeld & Nicolson,
an imprint of The Orion Publishing Group Ltd
Carmelite House, 50 Victoria Embankment
London EC4Y 0DZ

An Hachette UK Company

1 3 5 7 9 10 8 6 4 2

A CIP catalogue record for this book is
available from the British Library.

ISBN (Hardback) 978 1 4746 2083 3
ISBN (Export Trade Paperback) 978 1 4746 2084 0
ISBN (eBook) 978 1 4746 2086 4
ISBN (Audio) 978 1 4746 2089 5

Printed and bound in Great Britain by Clays Ltd, Elcograf, S.p.A

www.weidenfeldandnicolson.co.uk
www.orionbooks.co.uk

*In memory of David Held: scholar, mentor, cosmopolitan*

# CONTENTS

# PROLOGUE:
# WHERE WILL YOU LIVE IN 2050?

April 2020 will forever be remembered as the month the world stood still. Never in human history has the global population simultaneously coordinated a single act: the Great Lockdown. Almost all offices and stores shut. Streets and parks were empty. Cars, trains, and planes sat idle. Goats, deer, foxes, boars, ducks, kangaroos, and even penguins roamed freely through normally bustling cities from Edinburgh and Paris to Cape Town and Canberra. The *Economist* summed it up in one word: "Closed."*

The year of rolling global lockdowns that followed took an excruciating toll on billions of lives. Amid the chaos, one of the greatest ironies that surfaced was just how accustomed we had become to almost frictionless global movement. The year 2019 was a record year for tourism, with international arrivals topping 1.5 billion, the highest figure ever. More than 275 million people were classified as international migrants—from Indian construction workers and Filipino maids in Dubai to American executives and English teachers across Asia—also the largest number ever recorded. Then it all stopped.

Instead of migration and travel surging ahead, the lockdowns provoked a sudden reset of the world's population. From every corner of the world, tourists, students, and expats returned to their country of birth or nationality.

---

* As per the front cover of *The Economist,* March 21, 2020.

European countries dispatched planes to Africa and Latin America to repatriate their citizens. Asian students bought one-way tickets back home from the US, UK, and Australia. More than two hundred thousand Indian laborers were flown back from Gulf countries such as Saudi Arabia and the United Arab Emirates. This unprecedented repatriation of peoples artificially realigned location and citizenship. For the first time anyone could remember, nearly the entire world population was "home." But for how long?

A staggering share of our personal and professional lives hinges on mobility: the movement of people, goods, money, and data within cities and countries as well as internationally. Society only functions normally if we can move. Once you stop pedaling a bicycle, it quickly falls over. Our civilization is that bicycle. And move we will.

In the early 2010s, my colleague Greg Lindsay and I set out to answer the question, "Where will you live in 2050?" The answer could simply have been "high-tech cities," but which ones? Some will be sites of predatory surveillance while others will allow residents to preserve some privacy. Some will be in areas resilient to climate change, while others may well have been submerged by then. Some will have thriving service economies and lively culture, while others will have become the discarded "factory towns" such as those littered across Michigan. As we scanned the world for geographies that offer abundant freshwater, progressive governance, and could attract talent to innovative industries, we decided on . . . Michigan.

More broadly, we pointed to the emergence of a "New North," a collection of geographies such as the Great Lakes region and Scandinavia that are making significant investments in renewable energy, food production, and economic diversification. Not too long after living through Hurricane Sandy in 2012, Greg and his family moved from New York City to Montreal.


This seemingly simple thought experiment holds some valuable lessons. First, you don't get to choose your crisis: Covid, climate change, an economic crash, and political unrest can unfold at the same time—and even amplify one another in a downward spiral. Another takeaway is that places abandoned yesterday could be rejuvenated tomorrow. Rust belt cities across the Great Lakes region are the epitome of dystopian blight: Michigan today is still *losing* twice as many people per year as it gains (and losing congressional seats in the process). But Detroit may well be tomorrow's hot property market. Early signs of its comeback are already visible: a light railway, art museums, boutique hotels, artisan fashion, and sumptuous Arab and Asian foods. In the heart of Detroit there's now a sandy urban beach where young professionals kick back to enjoy lunch and drinks. Industrial firms are retooling Michigan's factories to crank out electric cars, and Alphabet's Sidewalk Labs is building a highway catering to autonomous vehicles between Detroit and Ann Arbor. Next may come plants for 3D-printed housing. Within a couple of decades, US-Canada relations may have progressed such that Detroit serves as the midway point in a seamless and thriving Chicago-Toronto corridor.

The opposite extreme could be represented by Hong Kong, a thriving global city being violently squeezed by Beijing. The former British colony has degenerated from Asia's premier capitalist hub into a battleground between native Hong Kong youth who cherish their freedom and a Chinese government that demands submission to its National Security Law. Long before 2047—the date Hong Kong was officially supposed to be fully integrated with mainland China—many of the city's youth will have taken their talents elsewhere and been replaced by millions of obedient mainland Chinese citizens.

To forecast which places will succeed or fail in the decades ahead requires taking a holistic look at political, economic, technological, social, and environmental factors, projecting how they intersect with one another, and building scenarios for how each geography may adapt to this unending complexity. Plenty of twists and turns lie ahead: lockdowns today, mass migrations tomorrow; populist democracy today, data-driven governance tomorrow; national identity today, global solidarity tomorrow—

or the reverse in some places, and flip-flopping in others. You may not know if you've made the right move—or moves—until 2050.

History is replete with seismic global disruptions—pandemics and plagues, wars and genocides, famines and volcanic eruptions. And time and again after great catastrophes, our survival instinct compels us to move. Humankind is embarking on the most extensive experiment it has ever run on itself: The pandemic is slowly beginning to pass, borders are reopening, and people are moving again. Which places will they leave and where will they relocate? What is the best way for *all* of us to cope with the complex interplay of political upheavals and economic crises, technological disruption and climate change, demographic imbalances and pandemic paranoia? The answer to these questions can be summed up in one word: *Move.*

The map of humanity isn't settled—not now, not ever. With this book I want you to consider scenarios for radical shifts in our geographic future—including your own location on humanity's next map.

# MOVE

# CHAPTER 1
# MOBILITY IS DESTINY

## *Geography is what we make of it*

Ask anyone who graduated from Georgetown's School of Foreign Service between 1990 and 2005 which one course they'll remember until the day they die. Their eyes will light up, a smirk will appear, and one word will come out of their mouths: "Map." A mere one-credit, pass-fail class quickly became so legendary that students intentionally failed its placement test just to take it. They were quickly joined by hundreds of other undergrads who just wanted to sit in, requiring larger auditoriums each year. All for the pleasure of witnessing the thunderous lectures of the encyclopedic and cantankerous Dr. Charles Pirtle, a human cannon of notable facts about every single country, capital, body of water, mountain range, and border dispute on Earth. In 2005, *Newsweek* magazine featured "Map of the Modern World" in its list of "College Classes for Masochists." We couldn't get enough.

Pirtle's noble objective was twofold: to combat geographical ignorance and, just as important, to demonstrate that the world map is an ever evolving collision of environment, politics, technology, and demographics. It's thanks to Pirtle that analyzing the interplay of these forces became my professional obsession. After all, high school geography class in the 1990s was hardly inspiring: It was basically earth science (mostly geology; no mention of climate change) with a static layer of borders on top. For most students, the study of geography sadly defaults to this *politi-*

*cal* geography, as if the most arbitrary lines on our maps (borders) are the most permanent. In reality, states are more like porous containers shaped by the flows of people and resources within and across them. Without these, what is a state even worth?

This is a book about the geography that matters most to us: *human* geography. Human geography investigates the where and the how of the distribution of our species across 150 million square kilometers of land on six continents. Think of it like climatology, a deep science of how we relate to one another and the planet. Human geography subsumes hot-button topics like demographics (the age and gender balance of populations) and migration (the resettlement of people), but goes much deeper into our ethnographic composition, and even our genetic adaptation to a changing environment. Climate refugees and economic migrants, intermarriage and even evolution—all are part of the grand story of our human geography.

Why does human geography matter so much today? Because our species is in for a rough ride, and we can no longer take for granted a stable relationship between our geographic layers such as nature (where the water, energy, mineral, and food resources are), politics (where the territorial borders are that demarcate states), and economics (where the infrastructure and industries are located). These are among the major forces that have determined our human geography for the past thousands of years—and in turn, our human geography has shaped them.

But never before have the feedback loops among these layers been so intense and complex. Human economic activity has accelerated the deforestation and industrial emissions that cause global warming, rising sea levels, and massive drought. Four of America's most important cities are most at risk: New York City and Miami may drown, while Los Angeles is running out of water and San Francisco is blanketed by wildfires.

The chain reactions slamming millions of people in America apply to *billions* in Asia. Consider this: Asia's spectacular economic rise in recent decades was propelled by breakneck population growth, urbanization, and industrialization, all of which have spiked its emissions output. This has contributed to rising sea levels that threaten the teeming populations of its coastal megacities on the Pacific Rim and Indian Ocean. So the rise of Asia is accelerating the sinking of Asia—which could cause ever more Asians to flee across borders and spark resource conflicts. We push the system, then the system pushes us.

This seems an appropriate moment to take stock of how badly out of sync these layers of geography have become. We have wealthy countries across North America and Europe with 300 million and counting aging people and decaying infrastructure—but roughly 2 billion young people sitting idle in Latin America, the Middle East, and Asia who are capable of caring for the elderly and maintaining public services. We have countless hectares of arable farmland across depopulated Canada and Russia, while millions of destitute African farmers are driven from their lands by drought. There are countries with sterling political systems yet few citizens, such as Finland and New Zealand, but also hundreds of millions of people suffering under despotic regimes or living in refugee camps.

Is it any surprise that record numbers of people have been on the move?

Children of the twentieth century know the adages "Geography is destiny" and "Demography is destiny." The former implies that location and resources determine our fate, while the latter suggests that population size and age structure are the most important factors. Together, they tell us that we're stuck where we are—better hope it's a well-populated and resource-rich country. Should we continue to buy into such determinism? Of course not. Geography is not destiny. Geography is what we make of it.

In my 2016 book *Connectography* I proposed a third axiom to explain the arc of global civilization: "Connectivity is destiny." Our vast infrastructure networks—a mechanical exoskeleton of railways, electricity grids, Internet cables, and more—enable the rapid movement of people, goods, services, capital, technology, and ideas on a planetary scale. Connectivity and mobility are complementary, two sides of the same coin, and together they give rise to a fourth axiom that will define our future: *Mobility is destiny*.

So what's stopping us from using our connectivity to the fullest? The root of our collective inertia lies in borders—physical, legal, and psychological. The world's political map looks the way it does mostly for contingent reasons: where ancient civilizations settled, where European empires conquered and divided, and where natural features separate populations. Borders are where they are because that's where they've been. But the Earth is *ours*—not America's or Russia's or Canada's or China's. The question is: Can we discover a new cartographic pragmatism that brings political geography more in line with today's needs?

The management guru Peter Drucker warned that "the greatest danger in times of turbulence is not the turbulence itself but to act with yesterday's logic."[1] We can no longer afford to be passive observers of how human geography unfolds. Instead, we must *actively* realign our geographies, moving people and technologies where they are needed while keeping livable places habitable. This requires an epochal shift in the organization of global civilization, a collective resettlement strategy for the world population. But if we get this right, we'll strengthen our odds of survival as a species, revitalize floundering economies, and forge a more sensible map of humanity.

Mass migrations are inevitable, and more than ever, they are necessary. In the coming decades, entire overpopulated regions of the world might be abandoned, while some depopulated territories may gain massively in population and become new civilizational centers. If you are lucky enough to be someplace from which you do not have to migrate— such as Canada or Russia—then chances are that migrants are coming your way. To paraphrase Lenin: You may not be interested in migration, but migration is interested in you.

The world of tomorrow is not only full of mobile people but is defined by the mobility of *everything*. Everyone has a mobile phone, meaning communications, Internet, medical consultations, and finance are all accessible anywhere; nobody goes to a "bank." Both work and study have migrated online; the ranks of digital nomads have exploded. Ever more people are living in mobile homes and other movable dwellings. Even "fixed" investments have become fungible: We can 3D print buildings, set up factories and hospitals anywhere, generate electricity from solar or other renewable sources, and have drones deliver us anything we need. As we move, so does the supply chain: Labor and capital can perpetually shift to new land, generating fresh geographies of productivity. Mobility is the lens through which to view our future civilization.

The concept of mobility blends the material and philosophical. It raises questions such as: Why are we moving, and what do those shifts reveal about our needs and desires? Then there are political and legal questions to explore: Who is allowed to move? What restrictions do we face on movement and why? And last but not least, there are normative questions: Where should people go? What is the optimal distribution of people around the world? Mobility is also an intangible and spiritual experience. Pause and appreciate how fluidly our anatomy carries us. Moving stimulates creativity, the process of witnessing ways of life coming together. Philosophers such as John Dewey meditated on the aesthetics of moving freely both in nature and the social milieu, eloquently arguing that such interaction imbued life with meaning. Walter Benjamin spent a decade reflecting on the significance of the glass-covered arcades built in mid-nineteenth-century Paris and the wandering *flâneurs* they invited. To move is to be free.

Are you ready to move? Is your welfare at risk from political and economic crises, technological disruptions, or climate change? Would circumstances be better for you and your family somewhere else? What is stopping you from going there? Whatever it is, you will need to get over it. For billions of people, perpetual mobility is becoming the norm. Movement may become an end in itself: One won't just move; one will *always* be moving. But perhaps, as we move, we will rediscover what it means to be human.

5

## Today's Human Geography

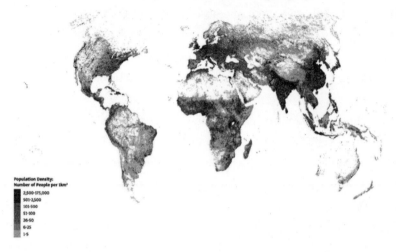

Population Density:
Number of People per 1km²
2,500-175,000
501-2,500
101-500
51-100
26-50
6-25
1-5

The current human population is just under 8 billion. Nearly 5 billion people reside in Asia,
1 billion in Africa, 750 million in Europe, 600 million in North America, and
425 million in South America.

## Migration makes nations

Most of humanity has never crossed a border. Even today, most people
live their entire lives within the country where they were born—but that
doesn't mean they're not migrants. Counting the number of people crossing borders is a terribly incomplete and skewed way to understand migration. According to the International Organization of Migration (IOM),
about three times the number of people migrate internally as internationally.[2] That includes those who have no choice but to uproot themselves:
the estimated 40 million internally displaced peoples (IDPs), mostly due
to political violence but also climate change, who have by definition been
forced to migrate domestically. The story of people on the move is equally
about these migrants as it is about the international jet set.

Arguably the greatest migration in human history has been un-
folding for decades just due to urbanization *within* countries. In 1960, only

1 billion people lived in cities; today that figure stands at more than 5 billion. For the vast majority of the world population, moving from countryside to city has brought unimaginable changes in life experience, from education to work to health.\* The influx of manpower into coastal Chinese cities doesn't just track to China's rise into an economic super-power—it was the engine. *China has more internal migrants than the world has migrants.* The same process is well underway in India as youth stream into Delhi, Bangalore, Hyderabad, and other up-and-coming commercial hubs. None of this appears in statistics as international migration, yet it has been one of the primary drivers of growth through wage gains and remittances to rural families. One doesn't have to cross a border to feel the power of migration.

Yet urbanization also feeds greater international migration. As the German geographer Ernst Georg Ravenstein explained more than a century ago, many people come to major cities as a stepping-stone to further opportunities abroad. With the relentless growth of the world's four-dozen megacities (those with more than 10 million inhabitants) and teeming second-tier cities, approximately 1 billion more people are predicted to move into cities in the coming decade. It's a safe bet that many will arrive there to get a passport.

## To move is human

The story of mankind begins with a single step. The first upright beings set foot out of Africa nearly 2 million years ago, crossing a land bridge to Eurasia in the geography of today's Red Sea and Sinai Peninsula. Over the thousands of millennia that followed, our protohuman ancestors interbred and gradually emerged as a unique species—*Homo sapiens*—

---

\* The gap between wages of people in cities and regions continues to grow and now stands at about 1.5 times higher in core cities. William Gbohoui et al., "A Map of Inequality in Countries," *International Monetary Fund Blog*, November 6, 2019.

about 300,000 years ago. Paleontologists believe that between 135,000 and 90,000 years ago, a severe African drought spurred *Homo sapiens* to fan out of Africa into the terrain of the Neanderthals in Europe. But unlike our Neanderthal competitors, *Homo sapiens* used their lighter, more upright bodies to cover longer distances when hunting and gathering with their bone (then stone) tools. Early man outran and outlasted his rivals.

We are told that speech is a key differentiator between humans and other primates, but why did we learn to speak at all? Linguists believe that human languages developed about a hundred thousand years ago, not incidentally because of the increasing interactions among these migrating *Homo sapiens*, who needed to communicate while covering several hundred kilometers of hunting range. Climatic events such as the Last Glacial Period of twenty-five thousand years ago pushed humans all the way across Siberia and over the land bridge to North America. But as northern latitudes once again became habitable just over eleven thousand years ago, intensifying Eurasian migrations gave rise to the entire Indo-European family of languages that boasts 3 billion speakers today.

Great migrations permeate all of recorded history and our oldest mythologies. According to the Hebrew Bible, the Jews suffered a long period of slavery under Egyptian pharaohs, until a great exodus miraculously returned them across the Sinai to their ancestral land of Canaan. We use the German term *Völkerwanderung* to describe the early centuries AD during which Germanic, Slavic, and Hun tribes invaded the declining Roman empire. Facing persecution in Mecca, the followers of the Prophet Muhammad sought refuge in the African kingdom of Abyssinia, but also became missionary conquerors, establishing the early caliphates and converting followers as far as Southeast Asia. The reason that allegedly up to 10 percent of Asian males between the Caspian Sea and the Pacific Ocean claim lineage to Genghis Khan is because the Mongols were nomadic and polygamous conquerors who intermarried with local tribes.

The fourteenth-century Black Death killed an estimated 100 million people and led to the splintering of the vast Mongol empire. In Europe, farmers and laborers moved to places where land quality was better and to towns where wages rose due to worker shortages. Up to 90 percent of the population in some Arab territories vacated their infected villages and fled to cities. During the centuries-long Little Ice Age that followed, expanding glaciers and crop failure pushed Eurasian populations to search for more reliable farmland, and also inspired the Dutch and Portuguese to undertake oceanic navigation, spurring their colonial expansion.

Migrations of the colonial era were both voluntary and involuntary. English immigration to establish colonies in America began in the late sixteenth century. Throughout the seventeenth century, these early settlers were joined by pilgrims in search of profit and Puritans and Quakers seeking religious freedom. Over the four hundred years of the transatlantic slave trade, an estimated 13 million Africans were shipped to North America, the Caribbean, and South America. In Asia, the British and Portuguese empires moved millions of Malay and Indian merchants across the Indian Ocean, and East Asians spread across the Pacific to both North and South America. More than a millennium of Chinese emigration into the Malay peninsula, across the Tang, Ming, and Qing dynasties, dramatically contributed to making Southeast Asia the ethnic melting pot that it is today.

The nineteenth century is widely referred to as the "age of nationalism" due to ethnonationalist movements resisting Europe's dynastic empires. Yet it was *also* the age of mass migrations, as the Industrial Revolution created huge demand for both agricultural and manufacturing labor. Millions of farmers were lured to factory jobs in cities, while steamships and railways transported millions of workers, slaves, and criminals across the British empire—especially across the Atlantic to North America. Sixty million Europeans moved en masse to America, including 1.5 million (40 percent of the population) fleeing

Ireland's potato famine, followed by several million Italians escaping rural poverty.

Nationalism had a phenomenal run of success in the twentieth century as well, with decolonization movements bringing an end to Europe's global empires and giving birth to dozens of new countries. And even though the end of World War II settled much of the world map—it did not settle the world's people. Millions of refugees shifted from Eastern to Western Europe, and from Europe to America. Both before and after the Holocaust, hundreds of thousands of Jews fled Europe to America and Palestine, with even more arriving after the creation of Israel in 1948. The partition of India and Pakistan in 1947 displaced an estimated 20 million Hindus, Muslims, and Sikhs—still the largest mass migration in human history.

Postcolonial ties brought millions of Indians and Pakistanis to England, as well as Vietnamese, Algerians, and Moroccans to France. During these postwar decades, severe labor shortages in Europe combined with high unemployment in Turkey lured waves of *Gastarbeiter* (guest workers) to Germany (and its smaller neighbors). In America, the 1965 Immigration Act repealed quotas on the national origin of immigrants, leading to a surge of Latinos from the Caribbean and Central America and waves of Asians from China, India, Vietnam, and elsewhere.

Recent decades have added yet more impetus for large-scale resettlement. Civil wars and state failures, such as Afghanistan in the 1980s and more recently Iraq and Syria, have forced millions to become refugees. The Soviet Union's collapse three decades ago continues to drive millions of people across its former republics spanning Eastern Europe and Central Asia. The Gulf oil boom brought millions of Palestinians and South Asian migrant laborers to Kuwait, Saudi Arabia, and the UAE. Migrants physically built some of today's most modern states. To move and to build—this is the essence of being human.

# MOBILITY IS DESTINY

## *Migrants make the world go round*

Many believe that protectionism, populism, and the pandemic mean we have reached peak migration, but let's look at the economics. Over the past half century, governments have borrowed to the tune of $250 trillion (more than triple global GDP) to finance everything from roads to retirement plans. While this has paid for modern civilization as we know it, aging countries are now staring down the barrel of economic stagnation unless they attract migrants and investors, and the tax-paying activities they bring. Without younger generations to make use of homes, schools, hospitals, offices, restaurants, hotels, malls, museums, hotels, stadiums, and other facilities, many countries risk permanent deflation—both demographic and economic.

Migrants are a small share of the world population, but their weight has only grown over time. By the late nineteenth century, international migrants represented a sizable 14 percent of humanity, about 225 million out of a total population of 1.6 billion people. Then World War I and the Spanish flu flattened those waves. A century later, we stand at approximately 275 million migrants, a lower share (3 percent) of a much larger population (8 billion). It might therefore seem that we have not come very far, yet today's figure in fact represents a far more meaningful accomplishment. Why? Because unlike nineteenth-century migration—comprised of the desperate exodus of Europeans and Chinese, as well as British colonial subjects forcibly circulated across the empire—today we have mostly voluntary movement of peoples among nearly two hundred sovereign nations. Furthermore, whatever their number, migrants today represent 10 percent of global GDP (slightly less than that of China or America), including almost $550 billion in annual remittances transferred across borders in 2019. (This figure also dwarfs total foreign aid, which has remained stagnant at around $100 billion per year since 1980.)

## The Rise of Remittances

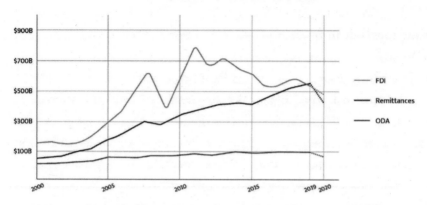

Remittances have been rising in lockstep with international migration, while aid has stagnated. Foreign Direct Investment (FDI) has been volatile due to financial crises and protectionist policies.

Unfortunately, humans have a much more difficult time moving across borders than money does. Countries have been open to the (relatively) free movement of goods and capital—but people, not as much. Migration is one of the primary, and most sensitive, arenas of sovereignty: controlling who comes in and out of one's territory. The US has imposed significant restrictions on asylum seekers and chain migration (especially Latino families), and Australia has set up migrant processing centers in the jungles of Papua New Guinea that have become semipermanent holding camps. Italy and other European countries have paid off Libyan militias to keep migrants from crossing the Mediterranean. The Universal Declaration of Human Rights doesn't guarantee anyone the right to reside in another country—only the receiving country decides that.

We do not have a binding global migration framework—and probably never will. But there are deeply rooted regional patterns in the flows of people, shaped by family histories, business needs, and cultural preferences. Half of all foreigners in America are Mexican or Latino; members of the European Union enjoy almost fully free migration and other privileges in one another's country; Southeast Asia has largely open borders, and most cross-border migrants are from within the region or from China and India. We use terms like "insider" and "outsider" to denote national distinctions, but in reality, our world is already a collection of regional mélanges.

## People on the Move: More Regional Than Global

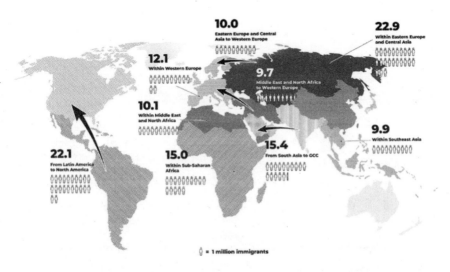

**10.0**
Eastern Europe and Central
Asia to Western Europe

**22.9**
Within Eastern Europe
and Central Asia

**12.1**
Within Western Europe

**9.7**
Middle East and North Africa
to Western Europe

**10.1**
Within Middle East
and North Africa

**9.9**
Within Southeast Asia

**22.1**
From Latin America
to North America

**15.0**
Within Sub-Saharan
Africa

**15.4**
From South Asia to GCC

◊ = 1 million immigrants

Most migration takes place within regions or between adjacent regions. The largest migrant stock remains among the former Soviet republics of Russia, Eastern Europe, and Central Asia, followed by the South Asian population in the Gulf countries

The largest flows of people in the world are *within* these organic regions. The former Soviet Union region spanning Eastern Europe and Central Asia represents the biggest migrant pool at 25 million people, followed by the circulation of primarily Latinos around North and Central America (20 million), sub-Saharan Africans within Africa (15 million), South Asians to the Gulf countries (15 million), EU citizens within the EU (12 million), Arabs and North Africans within the Middle East (10 million), Eastern Europeans into Western Europe (10 million), Southeast Asians within their ASEAN (Association of Southeast Asian Nations) group (just under 10 million), and lastly the fewer than 10 million Arabs and North Africans that have moved to Europe.[3] This also suggests that the two-tiered division of humanity into "North" (North America and Eurasia) and "South" (Africa and South America) persists. Five point five billion people live on continents with reasonable prospects, while 2.5 billion don't have a plan or opportunity to escape. Most migrants don't make it very far—yet.

## Voting with the feet

The coming age of mass migrations won't just be a continuation but an acceleration. The swirl of humanity will only get more intense as each of the forces shaping our human geography gathers steam:

- *Demographics:* Lopsided imbalances between an aging North and a youthful South able to provide the labor force the North needs

- *Politics:* Refugees and asylum seekers from civil wars and failing states, as well as those fleeing ethnic persecution, tyranny, or populism

- *Economics:* Migrants in search of opportunity, workers laid off due to outsourcing, or employees forced into early retirement by financial crises

- *Technology:* Industrial automation displacing factory and logistics jobs, while algorithms and AI make skilled jobs redundant

- *Climate:* Long-term phenomena such as rising temperatures and sea levels and falling water tables, but also seasonal disasters like floods and typhoons.

In day to day life around the world, all these parallel trends amplify each other—so much so that we can even state their relationship as an equation:

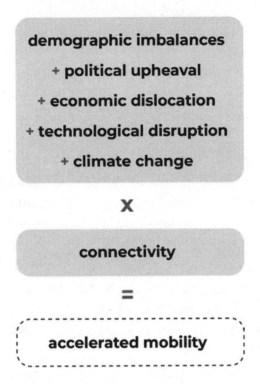

demographic imbalances
+ political upheaval
+ economic dislocation
+ technological disruption
+ climate change

x

connectivity

=

accelerated mobility

These variables also interact in complex and unforeseen ways. Pandemics wipe out millions of people within the span of a few years, while climate change does so cumulatively via droughts and other natural disasters. Both heighten economic and social uncertainty, which drives down fertility. So, too, do financial crises and labor automation, which also force people to move in search of jobs and an affordable life. The bottom line is that everything drives migration, alone and together.

The Covid-19 pandemic and its aftermath will reinforce these pre-existing trends. To be clear: The coronavirus lockdown was a stunning break from recent decades of intensifying resettlement—

but it was artificial and temporary. It did, however, prompt people everywhere to rethink where they live and begin looking for better options. People are ditching "red zones" with inadequate healthcare for "green zones" with better medical systems and "blue zones" offering greater climate resilience. *We are all in search of the right combination of latitude and attitude.*

The future of human mobility points in just one direction: *more.* The coming decades could witness *billions* of people on the move, shifting from south to north, from coast to inland, from low-lying to higher-elevation, from overpriced to affordable, from failing to stable societies.

No doubt there are billions of people who will die in the countries in which they were born. Indeed, let's assume that more than half of the most populous countries are too sedentary, old, infirm, unwilling, or unwelcome elsewhere to leave home. That means that at least 1 billion Indians, 1 billion Chinese, 700 million Africans, 200 million Brazilians, the same number of Indonesians, 100 million Pakistanis, and another 1 billion others remain geographically immobile. That still leaves *4 billion* people who may be both eager and capable of migrating.

Almost all of those 4 billion are young. Just over half the world's population was born in the three decades since the Cold War ended. This includes most millennials (Gen-Y) and all of Gen-Z. As of 2020, they represent more than *60 percent* of the world population. We often talk about a world that's aging, but right now, the world is more young than old—and the primary reason humanity is getting statistically older is because today's youth are barely having any children. Thus, when we talk about "the people," it's wrong to envision yuppie, middle-class, two-income, two-child households living in suburbia. That isn't true in America, Europe, China, or anywhere. The largest category of people in the world is best described as young, single, childless, and struggling in cities. If you are not one of them, you are in the minority.

Furthermore, if you are not Asian, you are definitely in the minority. Asia represents not only 60 percent of the global population (versus only 25 percent *combined* for North America and Europe), but also almost all of the countries with the largest number of young people in the world. *China and India each have more millennials than America or Europe have people.* In recent years, about two-thirds of Asian migrants have remained within the region, but as the West's demographic imbalances become more acute, Asians will be in ever higher demand worldwide. There are presently more Chinese outside of China than Indians outside of India, but soon that will reverse: Whereas China's population will soon begin to decline, India's is much younger and continues to grow—and with all of South Asia (including Pakistan and Bangladesh) much poorer than China, its youth are much more motivated to move. Geopolitically, the world seems like it's turning yellow, but demographically it's unquestionably turning brown.

Wherever they hail from, today's youth are the largest and most physically and digitally mobile generation in human history. Where they're going, how they're living, and what they're doing *today* reveals what social, political, and economic models will prevail—and which ones will fail—*tomorrow*. Countries that are losing citizens today are likely to wither tomorrow. By contrast, countries gaining youth today may well thrive tomorrow.

What will the *next* three decades—between now and 2050—hold for those under the age of thirty *today*? What geopolitical, economic, technological, social, and environmental circumstances will they face? Where are they going? Which societies will be the winners and losers in the twenty-first century? These and other great questions of our time are being answered as young people vote with their feet. To know the future, then, we must follow the next generation into it.

# MOVE

## *Survival of the mobile*

Baby boomers remember the Cold War "Doomsday Clock" that warned of impending nuclear destruction; scientists moved the needle closer to midnight as geopolitical tensions escalated. Today's youth are much more familiar with the "climate clock" that counts down to when the Earth's temperature rise hits two degrees Celsius. As climate activist Bill McKibben has written, "It is far too late to stop global warming, but these next ten years seem as if they may be our last chance to limit the chaos."[4] It's safe to assume we will fail to limit the chaos. Philosophers such as Roy Scranton tell us that we need to "learn to die." That's equally unlikely. The more interesting question becomes: What will we do to survive?

Mankind has long been on the move in search of the right climate, settling along rivers and coastlines in the temperate latitudes. As we learned to control fire, herd animals, build sturdy shelters, and pump groundwater, we spread more widely, with cities becoming the locus of populations and growth in the industrial era. But the intense resource consumption required to fuel urban life for billions of people has caused skyrocketing carbon emissions, scorching temperatures, and record ice melt, rendering ever more swaths of the Earth unlivable.

There are many ways to beat the heat and retreat from the sea—but no survival is possible without freshwater. Ancient civilizations of the Nile, Tigris, Indus, and Yellow River valleys were built on irrigation. Today two-thirds of the world's population lives near rivers, and agriculture consumes 70 percent of our freshwater. But with groundwater depletion accelerating and rainfall declining, rivers are drying up. Farmers from Brazil to Africa to India already face crop failure year after year. Those who are bonded to their land amass huge generational debts, commit suicide, flee to cities, or join the hordes illegally migrating across borders. One season without rain or one week of "zero day" water shortages is all it takes to push farmers and city dwellers to chase more fertile and hydrated lands.

## Rising Water Stress Across the Planet

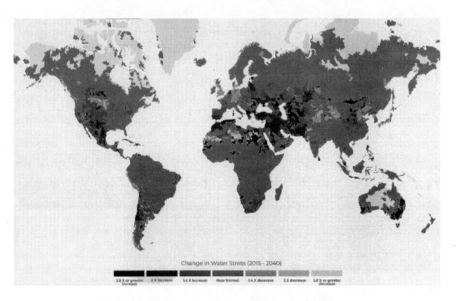

Change in Water Stress (2015 - 2040)

2.0 X or greater increase    2 X increase    1.4 X increase    Near Normal    1.4 X decrease    2 X decrease    2.0 X or greater decrease

Freshwater availability is projected to decline in almost all regions of the world over the coming two decades. The Middle East and North Africa, as well as the southern United States and eastern Australia, will be among the most affected geographies.

The term "Anthropocene" (defined by Webster as "the period of time during which human activities have had an environmental impact on the Earth regarded as constituting a distinct geological age") initially gave us a false sense of control over the environment, but now we see that it signifies a self-destructive feedback loop.* Even if some of today's most ambitious proposals are undertaken immediately—stopping all coal-powered electricity generation; replacing fossil with nuclear, hydrogen, wind, and solar power; and planting 1 trillion trees across Russia, Canada, Australia, Brazil, and America—greenhouse gases already accumulated in the atmosphere may have an even more severe impact on planetary life than they have had to date. For billions of people, staying put means

---

* Georgetown environmental historian J. R. McNeill has methodically documented this "great acceleration" of the man-technology-nature nexus.

inevitable suicide. Political sovereignty has been a defining feature of our geography for only three centuries—but our seas will be rising for the next several centuries. Ask yourself which force will give way.

The climate doesn't care about our political boundaries, and people too will clamor ever more to overcome them. Climate stresses cause migrant swells. The 50 million climate refugees today already outnumber political ones. According to the National Academy of Sciences, another degree of temperature rise could push 200 million people out of the "climate niche" to which they have become accustomed.[5] And a further degree beyond that could mean the decimal place moves one further, turning 1 billion or more of humanity into climate refugees.

## How Fast Will It Get Hot?

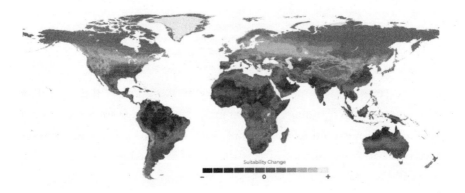

The optimal geographies for human habitation are shifting as temperatures rise. Regions in black will have average daily temperatures above thirty degrees Celsius and become unsuitable for human habitation by 2070 or sooner. Lighter shaded regions will become more suitable for settlement over time.

Mitigating the effects of climate change no longer appears plausible, and few will wait until the worst case scenarios come true to abandon wherever they have called home. We must focus instead on adaptation—and for most people, to adapt will mean to move. Poor Central American farmers who lose everything in a cyclone and Africans wiped out by drought will simply take what's left and move north. As the rich lose a home in a forest fire or a yacht in a typhoon, they invest in land and bunkers farther inland and at higher elevations, or in Norway and New Zealand. Whether rich or poor, ever more people are, like our ancient ancestors, chasing the climate niche.

## Running from the robots

While climate change drives us away from our traditional habitats, robots are chasing us away from the stable jobs we once knew. Outsourcing and automation have already devastated America's industrial workers, forcing them to move to cheaper places in search of new jobs. Asian workers were the beneficiaries of supply chain shifts, but today no country is investing more in ramping up industrial robotics than China, pushing tens of millions of Chinese workers into the rootless gigonomy.

Covid-19 will accelerate automation efforts worldwide as companies seek to reduce dependence on vulnerable humans. In the US, up to 3 million truck drivers could lose their jobs to autonomous vehicles, and 2 million real estate agents to proptech apps. Amazon's warehouses will eventually manage themselves without people. The unsung heroes of the Covid lockdown were undocumented migrants laboring on farms and in meat processing plants, but they won't be rewarded: They will be automated by machines that can crush weeds, plant seeds, and pick crops. Latino farmhands might as well move on to Canada to help expand farming there, and Romanians to Russia.

Many current job creation engines will be wiped out before today's youth even join the labor market. There's no point in aspiring to install 5G telecom networks or solar panels when all of that will have been done already. Other major sectors, from education to hospitality to retail, have yet to be digitally overhauled—but they *will* be. One estimate suggests that at least 375 million people will have to switch "occupational categories" due to artificial intelligence and automation. Will their new job be located where their old one was? Not likely.

The race against the machines is survival of the richest. Coders, engineers, and others with top-tier skills stay ahead of robots and algorithms by designing them, while poor workers serve as cogs in the manufacturing, logistics, or retail machinery until they become disposable. At the same time, young people don't want to work like robots either. In France, village bakeries are being replaced by semi-automated grocery stores and even baguette vending machines. Youth aren't interested in waking up at 3 a.m. to bake bread anyway, so they move.

If countries tax corporate robots and redistribute profits, they can become more equitable welfare states without needing larger populations. Today, however, only Germany and Japan could conceivably muster the political will for such a move without their companies rushing to outsource. Either way, they remain migration magnets because they offer jobs in finance, media, education, tech, medicine, logistics, entertainment, retail, and other professions. According to the Small Business Administration (SBA), US states where these sectors are growing are the same states where populations are growing: North Carolina, Oregon, Washington, Virginia, Georgia, Utah, Colorado, California, and Texas.[6] The lesson is clear: Follow the people.

### A quantum future

Over the past two decades, millions of Americans who abandoned rust-belt districts of Michigan, Pennsylvania, Ohio, and other northern states wound up in California, almost by default. Since 2015, however, California has been losing residents, especially to lower-tax Texas and Arizona. Yet the entire southwestern US is suffering from intensifying heat waves, water shortages, and volatile immigration policy. Despite the popularity of Las Vegas, Phoenix, and Tucson, large tracts of America's desert regions might need to be deserted—and those who fled the Great Lakes may well return sooner than they think.

To end up where one started seems a pointless circularity. And yet over a certain time horizon, we can engineer the logic behind it. Take another example: The UK's 2016 Brexit decision pushed business and investment away from the country, with British talent taking their skills and money to Canada, Portugal, the Netherlands, Switzerland, Sweden, and a half-dozen other countries. But Britain has an educated population, a large economy, ample freshwater, and will fare far better than most places as climate change accelerates. So those that Brexit pushed away may eventually return despite Brexit—along with a new wave of migrants recruited by a wiser government.

Human geography is getting fuzzy. As people find themselves regularly on the move, we are experiencing a phase shift like when matter transitions from solid to liquid to gas: molecules heat up and loosen from one another, vibrating more rapidly. One might even say that humans are becoming like particles in quantum physics, their velocity and location always in flux. It would be nice to return to some semblance of stability, but that's not how things work in a quantum world. Instead, the complexity of today's world makes it increasingly difficult to settle permanently anywhere. Highly paid digital nomads and billionaires with multiple passports as well as the migratory underclass of Filipino maids and Indian construction workers are all part of the diverse and growing global demographic of quantum people.

There's also no reason to believe that the rising tide of political refugees and asylum seekers will stop—but plenty more reasons suggesting it will continue. Across the postcolonial landscape of Africa, the Middle East, and parts of Asia, nations began to decay from overpopulation and corruption almost as soon as they were born. In recent decades, the multiple Iraq wars and the Arab Spring have pushed millions of Arabs from North Africa to Syria into Jordan, Turkey, and most recently Europe—perhaps never to return to the home nations that have been shattered beyond recognition. As Paul Salopek wrote in *National Geographic* in 2019, "More than a billion refugees and migrants are on the move today, both within countries and across borders, fleeing mass violence and poverty. This is the largest tide of rootlessness in human history."[7]

The term "refugee" implies a narrow and transient group, but what we have is semipermanently resettled people, such as Syrians in neighboring states, Palestinians in Jordan, Afghans in Pakistan, and Somalis in Kenya. In Turkey, nearly 4 million Syrians hold "temporary protected status" but in reality may never leave. At the same time, they're always at risk of being deported as a bargaining chip to extract concessions from Europe—as Turkey did in 2020 in pushing another wave toward Greece. These refugees regularly shift within Turkey, meaning more steps in their perpetual movement—and for those who are deported, yet one more. There are few safe bets for tens of millions of refugees, asylum seekers, and undocumented migrants. The US has pushed several million Mexican and Central Americans back across the border over the past decade, Spain continues to expel North Africans, and China booted Burmese migrants back into Myanmar as the coronavirus struck. They thought they had made it—until they were forced to move again.

Violence and resource stress are daily facts of life in the teeming megacities of Latin America, Africa, and South Asia. Today's fastest growing cities are not those in China's hyper-modern Greater Bay Area but cities such as Lagos, Karachi, Cairo, Dhaka, Manila, Istanbul, Jakarta, Mumbai, Kolkata, São Paulo, and Bangkok—most of which rank worryingly low in climate resilience. The vast slums in these and other megacities are home to an estimated 1.5 billion people. Cities that recycle shipping containers or subsidize 3D-printed housing, offer mobile health clinics, and create jobs in urban farming and installing solar panels may pacify the poor underclass. But such initiatives are still few and far between. In the coming decade, we will either see such innovations scale or we will witness large-scale revolt against marginalization and oppression. There is also a third scenario—mass exodus—as people flee to towns closer to resources and at higher elevation. Which will it be? The answer is: all three.

How do we know which places will gain or lose people in the years ahead? Some places have every strike against them: They have too few young people, are politically volatile, economically uncompetitive, and ecologically vulnerable. These are the places from which people want to flee. At the other end of the spectrum are places that have it all going for them: robust demographics, stable politics, prospering economies, and environmental stability. Those are the places everyone wants to go to. The catch is: How we would describe one country today may not be true tomorrow. What place can be sure of its stability when so many newcomers arrive? Its own desirability could quickly destabilize it. This is what some feel has already happened to Europe and America; Canada could be next.

But unpredictability is no reason to stand still. On the contrary, it's precisely why so many people move in the first place—and find themselves moving again and again. Mobility is our response to uncertainty: flight from what we cannot fight. The future is a moving target—and so are we.

## One Future, Four Scenarios

I'm not the daydreaming type, but sometimes during a long hike, I fall into a light trance. My mind slips into visions of a world in which disparate communities across the globe freely and peacefully connect and exchange, and people circulate as they please. Sadly, we are a long way from that dream today. At the moment, our human geography is emerging more by accident than design. That leaves us little choice but to build a range of scenarios for how the combinations of mobility, authority, technology, and community will unfold in the years ahead.

The four scenarios depicted here represent divergent visions for our future playing out along the axes of migration and sustainability.

## Which Path Will the World Take?

**More Sustainability**

**Regional Fortresses**

A self-sufficient North American Union drifts from Eurasia, where a stronger EU partners with Russia to ward off migrants. But northern powers supply the south with technologies to conserve their ecosystems.

**Northern Lights**

An archipelago of sustainable Arctic settlements absorbs two billion climate migrants with international agencies enabling frictionless seasonal migration. Demographic revival and cultural assimilation flourish amidst an economy built on human-centric innovation.

**New Middle Ages**

A return to hunter-gatherer localism contrasting stable city-regions and chaotic provincial decay. Allied territories pursue military and commercial networks but fortify themselves against climate migrants.

**Barbarians at the Gate**

Cascading climate crises crash the global economy while great powers clash over watersheds. Elites buy up fertile geographies while uncontrolled mass migrations overrun borders and overwhelm government capacity. Civil wars erupt as ethnic enclaves harden.

**Less Sustainability**

**Less Migration**

**More Migration**

Four scenarios for the future. All are likely to play out simultaneously in different parts of the world.

In the upper left, "Regional Fortresses" most closely resembles today's status quo. Clean energy investments are ramping up, but migration is limited. The rich countries of the North are far more focused on their own climate resilience than supporting deprived regions. They selectively promote sustainable farming or other survival measures in impoverished regions, but mostly to bribe their people to stay away. North America, Europe, and Northeast Asia drift into self-contained systems with limited interactions, though they may coordinate where necessary to limit encroachment from the South. They could also be at perpetual war with one another as in George Orwell's *1984*.

Another low-migration scenario portends the emergence of a "New Middle Ages" of even greater fragmentation. In this scenario, sustainability investments are abandoned and militaries forcibly seize water and energy resources from their own citizens or across borders. Waves of natural disasters and man-made ecocides kill off large portions of the world population. Those that remain converge upon feudal city-regions that form alliances akin to the medieval Hanseatic League. This landscape has been captured in countless films, from *Hunger Games* to *Mad Max*. (Throw in killer robots and you get *Terminator*.)

In both these low-migration scenarios, the world population as a whole is clearly not better off. Climate change may be less devastating in a world of regional fortresses, but even with lots of robots supplanting foreign labor, we may lack the young workers needed to rejuvenate our societies and lead a more convenient life. If we're headed into a new Middle Ages, then the world will be much less than the sum of its parts—and potentially on the fast track to human extinction.

Moving to the bottom-right quadrant, we find a world similarly unable to coordinate sustainability efforts but with far more "Barbarians at the Gate." Climate change wreaks havoc on the global economy, "water wars" break out over watershed regions, and masses of migrants force their way into livable regions, their overwhelming influx ruining habitats. At the same time, the rich buy up climate oasis zones for themselves and their dependents, building armed moats around them. The sci-fi disaster film *The Day After Tomorrow* perhaps best captures this combination of political and climatic chaos.

Only one scenario, "Northern Lights," involves advanced planning for large-scale human resettlement and environmental regeneration. Economies move rapidly toward carbon-neutral energy, vast tracts of transnationally financed and governed zones (mostly in the northern hemisphere) absorb billions of migrants, and large investments are also devoted to rehabilitating the southern hemisphere. The world achieves both resource efficiency as well as managed cultural assimilation. No movie has yet been made about this scenario. We will have to write the script.

What might be the pathways and stages for getting to a Northern Lights world? In the first phase, today's populism and pandemic restrictions may limit migration to the national and regional level. But within a decade, as economies recover and baby boomers retire, labor shortages will worsen and a younger generation of more migrant-friendly leaders could take the helm. At the same time, climate effects may kick in even more severely, compounding the need for migrants to relocate and governments to deploy them to cultivate habitable terrain. Serious geoengineering efforts will get underway to limit $CO_2$ emissions and solar radiation, as well as fortify the ecology of devastated regions. Eventually, we might well stabilize the environment and safely repopulate the Earth.

But the future won't give us the luxury of following one neat, predictable path. Plausible scenarios are never mutually exclusive; reality takes a zigzagging path, with elements of all four visions undeniably present. For example, environmental restoration may occur through conscious planning in a Northern Lights scenario but also via mass death in the New Middle Ages. Some degree of innovation, fragmentation, and inequality pervades all scenarios.

Importantly, we must never think that the collision of so many variables will play out evenly, either geographically or chronologically—which is why, as disparate places lurch across these scenarios, we move in search of a better life. Indeed, within a single vast country such as America, one can easily imagine elements of all four scenarios coming to pass in different regions at different times. This begs the question as to whether we can continue to rely on "the nation" as the anchor of our future. What matters more: places or people?

## CHAPTER 2

# THE WAR FOR YOUNG TALENT

### Welcome to "peak humanity"

On October 16, 1975, national security advisor Henry Kissinger presented a memo to President Gerald Ford seeking approval for NSSM-200: "Implications of Worldwide Population Growth for US Security and Overseas Interests." The proposal called for enhanced support for family planning and other population control measures in a dozen countries, such as India, Pakistan, Bangladesh, Nigeria, Ethiopia, Indonesia, Mexico, and Brazil. The White House hoped to steer the world population to 6 billion by 2050, "without massive starvation or total frustration of developmental hopes." Those countries clearly never got the memo. When the world population did reach 6 billion (in 1995), the United Nations still forecast nearly perpetual growth toward *15* billion.

Today, however, the outlook is different. We can now foresee with confidence that the world population may peak as soon as 2045 and perhaps never reach 9 billion. How could we have miscalculated so badly? The answer is that we were wrong because we were right: Warnings about the economic and ecological perils of overpopulation are what prompted poor countries with high fertility to take measures to curb their breakneck population growth. Were it not for this feedback loop, world population may already have crossed 10 billion.

Even getting to 9 billion actually hinges on what are likely erroneous predictions of a continued population explosion in highly fertile countries such as Nigeria, Ethiopia, Uganda, Tanzania, Congo, and Egypt in Africa, and India, Pakistan, and Indonesia in Asia. Instead, rapid urbanization, female empowerment, and depleting water supplies will surely impact family planning in those places. Parents in developing countries used to consider having more children a good investment in the future labor force. Today, it just creates more unemployment.

## A Brief History of the World Population

Over the millennia of humankind's wanderings across the planet, the total human population remained relatively constant. By the year 1 AD, it was estimated to be somewhere between 200 and 300 million people. One thousand years later, it remained about the same. Even by 1500 AD, perhaps only 100 million people had been added. Then came the eighteenth-century Industrial Revolution, during which fossil fuels replaced human and animal muscle as the primary source of power. The cotton gin and wheat thresher made farms much more productive, while steam engines and railroads carried food long distances. Better sanitation curbed the spread of diseases, ensuring that people lived longer and more children reached adulthood. All of these innovations helped push the world population to 1 billion by the year 1800.

Witnessing the surging population enabled by the Industrial Revolution, the English scholar Thomas Malthus famously predicted in 1798 that an ever more crowded world would face a crisis of insufficient food supply. But better nutrition and healthcare (such as vaccinations) worked in tandem to extend our lifespan while helping more children survive childbirth and infancy, all together expanding the total global population to 1.6 billion by the end of the nineteenth century. After World Wars I and II, the Green Revolution introduced fertilizers and pesticides that massively boosted global food supply for developing countries such as India, catapulting the global population from just over 2 billion people in 1945 to nearly 4 billion by 1970.

Despite the incredible gains in agricultural output, some experts became worried that Malthus's prophecy was finally coming true. In 1972, the members of the Club of Rome (a group of financial, political, and academic elites) published a manifesto, titled *The Limits to Growth*, arguing that our planet has finite resources and could not sustainably support such a fast-growing population. They advocated for stronger population control policies, such as easing restrictions on abortions and promoting contraception. This neo-Malthusian thinking was so influential that China launched a one-child policy and India began forced sterilizations of men and women.

Around the same time, contraception—in the form of condoms and diaphragms, as well as the advent of the birth control pill in the 1960s—helped drive down global fertility. The latter was also crucial to women's empowerment in homes and schools, in communities and the workplace. Equally significant, urbanization rapidly accelerated. In 1960, 2 billion people lived in rural areas and only 1 billion in cities. Fifty years later, in 2010, the urban population eclipsed the rural. When families move to cities, women get access to healthcare, education, and jobs—but living in cramped apartments with high rental and other costs also means less money and space to have eight or more children.

And so, here we are: a planet of 8 billion people today creeping toward 9 billion—but likely not more. Instead, it turns out that *our demographic destiny is no longer to multiply but to shrink.*

## Peak Humanity

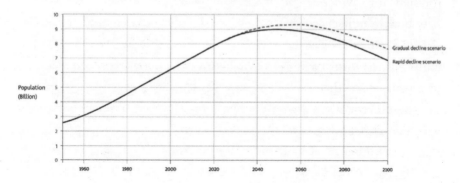

The world population is nearing its zenith and will begin to decline. The only question is how quickly.

How else can we explain our reproductive anxiety? Malthus feared population growth outstripping food supply, but today about 30 percent of the world population is *obese*, and only 13 percent malnourished. This is one sign that humankind is a victim of its own success. Money is also a major factor inhibiting fertility. Since the 2008 financial crisis, stability has given way to angst. In America, birth rates had been rising slightly for five years until the crisis, after which they plummeted. In fact, the entire world—rich *and* poor—saw fertility rates decline markedly in the decade plus since the crisis.[1] Globally, as of 2020, there are more human beings aged sixty-five and older than there are children aged five and younger. Higher life expectancy also paradoxically contributes to declining fertility: Now that we consciously manipulate our biology, we must save more money to take care of ourselves during longer and more active lives.

In addition to longevity and money, there are ethical dilemmas. Even millennials who could afford to have more children tend to subscribe to postmaterialist values—the most significant of which is a focus on the climate. Gen-Z carries a self-conscious guilt about how to cope with the fragility of the planet: They're far more concerned with civilizational survival than with having children. To many, bearing children is not only an economic luxury but is considered immoral given the volatile environment into which the children would be born and the damage each new human inflicts on our fragile ecosystems. A popular infographic circulating online shows that having one less child would save more $CO_2$ emissions than not having a car, avoiding long-haul flights, and shifting to a plant based diet—*combined*. In a world that's increasingly secular—or where eco-consciousness surpasses any religion in adherents—most youth don't believe that it's God's will for them to get married and have multiple children.

### The Great Baby Bust

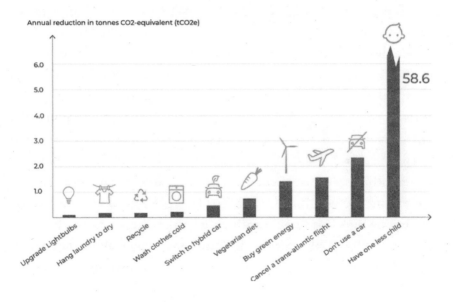

Environmentally conscious millennials and Gen-Z take many steps to reduce their carbon footprint, but the biggest emissions reduction by far would come from bringing one less child onto the planet.

All of this was happening *before* the Covid-19 pandemic. With an economic contraction far more severe than the 2008 financial crisis, we can expect Gen-Z's fertility to crash in the same way that millennial fertility did after 2008. During the pandemic, governments hoped that couples being forced to shelter in place would lead to elevated childbirth, but instead, condom sales surged early in lockdown and divorce rates spiked when it lifted. Another baby bust. The Brookings Institution estimates that as many as 500,000 *fewer* children were born in the US in 2021 as in 2020. And in the years ahead, should the world experience any major world war or natural disaster—or another pandemic—it would only further hasten our demographic reckoning.

Humanity has recovered from numerous instances of mass death, such as the Mongol conquests of the thirteenth century and the fourteenth-century Black Death. It has also been resilient to other events that caused large-scale fatality, such as the devastation of the native peoples of the Americas by European colonialists and their exotic diseases, centuries of civil warfare across dynasties in China, the Little Ice Age of the 1600s (during which one-third of the world population perished), the centuries-long Atlantic slave trade, World Wars I and II, the Spanish flu pandemic of 1918, and the politically induced famines during the time of the Soviet Union and under Mao in China.

But this time is different. Right now, millennials (born 1981–1996) and Gen-Z (born 1997–2014) represent 64 percent of all human beings. But these youth aren't producing a larger batch of offspring: Gen Alpha (born 2015 onward) may not be as large as Gen-Z. As a result, today's younger generations constitute most of *tomorrow's* population as well. In other words, they are *both* the present *and* the future. By 2050 they'll be thirty-somethings to sixty-somethings who *still* represent most of the total global population because today's elderly will have died off and few children will have been born. When Jack Ma and Elon Musk shared the stage in August 2019, they couldn't agree on the future of AI, but they resoundingly agreed that the greatest challenge of the next twenty years is global population *collapse*.

## The Last Great Generation?

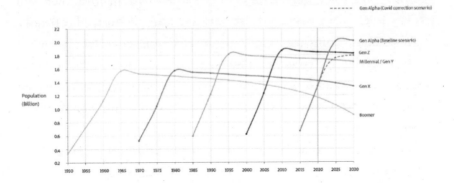

For nearly a century, each generation has been larger than its predecessor. But economic crises and Covid-19 may bring down Gen Alpha's total size to slightly less than Gen-Z.

## *Rich countries, vanishing people*

Amid US president Donald Trump's multi-year campaign to erect a wall on the Mexican border and roll back immigration, he paused to declare, "Our country is full." But his own chief of staff Mick Mulvaney begged to differ. At an event in early 2020, he confessed, "We are desperate, desperate for more people." The simple arithmetic behind his statement is telling: Even if America brings in five hundred thousand new migrants per year, in 2030 its GDP will still be $1 trillion *smaller* than it was in 2020.[2] And right now, even half a million migrants would be a big stretch. After five consecutive years of gaining more than 1 million new migrants annually, net migration plummeted in 2019 to just over two hundred thousand. America isn't even taking in enough migrants to replace its existing workforce: More than 1 million baby boomers (out of 80 million) are retiring each year, hence almost all counties are suffering a decline in the number of workers.[3] Given America's low fertility and rapid aging, immigration is the only reason the population is growing at all.

We don't have to wait until 2040 to witness peak humanity. Much of the world feels that way already. North America, Europe, and Northeast Asia—the three richest zones of the world—have sub-replacement fertility levels.* No country better exhibits the dilemma of a vanishing population than Japan. Life expectancy for Japanese born today has reached 107, but the country is losing a net of five hundred thousand per year from its current population of 125 million. It has the world's highest dependency ratio, meaning the number of old people each working-age person supports financially. Adult diapers now outsell those for babies, and Panasonic is making hospital beds that transform into wheelchairs. South Korea's fertility rate is even lower than Japan's: below one child per woman. The country has built high-tech new cities, such as Songdo near its main airport at Incheon, but there are few young people interested in moving there.

China is still the world's most populous nation with 1.4 billion people, but its population will peak and begin to decline this decade. Like Japan but with *ten times* the population, China is aging rapidly without enough children willing to care for the elderly. In 2020, China's social security fund payments began to exceed its inflows, and by 2040, China could have twice as many elderly people as children under the age of fifteen. Hence some call China the "world's largest nursing home."

Europe's future is also starting to look like an unplanned version of the one child policy. Europe's median age of forty-three is ten years above the world average, and its population is projected to shrink over the course of the 2020s *despite* immigration. From Ireland to Slovenia and Finland to Italy, almost every European nation faces the untenable combination of *rising* spending on pensions and elder care and a *shrinking* workforce. Spain and Italy, whose citizens enjoy longevity similar to the Japanese, have similarly low fertility. Italy's population has declined for the first time in a century and now stands at 55 million; 80 percent

---

* In total, half the world's population lives in countries falling within this so-called "fertility trap" of sub-replacement birth rates (anything less than two children per mother).

of Spanish towns have experienced population decline as people cluster into larger cities. By size and population, Italy and Spain are relatively large countries, yet many of their provinces are effectively vacant. Fellow Catholic countries Ireland and Poland also have birth rates below two and falling.

A declining population makes abstract economics suddenly seem worryingly finite. Who will pay taxes to fund hospitals and sanitation? Who will care for the elderly? Who will attend school? Who will go out to restaurants and shop in stores? Smaller (and poorer) populations mean less consumption and less investment (both domestic and foreign). As populations deflate, property values plummet. Demographic decline is worse than zero-sum: it's *negative-sum* as communities suffer irreversible decay. Companies tend to make tangible investments where they see the potential for rising consumption. In other words, where there are people.

## Come one, come all

In April 2020, Donald Trump signed an executive order to heavily restrict immigration, especially for Latinos and Asians. Ironically, at the same time, amid America's mounting coronavirus body count, US embassies and consulates all over the world were instructed to find doctors and nurses to be fast-tracked for immigration. Thirty percent of America's doctors and surgeons are immigrants, as well as nearly 25 percent of the overall healthcare sector. Tens of thousands of lives would easily have been saved if America's immigration policy were guided by supply and demand rather than ideology.

Similarly, over the past decade, British citizens have grown accustomed to hearing Brexiteer Nigel Farage pontificate on "the number one issue in British politics"—immigration—and how "we have lost control of our borders." Though Boris Johnson rode these slogans into Whitehall, it didn't take long for euphoria to give way to brute facts: a shortage of more than a hundred thousand doctors and nurses in the National Health System, and a record 4.5 million patients on waitlists for treatments—and that was before Covid-19 struck. By mid-2020, the government had changed its tune. Boris Johnson pledged to put "people before passports," and home secretary Priti Patel promised to fast-track visas for doctors, nurses, midwives, full-tuition paying students—basically anyone with a pulse and some skills or money.

The great irony of global migration today is therefore that countries with the largest labor shortages have had hostile anti-immigrant politics. But such populism is merely a blip compared with their overwhelming imbalance between old and young populations, and the labor shortages that need to be filled for social and economic life to function. Populism and the pandemic have hardened some borders, but they are also softening again to allow people with skills to circulate. Much as the world is in a transition from rapid population growth to decline, today's misguided immigration policies are giving way to an all-out war for talent.*

Make no mistake: Immigration *is* an economic stimulus. From Washington to London to Singapore, conservatives decry an overdependence on foreign labor. But immigrants actually raise output by allowing professionals to be more efficient. They also rent and buy homes, and their children earn more and contribute more to the tax base than the native-born themselves. America's economy is consumption-driven and dominated by activities such as retail, grocery, healthcare, and entertainment. The country's financial titans should therefore be rabidly pro-immigration, both for the supply of cheap workers it brings as well as to import a new generation of consumers. What strategy do those opposing migration have to revive growth, since restricting migration tends to do the exact opposite? At a time when America needs a massive infrastructural overhaul, imported labor will be essential to getting it done.

---

* The Global Talent Competitiveness Index ranks countries by their ability to attract skilled workers and retain them. Its top performers include Switzerland, Singapore, the US, Britain, Sweden, Australia, and Canada, with all the other top scorers being European.

It's also a mistake to believe that innovation-driven economies need only highly skilled migrants.[4] In fact, from construction and manufacturing to farming and nursing, entire industries would grind to a halt without low-skilled immigrants, while rising prices for many goods and services would drive inflation upward. Anti-immigration advocates argue that a government's first duty is to its own citizens, but who's the loser when hospitals are short-staffed? Rectifying America's haphazard immigration policy couldn't come soon enough given the need to care for the more than 10 million infected with Covid and the long-term effects that those who survive will suffer.

There's no fundamental tension between upskilling the unemployed while inviting in foreigners who add value. Domestic and foreign labor largely belong to different professions and rarely compete for jobs. Not enough Americans will pick fruit and cotton to replace Latinos, nor become nurses and nannies to replace Filipinos, nor substitute for all the Indian coders. Some of the fastest growing jobs categories, such as home health assistance, food preparation, sanitation services, and so forth, require little or no education but make life far more convenient for the rest of society, especially the elderly and the middle class.

Indeed, working Gen-X women in Western countries suffer the most of anyone when they have to care for the generations above and below them at the same time with little or no help. During the Covid lockdown, mothers were run ragged managing the kids' online schooling (to the extent there was any) alongside their jobs, while also checking in on their aging parents and managing the usual housekeeping. It doesn't help that the divorce rate has risen among Gen-X, meaning typically mothers have to manage childcare with even less support at home. Meanwhile, there is massive undersupply of affordable hospices, elderly care homes, and active adult communities, as well as child-minders and babysitters.

The "motherhood penalty" has returned with a vengeance in America, forcing rising numbers of women to drop out of the workforce. By contrast, women comprise a larger share of the corporate executive class in Hong Kong and Singapore, where middle-class households can afford maids, cooks, cleaners, and nannies. Being an exhausted "soccer mom"— or "rage mom" in the age of Covid—is a political choice, a malady for which migrant labor is a large part of the solution.

When America loses immigrants, it also loses the hundreds of billions of dollars in investment they are willing to make in the economy. More than one-quarter of the approximately $250 billion in foreign direct investment (FDI) the US received in 2019 went into real estate, with cash-rich migrants fast-tracked into green cards followed by citizenship. The US EB-5 and other schemes steer foreigners to buy properties in disadvantaged areas (such as "opportunity zones") or to lend to property developers so they can complete condos in which they have purchased an apartment. EB-5 has been popular across administrations, and not surprisingly was spared Trump's erratic immigration policy since his own sons actively promoted it to Chinese investors.[5]

Immigrants have fueled property markets such as Los Angeles, San Francisco, Seattle, Denver, Dallas, Houston, Miami, Atlanta, and Washington, DC, as well as sagging ones such as Akron, Indianapolis, Orlando, and Jacksonville. In these cities, immigrants have arrived just in time to buy homes, put kids in schools, and take over from white opioid addicts in local jobs. Tens of millions of Americans are not living up to the potential embodied in American ideals, while tens of millions of immigrants are doing much more to keep America great. America should be grateful when they come.

### Get them while they're young

Students are the most visible free agents in the war for talent. After the 9/11 terrorist attacks in 2001, Muslim (particularly Arab) students were targeted in America's immigration restrictions. Over the two decades since, many developing country elites' desire to study in America has diminished in lockstep with both the growing difficulty of doing so and competition from elsewhere. As of 2019, there were an estimated 5 million international students up for grabs. The US used to attract one-fifth of them, but geopolitical tensions with China and xenophobia toward Asians more broadly have taken their toll. Since the mid-2010s, Chinese students (representing up to a third of total foreign students in the US) began to return home in growing numbers, especially after they were forbidden from sensitive technical subjects and their access to the optional practical training (OPT) visa extension terminated. Similarly, the uncertainty over the H1-B visa program, which had mostly benefited Indian professionals, pushed away many Indian students as well. The losers, of course, are not Asian students but the American economy and universities—especially in California, which gets one-fifth of all foreign students coming to America.*

The rest of the Anglosphere wasted little time in capitalizing on Trump's xenophobia and botching of the coronavirus. The UK offered four-year residency visas to all Indian graduates, Canada deployed an all-digital student visa system, and Australia fast-tracked travel immunity for Asian students. The number of foreign students admitted to UK universities in 2020 doubled to more than forty thousand despite the country's similarly poor handling of Covid-19. Whatever happens in American politics, these other countries offer equally high-standard universities at much lower cost, and are safer countries with good job prospects for graduates as well. American universities themselves have wisely capitalized on students' uncertainty about traveling to the US by setting up world-class campuses abroad, such as Yale-NUS in Singapore and NYU Abu Dhabi in the UAE.

Every March and April I get antsy emails and phone calls from

---

* In the three years after 9/11, international student applications to the US dropped by 30 percent, and a decade later net enrollment of foreign students had fallen by 2.4 percent. Burton Bollag, "Foreign Enrollments at American Universities Drop for the First Time in 32 Years," *Chronicle*, November 10, 2004.

friends in London, Dubai, Hong Kong, and Singapore whose children have just been admitted to numerous fill-in-the-blank universities in America, Canada, Britain, and elsewhere. After debating the merits of the schools and countries, they thank me and go back to fretting about their kids' future. Over the past few years, I've noticed a more frequent leaning toward sending their children to Canada. While American college graduates remain unsure what to do with their degrees, Canadian universities such as Waterloo have blended apprenticeships into their curricula as a requirement for graduation.

In the war for talent, countries that offer the most hassle-free migration will get the edge—and make no mistake what they mean by talent: *youth*. Points-based immigration systems universally favor young people. For Canada, applicants aged eighteen to thirty-five get twelve points toward their total score; those above forty-five get only two points. Talent migration is ageist and Gen-X might as well not apply. Millennials and Gen-Z, however, should pack their bags.

Grabbing students has an uplifting effect on the economy because the frugal college kids of today are likely to become the entrepreneurs of tomorrow. That's why foreign students should be given green cards alongside their diplomas. If they remain where they studied, they'll revitalize university towns, and when they move, they'll turn rust-belt towns into hubs for digitized industrial design and advanced manufacturing. Only one-third of America's immigrants have bachelor's or master's degrees; that could easily be doubled if policies were aligned with the demands of the country's high-tech industry. If America doesn't take global talent, the rest of the world is happy to—and increasingly will get them first.

Old truisms die hard: Whereas once it could plausibly be claimed that America received the lion's share of the world's best and brightest, today that's little more than a cliché. While this is a golden age for English as a universal language, there's an ever growing roster of countries where one can get a quality English language degree without the side order of Anglo-American populism. Germany, the Netherlands, Sweden, Japan, and other countries have switched many programs to English precisely so that they can directly compete with the US, Britain, Canada, and Australia.

As in America, European leaders speak of seeking only skilled migrants, using points-based systems to favor people with good education, work experience, and financial independence. But much like America's misalignment of its visa policies, top European universities such as ETH-Z in Zurich spend millions per year on scholarships for Asian students only to give them a mere three months to find a job before their visas are terminated. Instead, European governments should give them at least three *years* during which they'll surely make positive contributions. Doling out European blue cards en masse to boost investment is a better plan than spending taxpayer money on talent and then tossing it out. Whichever countries untangle their contradictory immigration policies first will get the edge in the war for young talent.

## Winning Young Hearts and Minds

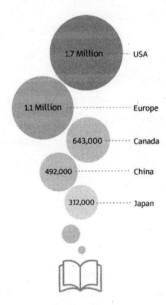

Each year nearly 5 million students go overseas for study. Europe has the largest number of cross-border students, while the US traditionally receives the largest number of Asians. Canada is now actively competing with America for foreign students, while Japan is expanding its English-language programs to capture more Asians.

# Women make their move

After Iceland's economic nosedive in the financial crisis, an almost all-female cabinet took over to clean up the mess. Finland's prime minister Sanna Marin entered office in 2019 at age thirty-four, at which point four of the country's five major parties were run by women in their thirties. Europe is the only region of the world where parity for women has been both legislated and effectively achieved. European women are empowered to follow their hearts or follow the money—which often means leaving Europe despite its comforts. Profiles of twenty-something au pairs from almost every European country seeking placements in Asia overflow on websites. Worldwide, women are getting better educated and having fewer children, making them among the most eagerly mobile of global youth. But sadly, most of the world's forced migrants are women from Asian and Arab countries. Recruited as household workers, they're exploited and underpaid (if at all), trafficked as prostitutes, bonded domestic laborers, dancing girls, or other forms of servitude.

Ever more of the world's migrant pool may be comprised of Chinese and Indian women. After decades of gender selection and female infanticide, both countries have massive male surpluses competing for fewer women. In India this means rampant sexual violence and bonded labor; in China, women have been encouraged to take multiple husbands. No wonder many go abroad as soon as possible. At the same time, though, Chinese women make up 20 percent of VC partners in China (versus only 8 percent in Silicon Valley). Such high-earning East Asian professional women (whether unmarried or divorced) have been big spenders in the property markets of New York, Singapore, Hong Kong, London, and Vancouver. In India, 44 percent of STEM graduates are women, higher than in the US (34 percent) and other Western countries. A female Indian IT professional is surely the least physically threatening immigrant a country could wish for.

They may soon be joined by Saudi women making their first forays abroad after generations of suppression. As of 2015, more Saudi women are enrolled in the country's universities than men. Now they can also get passports without the permission of their husbands. From Dubai and Beirut to London and Paris, Saudi women will increasingly feature in the professional landscape as well. The more women are able to work, the more independent they will become, the fewer children they will have, and the more qualified and willing they will be to migrate abroad.

## The real migration problem: emigration

"Are we a country facing extinction? Unfortunately, yes. A country that doesn't create children is destined to die." Few Italian leaders have garnered as many headlines as Matteo Salvini, leader of the country's Northern League party who briefly served as deputy prime minister. Salvini fancies himself a charismatic Gen-X political icon. His stump speeches, shirtless rallies, and selfie sessions last for hours. He even DJs.

When it comes to fertility policy, however, his record is lighter than the country's signature white truffle flakes. Even though he pushed for the creation of a "family ministry" to support women having more children, the number of professional Italians—men and women—leaving the country has risen every year since 1980. Countries that get their demographic house in order could benefit from lean populations if it means higher wages and empowered women, but today not a single country in southern Europe fits that description.

Immigration has been a lightning rod issue in European politics for over a decade, but someone forgot to tell the region's populists that the far greater existential threat they face is *emigration*. Europe is half the size of America, with twice the population, yet so much of it feels vacant—because it has been *vacated*. Between low fertility and emigration, no region of the world is shrinking more rapidly than Eastern Europe. Since

Romania joined the EU in 2007, an estimated one-quarter of the country's population (about 5 million people) have headed west and never returned. Experts make obvious suggestions to countries such as this: improve infrastructure, offer more childcare, invest in education—but little is done. Such reforms probably wouldn't be enough to keep young Bulgarians from leaving to study or work abroad, which is why (alongside a high death rate and low birth rate) Bulgaria is the most rapidly depopulating country in the world. A razor-sharp fence currently inhibits easy crossing of the 270-kilometer-long border between Bulgaria and Turkey, but soon enough there won't be anyone left to police it.

There is no end in sight to the brain drain of southern and eastern Europe—and that's before Balkan countries such as Serbia, Bosnia, and Albania eventually achieve EU membership, which will likely accelerate emigration even further. These emigrants also have no plans to return, since they also rightly believe that their children will have better economic opportunities elsewhere. And once their parents back home pass away, their remittances will stop as well, severely crippling these already shaky economies. Clearly, we are as much creatures of economic necessity as tribal identity.

For much of history, place—one place—has been the source of identity and stability. But growing up in societies offering few jobs while excelling at incompetence and corruption, youth have to take matters into their own hands. Surveys suggest they hold the privilege of mobility to be more important than the right to vote. Mobility is a higher virtue than belonging—especially if your country's leaders espouse archaic social attitudes. This is why studying migration is more useful than indulging in today's populism. Young people's response to political turmoil and economic malaise is not to "tough it out." They have no interest in clinging to the mast of a sinking ship when they can swim to sturdier ground. Following youth thus illustrates that nationalism and migration are not antithetical at all: Nationalism does a superb job of driving people *away* from the states of which they're supposed to be proud.

Geographers and anthropologists alike urge us to overcome the "territorial trap" of conflating identity with nationality. Appreciating the far-reaching yearning for mobility is a good place to start. For most people, migration—not nationalism—is liberation.

## America: land of emigrants?

History's biggest winner in the war for talent is, of course, the US. Its greatness derives as much from immigrants as natives—less than a quarter of whom are actually descended from the original English settlers, meaning most "natives" have immigrant roots as well. Nearly 40 percent of America's scientists, one-third of its doctors and surgeons, half of Silicon Valley's tech company founders, and more than two-thirds of its tech employees, are foreign-born, mostly from China and India. These migrants are a reminder that an America of only "Americans" would be nothing like America with non-Americans who have become Americans.

But even as America continues to receive a large number of immigrants annually, it has also become a growing source of *emigrants*. Since the 2008 financial crisis, the number of American expats has *doubled* to more than 9 million. Frugal retirees have moved to Mexico or the Caribbean, while thousands of the well-heeled have moved abroad with their money and given up their citizenship to avoid US global taxation. Gen-Xers and millennials have planted roots in Canada or Europe to escape political dysfunction or in Asia for higher expat salaries and entrepreneurial dynamism; Gen-Zers have fanned out abroad as English teachers or just to avoid crushing student debt. All have left their countrymen behind to deal with polarized politics, obscene inequality, crumbling infrastructure, and culture wars.

Could the combination of economic recession and unemployment, fractured politics and ethnic xenophobia, turn the tables on history's greatest immigration story? Geneticist and former *National Geographic* explorer-in-residence Spencer Wells forecast that future demographic historians would look back at 2020 as the year America's population peaked at roughly 330 million. America in the 2020s could be like Ireland in the 1850s—at least when it comes to attracting the best and the brightest. Unlike previous generations for whom America represented the pinnacle of migrant achievement, today America has to compete for talent in a global marketplace—and even to keep Americans at home.

## Nationalism heads to the grave

For centuries, nationalism has promised political liberation and a secure homeland. Who could argue against such a proud tradition of secular and civic state building? In fact, there are still tens of millions of stateless people fighting for nationhood, whether Palestinians or Kurds. For them, nationalism remains an existential mission. If we stick to nationalism as applied to these causes, it is a worthy ideology indeed.

Yet recent years have also witnessed pundits proclaiming the rise of a "new nationalism" that combines patriotic pride with prejudice against others. From America to Turkey to India and China, ethnochauvinists have seized upon the slogan to scapegoat minorities and foreigners. Governments that have done little to upgrade industries and infrastructure naturally find it easier to blame immigrants and China for their failures.

The new nationalism, then, is all about deflecting hard truths without creating a workable plan for the future. It used to be that only the postcolonial societies of Africa, the Middle East, and Asia would blame colonialism and capitalism for their woes. But in an ironic twist, many postcolonial countries have given up on such futile self-pity and are now busy bootstrapping their way into modernity. For the most part, Asians are justifiably patriotic, as they have rapidly cut poverty and grown their economies. But their nationalism reinforces a desire to catch up to and supersede the West, not to punish it. One wonders how different American or British "nationalism" would look if those two governments had spent what Japan or South Korea do on worker retraining, affordable housing, and high-quality infrastructure.

Especially in America and Britain, the new nationalists have also drawn battle lines between themselves and globalists, who believe that global markets are beneficial and global coordination is essential to confront planetary challenges. Once again, the real divide is actually *within*: urban versus rural, wealthy versus underclass, and young versus old. Urban youth strongly voted against Trump in the US and Brexit in the UK. Neither Brexit nor Trump therefore presents compelling evidence of a durable new nationalism, though both reveal the fragility of consensual democracy in countries so divided by geography and generations.

This is a reminder that the new nationalists (especially in the West) cater largely to an older generation, with one foot in the grave—and will follow them into it. They represent the last hurrah of a white overclass that managed to masquerade its identity politics as the national interest. The Pakistani novelist Mohsin Hamid poignantly captures this seductive nostalgia:"We are told not only that movement through geographies can be stopped but also movement through time can be too, that we can return to the past, to a better past, when our country, our race, our religion were truly great. All we must accept is division. The division of humanity into natives and migrants."[6] But the only certainty in this thesis is that its advocates will soon be dead. Elderly xenophobes are headed for what Hamid terms the "big Brexit in the sky."

By contrast, today's youth can hardly be considered chest-thumping nationalists. According to the US Election Survey, only 45 percent of American millennials even consider their national identity important (versus 70 percent of boomers and 60 percent of Gen-Xers). Furthermore, half of American millennials believe the US is no greater than any other nation, a significant drop from the 75 percent of boomers who view America as exceptional. (PragerU's vacuous five-minute video titled *Why You Should Be a Nationalist* has fewer than 4 million views.) In previous generations (or centuries), one might have assumed that ungrateful youth would eventually mature into nationalist attitudes, but today's young have far better access to information and can judge for themselves whether their nation is actually deserving of gloating self-praise.

Just as important is the fact that today's young populations hold demonstrably pro-globalist attitudes. In a survey covering twenty Western nations, an overwhelming 77 percent of respondents aged eighteen to twenty-four felt that "globalization is a force for good" versus only 11 percent taking a negative view.[7] The more youth move and mingle, the more globalism is entrenched and nationalism recedes. The work of scholars such as Ronald Inglehart and Jonathan Haidt suggests that educated youth carry globalist traits and society's values evolve with them. Maybe the difference between a globalist and a nationalist then is that the former accepts reality and the latter does not.

Youth are also wise to believe that populist politics are a bigger threat to national stability than immigration is. As with nationalism, populism is much more a political movement to exploit grievance than a platform to actually address it. The history of populism is a lengthy roster of regimes skilled at rallying voters behind alarmist rhetoric and calls for drastic reforms—but achieving next to nothing. From Latin American socialists to Arab Islamists, populists have never failed to fail. The worst Covid-19 infection rates were in countries with populist nationalist regimes such as the US, UK, India, and Brazil.

Poland and Hungary have most frequently been held up as harbingers of a pan-European populist wave. In Poland, the right-wing, anti-immigrant Law and Order Party barely clings to power after being clearly rejected by the country's youth in the July 2020 election. Hungary's Victor Orban, icon of Europe's illiberal strongmen, made anti-immigration a pillar of his agenda (not that migrants actually wanted to stay in Hungary with Germany so close). But predictably, once worker shortages meant that ordinary Hungarians had to work overtime and weekend shifts (without pay), public rallies quickly turned against him. Meanwhile, young, green, and technocratic liberals have swept the mayoral elections in Warsaw, Budapest, Prague, and Bratislava. In small countries, there's only one job bigger than being mayor of the capital—so we won't be referring to their countries as nationalist strongmen regimes much longer.

The megaphones utilized by populists are their own undoing. Whether on the left or the right, those who gain the spotlight by preaching populist messages make clear on a daily basis where the buck stops. High on emotion and low on substance, they claim to represent a backlash against "business as usual," yet quickly invite a backlash against themselves. In Italy, the grassroots Sardines movement, for example, has been credited with taking the wind out of Matteo Salvini's sails with a message that *they*—ordinary, centrist, working-class—are the people, not the bombastic fringe.[8] Instead of wannabe DJ drop-outs, Italy's most recent prime ministers have been the academic lawyer Giuseppe Conte followed by central banker Mario Draghi. Similarly, after a decade of playing "Grexit" chicken with Brussels, the music has stopped on Greece's merry-go-round of populist parties. (The neo-Nazi Golden Dawn party also disappeared, exposed for murderous thuggery, its true vocation.) In their place, the New Democracy Party is focused on what a government should do: encourage investment and create jobs. Technocrats may be less sentimental, but populists' incompetence guarantees a short political lifespan. And remember that in the largest and most important European states—Germany and France—technocratic pragmatism prevails. Angela Merkel, Europe's elder stateswoman, used the seventy-fifth anniversary of the end of World War II to denounce the very idea of "the nation-state alone."

Europe—the birthplace of the ethnically defined nation-state—is also where nation-states are being most rapidly diluted through demographic decline, migration, intermarriage, and legal changes to citizenship rights. Europeans once divided themselves violently by nationality;

now they have a generation of "Erasmus babies" born of Gen-X parents who met during cross-border exchange programs—the first generation of post-national Europeans. Furthermore, both the number of migrants into Europe and the diversity of where they come from are growing. No matter what you hear from far right political parties today, supply and demand remains a far more powerful force than any populist movement in history. If there is a deep and irreconcilable tension between eth-nonationalism and immigration as economic necessity, *not a single Western country* ultimately lands in the former category.

There is an extreme scenario in which demographic expansion goes further than societies can politically and culturally manage. By that point, however, turning back the demographic clock won't be possible; the choice will be between building an inclusive new national identity or civil war. An older generation may well cling to their nostalgic notions, but that's a luxury today's youth and future generations can't afford.

America has never been more ethnically diverse than today. In fact, the only counties in America that have become *less* diverse are those that were already mostly Hispanic populated and have become even more so, such as around Miami or along the Mexican border of Texas. Year after year, the US, UK, Canada, and Germany rank as the world's top immigrant destinations. This is both a reminder that populism is fated to fail but also a warning that it's here to stay, since the presence of migrants gives populists something to rail against. But the fact that populists remain sufficiently obstinate in democratic politics to prevent political progress is precisely why more and more people—particularly the young—want to have an escape hatch. If their countries tilt too far toward political extremism in either direction, they'll rush for the exits.

Young people choose destinations not based on exclusive identity but rather, as nation branding expert Simon Anholt explains, whether a country is admired or scorned. Not surprisingly, there is an inverse correlation between those countries most chauvinistic about their identity and the admiration they command worldwide. A hypothetical world in which each person could choose only one citizenship would be deeply embarrassing for the nationalist leaders in Turkey, Russia, and Brazil, given how keen their youth are to abandon ship.

This is what makes the currently vogue notion of "civilizational states" bent on ethnocentric imperialism little more than a pseudointellectual abstraction. In reality, their underlying demographics often point to dilution rather than purification. Russia and Turkey are most conservatives' poster children for civilizational revanchism. But Russia has a *growing* population of Muslims and Turkic minorities from former Soviet republics, while ethnic Russians have the highest death rate. As much as Putin would hate to admit it, he can't rebuild the Soviet Union without accepting the Soviet Union's vast ethnic diversity from Baltic to Asiatic peoples. For its part, Turkey has *more* Kurdish citizens and Arab migrants than ever. If Erdogan genuinely wants to resurrect the Ottoman empire, he'll also need to do so demographically, for the Ottomans presided over a dizzying array of ethnicities and faiths, from the Balkans to Iraq to Egypt. As with Russia, minorities are scapegoated in bad economic times, but long-term success hinges on turning them into assets.

History rewards empires who forge shared identity and punishes civilizations who put themselves above the rest. Throughout history, successful empires, such as the Romans and Mongols, have been built on diversity and inclusion rather than singular ethnic dominance. A "civilizational state" in demographic decline will in due course not amount to much of either a civilization or a state.

Strongmen pursuing an agenda of civilizational pride may want to reset the clock to a time when there was a coherent national identity, but younger generations have no idea what that looks like other than in grandparents' photo albums. Inevitably, each generation is ever less anchored in a single dominant tribe. The nation doesn't make people; people make the nation.

## Diversity with harmony?

All of this applies in spades to the world's most ethnically diverse large country: India. Its present leader, Narendra Modi, is a majoritarian populist who speaks of a "New India" that is Hindu-centric rather than secular.* The 2019 Citizenship Amendment Act (CAA) denied millions of Muslim migrants from Bangladesh the right to citizenship, while the National Registry of Citizens (NRC) turns Muslims without formal birth certificates into second-class *noncitizens*. But for all Modi's assaults on Muslim freedoms, India remains on track to have the largest Muslim population of any country in the world (more than Indonesia or Pakistan) within the next two decades. Indian Muslims are moving to more Muslim-populated areas, including villages—but they're not leaving India. A dozen Indian states have declared they won't back the CAA, making them potential magnet destinations for Muslims. Meanwhile, the electorate is more interested in economic reforms than cultural tutelage. Indian youth rallied behind Modi for his infrastructure investments, focus on job creation, non-dynastic background, and bootstrapping swagger, but now many have turned on him just as quickly for his economic follies and divisive chauvinism. They don't need their identity prescribed to them. India's masses of disgruntled farmers were similarly unfazed when Modi labeled their protests "anti-national." Modi will learn that if he overplays his hand, he could perversely accelerate the very fracturing he set out to reverse.

China also has several dozen ethnic minorities, but neither they nor foreigners taken together represent more than a tiny percentage of China's 1.4 billion mostly Han population. Han nationalists are nonetheless bent on denying the prominent role that Mongols, Manchus, Sui,

---

* This has already impacted regional migrations: Those Hindus who remained in Pakistan after Partition have been returning to India in record numbers—doubling every year to more than twelve thousand in 2018.

and other ethnicities have played in China's historical success and the genetic diversity embedded in the society's fabric. The ongoing pogroms to cleanse Tibetans, Uighurs, and Mongolians of their identities will lead many more to flee to India, Kazakhstan, and Mongolia respectively. China is an empire, but historically a more multi-civilizational one than its current leaders are willing to acknowledge.

## Conscription: The test of nationalism

When I finished high school in Germany, all my (male) friends were required to report to the *Bundeswehr* for military service, with a minority opting instead for *Zivildienst* (civil service). Skipping out on military service was unthinkable. Only a very good medical excuse—or serious claim to be a conscientious objector (*Wehrdienstverweiger*)—could secure exemption and a route to civil service instead. Based on letters I received, it seems both military and civil service were equally monotonous. After all, it was the mid-1990s and Western Europe was enjoying the post–Cold War peace. Pressure had been steadily mounting to reduce the term of military service from eighteen months to one year or less. By 2011, the inertia—and the lacuna—could no longer hold. Germany switched to an all-volunteer army, making it (as in America) a career choice, often a very temporary one. In 2018, Germany's CDU party floated the idea of bringing back military service to compensate for plummeting troop numbers, mostly as a gesture pandering to the far right that supported the move. It was ridiculed by everyone else.

Attitudes toward conscription present the most damning picture of the so-called "return of nationalism." Perhaps no issue more clearly embodies the gaping generational divide across many societies—both East and West—than the duty to protect one's country. Bertrand Russell defined patriotism as the "willingness to kill and be killed for trivial reasons." By that measure, today's youth are the most unpatriotic generation in history.

Across Europe, youth have rejected any whiff of government imposition in their sacred post-adolescent lives. Conscription has been abolished or the time commitment heavily reduced. Even Switzerland—of which it was famously said: "Switzerland does not have an army; it *is* an army"—has rapidly declining rates of military participation. For the older Swiss generation, bonds formed during military service translated into lucrative jobs in the banking industry. But with youth today more interested in entrepreneurship and civic pursuits, suddenly national service appears a waste of time. Individual opportunism trumps collective commitment.

Americans are no more patriotic than any other nation when it comes to taking up the burden of military service. The US returned to an all-volunteer army after the Vietnam War, and today less than one-third of Americans under the age of thirty have a relative serving in the military.* All-volunteer armies represent a sea change from military service as a patriotic duty and rite of passage. According to a 2018 survey by the RAND Corporation, occupational motivations (meaning needing the military as an employer) far outweigh institutional motivations (the value of military service) in the US. Enlistees are primarily interested in getting out of an unhealthy environment and gaining financial and educational benefits, whereas serving one's country tends to motivate primarily those who have a family history of military service. Two decades after the 9/11 terrorist attacks, the trauma suffered by Iraq and Afghanistan war veterans has discouraged would-be recruits across the board. These "forever wars" have fared so badly that youth today will do anything to avoid being sent to die in wars they don't believe in.

---

* Veterans, including those who have served over the past twenty years in Iraq and Afghanistan, constitute their own social class of families, settled perhaps not far from the bases they served at, their families dependent on social services and welfare provided by military benefits.

Even if they wanted to, much of the American public isn't fit to fight. Seventy-one percent of Americans are ineligible for military duty due to health issues (such as obesity), criminal records, or insufficient education. A series of US Army reports from the 2010s carried ominous titles such as *Too Fat to Fight*—followed by *Still Too Fat to Fight*—warning (repeatedly, it seems) of the threat obesity poses to American national security. (You can't make this stuff up.) If time spent on social media and gaming constitutes preparation for a career in cyber warfare, however, then the army of the future has plenty of recruits to tap. This is perhaps why it began actively using TikTok to recruit more Gen-Z volunteers (until TikTok fell out of favor). In early 2020, rumors that the army wanted to reinstate the draft led to the Selective Service website crashing as fearful youth nervously Googled it. The call to fight is one today's American youth are not going to answer.

Russia would seem an obvious case of a nationalistic country for which a strong army of loyal soldiers is vital to ensuring its stature. But Russia too slashed its mandatory conscription, from two years to one, in 2008, and one of the only pledges that has maintained Putin's standing among youth is his promise to abolish conscription entirely as soon as Russia can afford to replace it with a professional army. As of 2016, only 260,000 new draftees enter the Russian army each year, versus nearly 400,000 contract soldiers—effectively domestic mercenaries of all ages looking for a job, whether maintaining military installations across the country or occupying foreign ones. As in America, Russian youth enter the military profession mostly if they need the money.

Even in tougher neighborhoods such as the Middle East and Asia, youth have no appetite for military service. For example, Turkey and South Korea are both patriotic societies facing genuine strategic risks. As in Europe, public pressure in Turkey has already led to military service being reduced, from one year to six months. But even that's too much to ask. As of August 2018, the Turkish government allowed young men to buy their way out of the six-month service and do just three weeks by paying 5,000 lira (about $900). Within the first two weeks of the registration portal going online, 340,000 Turkish men had applied for the exemption. That year, an additional 180,000 men failed to report for military service. Saving up to bail out of national service has become the most significant savings priority for any Turkish teenage male. It's that or get sent to Syria. In 2020, Turkey signed an agreement offering citizenship to Pakistanis who would serve in its military as they have for Saudi Arabia in Yemen.

The situation is similar in South Korea, where 83 percent of men say they would dodge conscription if they could. Poor retention has shrunk the army to just eighty thousand. Older South Koreans are prone to viewing North Korea as an existential threat, while the younger generation supports President Moon's agenda of reunification. Indeed, one of the government's motivations in opening North Korea is to create jobs for legions of unemployed young South Korean males who would be sent to North Korea not as soldiers but nation builders. Seoul has recently dabbled in trying to recruit more women—something men also strongly support, as revenge for the country's strong #MeToo movement. Given their low fertility rate and trending #NoMarriage meme, women can't use family life as an excuse. The same is true in Japan, where the fertility rate is so low that the Self-Defense Forces have tried appealing to women, to little avail.

How about China? Chinese youth are constantly exposed to nationalistic dogma, but overall they're far more materialistic than militaristic. They know China may have to fight America to expel it from their neighborhood, but wouldn't want such a conflict to disrupt their comfortable existence. After the Tiananmen Square massacre, China expanded its one-year military service program in the name of building nationalism. But soon after, it was reduced to two weeks of lectures and fitness training at the beginning of the first year of university.

Why have militaries at all? Countries such as Mexico are weighing disbanding their armies, replacing militaries with stronger national guards focused on fighting drugs and crime—and controlling migrants. Washington compelled Mexico to deploy more robust forces to block Central Americans from reaching the Rio Grande, resulting in hundreds of thousands more Guatemalans and Hondurans staying within Mexico's borders. Officially, the country has less than 2 million foreign-born residents; the unofficial figure is twice that. Brazil, too, faces no international military threat; its largest military deployments have been to protect the Amazon. Meanwhile, Kenya and Ethiopia are marshaling their air forces to combat swarms of billions of locusts rather than each other. Across the world, militaries played a crucial role in combating the coronavirus as warships became hospitals and armies erected medical tents.

America's military also needs to refocus on existential *domestic* missions. As ever more bases, from Florida to Nebraska to Alaska, are threatened by floods, hurricanes, and wildfires, the armed forces are spending more time and money simply keeping themselves operational.[9] After an embarrassingly and deadly year of Covid-19 mismanagement, it was the capable and disciplined Defense Department that accelerated Operation Warp Speed in support of vaccine manufacturing and deployment. Perhaps nationalism should be redefined as recognizing that we are often our own worst enemies and doing something about it.

Most countries can and should have a one-year national service requirement for both men and women, to take care of urgent contributions to social cohesion and civic culture such as elder care, migrant assimilation, and helping unfit people get into shape. Bill Clinton made national service a centerpiece of his presidential campaign in 1992. Thirty years later, America still has no such mandatory program. Teach for America is both competitive and respected, but it's also small and underfunded. There are countless ways to blend patriotism with pragmatism. Societies with national service have more solidarity—and without that, nationalism ultimately means nothing.

# What about religion?

If nationalism is overstated as an animus today, then so too is religion. Religious identity is by definition stateless. Christians and Muslims can be considered the largest communities in the world with an estimated 2.2 billion Christians and 1.8 billion Muslims spread across the planet. In practice, however, most Christians and Muslims (or adherents of any other faith) identify as or more strongly—or weakly—with their nation as with their religion.* What nationalism and religion hold in common is that for most people they are spectator sports—and most people actually devote far more time to actual sports (whether playing or spectating). This helps explain why ever more young Arabs have taken refuge in Malaysia and Indonesia, where they can be practicing Muslims without the oppressive politics.

It has been demonstrated time and time again how weak religion is as a geopolitical agent. The most obvious example is the plight of the Palestinians, who despite all rhetoric evoke far more sympathy than action from their fellow Arab Muslims. Their feeble response to Jewish territorialism has had grave consequences for Palestinians, with both Muslims and Christians seeking refuge abroad. And as Israel annexes the Jordan Valley while explicitly denying its residents Israeli citizenship, ever more Palestinians will move to Jordan itself, already home to more than 2 million of their refugee diaspora. Nor have Muslim states made anything other than perfunctory statements of concern about China's internment of Muslim Uighurs in Xinjiang. In fact, in 2019 many signed a declaration supporting China's tough stance against the risks of religious extremism—something they fear as much as China does.

---

* This is in itself evidence that identities are multiple and overlapping. It's ironic, then, that nationalists accuse many ordinary religious people of being extremists when they are in fact most familiar with the challenge of holding manifold identities. It's nationalists who are the extremists, prisoners of the simple-minded mentality of a singular identity.

Religious majoritarianism is a very useful tool to mask what are more secular and territorial agendas. Religious persecution has driven large numbers of Christians out of India and China as well, eliminating what is much more a political than a spiritual nuisance. More than 1.1 million Muslim Rohingya have been expelled from Myanmar and live precariously as refugees in Bangladesh. There and in Sri Lanka, militant regimes have persecuted ethnic and religious minorities not because their faith poses a threat but because of the land and resources on which they sit.

The coronavirus pandemic also forced religion to take a backseat to secular priorities. From South Korean churches to mosques in Pakistan to temples in Israel, religious sites were superspreaders of disease. Saudi Arabia was even forced to close Mecca to Muslim pilgrims. Buddhists view the pandemic as one of several varieties of scourge including poverty, war, greed, and drought. In the face of the apocalypse, will people return to religion, praying that each season doesn't bring even greater calamity? Some certainly might, and it will surely make the news. Most people, however, will save themselves in a more tried and tested way: They'll move.

# CHAPTER 3
# GENERATION MOVE

## *The first global generation*

Exactly twenty-five years ago I was a card-carrying intern in the United Nations Youth Unit—and the only actual youth on the team. Most of the unit's budget was spent on convening and training young activists to lobby their governments to include their views when making social policy. Those millennials have gone on to become progressive mayors and ministers, "cause-mopolitans" running social justice groups, managers at multilateral humanitarian organizations, and corporate "intra-praneurs" advancing stakeholder engagement, sustainable supply chains, and impact investment funds. So many youth want these jobs that business, law, and policy schools have undergone massive curricular upgrades to cope with the demand.

One unshakable observation I recall from those youth-focused internships in the 1990s was that even though each delegate was focused on national change at home, their camaraderie was generational. The same is true of political identity: It is now more generational than national. As Karl Mannheim explained in the 1920s, generations are not just biological but also sociological: shared experiences shape their psychology.[1] But only in the past thirty years have truly global events served as generational milestones: the collapse of the Soviet Union in 1991, the 9/11 terrorist attacks in 2001, the financial crisis of 2008, and the coronavirus pandemic of 2020. During this same time frame, migration exploded, mobile phones and the Internet reached universal scale, and climate change became an existential planetary threat. The late sociologist Ulrich Beck was correct that technology has enabled self-awareness beyond geography and class. The 1968 student demonstrations were neither as global nor as inclusive as today's #MeToo, climate action, and racial equity movements.

In fact, today's youth hold common views across geography far more than they do with older people *in their own countries.* We tend to think of nations as having a common mindset, but millennials and Gen-Z share values on a global scale—especially the right to connectivity, mobility, and sustainability.[2] For no previous generation could we so confidently pinpoint these or other common traits as we can for *billions* of young people today. The great divide in the world is therefore not East versus West or North versus South but *young versus old.*

I have great sympathy for the youth predicament. Over the past twenty years, I've queried countless entrepreneurs and activists, students and professors, politicians and journalists, fixers and translators about what life is like for the young in their countries. During the past two years of research and workshops, I've had the chance to speak with hundreds of young professionals in small group discussions. What I found is that almost nothing looks the same through their eyes: geopolitical rivalry (irrelevant), financial capitalism (hate it), electoral democracy (nonessential), home ownership (a drag), marriage (later, if ever), or even a college education (too expensive).

## The best form of government . . . ?

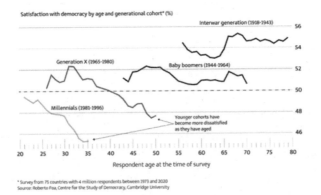

Younger generations have been increasingly disillusioned with democracy; millennial respondents exhibited the lowest level of satisfaction with their government.

In all these sessions, the one question they always ask me is: What is the one skill most essential for their success? More than ever, my answer is: Whatever skill you have, make sure it's portable. Be ready to move. I suppose I might know a thing or two about moving. On average, I've moved every three to four years of my life. My family moved around regularly even when we didn't have a powerful passport (Indian). Every move I've made since my teenage years, between the US, Europe, and Asia, has reinforced the intellectual and professional benefits of shifting geographies.

We underestimate people's willingness to leave their home country, perhaps out of some unconscious bias that others may be as comfortable in their homes as we are in ours. It's true that, historically, people have tended to settle near their national tribe; even many who ventured abroad returned to care for elderly parents or to start a family. Overseas Chinese, for example, speak of such "cultural recognition" or "searching for my roots" that lures them back home. But youth who don't have children don't need to go "home" to raise them a particular way, nor do they need their parents to help out. In any case, today's grandparents don't expect their children to return, so they're moving into professional care centers and can't be full-time babysitters. Perhaps most of all, today's world is full of places where youth can co-create their social milieu rather than submitting to a predefined culture.

Even across countries with very different standards of living, youth face similar economic challenges. For example, American wages have stagnated since the 1990s while home prices have doubled, healthcare costs have risen by 280 percent, and college tuition by 500 percent. American millennials and Gen-Zers owe about $1.5 trillion in student debt and even more in credit card debt. A 2019 Federal Reserve report states that millennials "are less well off than members of earlier generations when they were young, with lower earnings, fewer assets, and less wealth."[3] Despite its military might, deep financial markets, innovative talent, and entrepreneurial dynamism, America is also a nation of listless youth with low savings and weak confidence in the future.

By contrast, Chinese youth are far better off than even their parents could ever have imagined. The 1980s reforms of Deng Xiaoping rapidly elevated China into the factory floor of the world and the fastest growing economy, achieving the most extensive mass poverty alleviation in history, with the bottom 50 percent seeing their incomes quadruple. Yet overall they share the same daily concerns over the lack of quality jobs and rising living costs as Americans.[4] The only affordable homes in Beijing are outside the city's fifth ring, and a thirty-year mortgage takes a whole extended family to pay off. Chinese loan sharks have also exploited a cash-strapped generation, plunging millions into debt as they borrow from one digital lender to pay off the others.

For the young, urban, and skilled, China remains a land of opportunity. Educated and childless millennials can spend their money anywhere here; their vast domain is (like America) one enormous domestic market. They bounce from job to job among China's megacompanies or startups without hesitation. But they're also willing to decamp from first-tier cities if need be. China has so many growing cities that youth arrivals turn second-tier cities into the next first-tier cities. Changsha, Kunming, and Chongqing are becoming like Austin, Pittsburgh, and Atlanta—except more than ten times bigger. Chinese youth prize the national stability that enables this physical and professional mobility. That's why, according to Oxford historian Rana Mitter, many of them have been drawn to Maoism—millennial socialism with Chinese characteristics.

Millennials worldwide also report being overworked by the grind of the gigonomy. Journalist Malcom Harris describes this young American *precariat* as "buzzing clouds of freelance servants, always in motion."[5] Many are bowing out and starting over at a slower pace somewhere else. Those that are unemployed have even less to lose by moving to cheaper places. Similarly, China's iconic mogul Jack Ma has glorified working "9 9 6"—meaning 9 a.m. to 9 p.m., six days per week—while millions in China's "ant tribe" can't find good jobs to match their education, so they eke out a minimum wage existence on the margins of city life. Even in Japan, where century-old companies have long dominated the rigid labor market, 35 percent of youth are now temps farmed out part-time so that big firms can pare down overhead costs. Korea's "dirt spoon" youth (as opposed to wealthier "golden spoon") have suffered rising inequality despite promises of greater social mobility. No wonder Bong Joon Ho, director of the Oscar-winning film *Parasite*, has said, "Korea seems glamorous, but the young are in despair."[6]

Sluggish economies, corporate downsizing, and automation have resulted in self-employment becoming the norm for Gen-Z. A career is nothing more than an assemblage of gigs and fees, whether delivering food or running errands for rich people. From San Francisco to Jakarta, "wealth work" apps pair people who are money rich and time poor with those who are money poor and time rich. Being a gigonomist becomes tedious after a decade, but that doesn't mean full-time work will offer itself to everyone. No wonder youth blogs repeat the worn phrase "The only certainties in life are uncertainty and death."

Most American youth have yet to start saving meaningfully for retirement—but they will have to move to more affordable places in order to ever retire at all. Many millennials who are earning decently and saving aggressively are moving out of expensive states such as California to cheaper ones such as Oregon or Arizona. Being mobile—and having few possessions and no children—is the surest way to stretch one's savings.[7] For Gen-Z, stability is even more elusive. Even before Covid, they were fated to lag behind millennials and Gen-X in net worth and housing assets. The coronavirus has made their situation unfathomably worse. No wonder so many Gen-Zers have sought psychological counseling or turned to drug abuse. When I asked a friend where he thinks his Gen-Z kids would be a decade from now, his deadpan answer was "Rehab."

## Globalism without apologies

Where do today's youth belong? Where can they feel like citizens, not only in the sense of legal membership and obligations, but pledging allegiance irrespective of their actual nationality? Can one be a "global citizen" or "citizen of the world"?

The terms are related but distinct. The phrase "global citizen" generally refers to one's identification with our common humanity and concern for global interests such as human rights or the environment. Today there are many organizations and movements bearing the name "Global Citizen," from NGOs combating poverty to youth leadership training programs that advocate for more civic engagement.* From Montessori nurseries to elite international schools, youth are being raised to think of themselves as global citizens through the growing number of schools teaching "global citizenship" classes and the increasingly popular international baccalaureate (IB) curriculum being adopted in high schools around the world.[8] The United World College (UWC) movement has more than one dozen IB schools around the world, with thousands of students who are self-aware of their membership in a larger community. Being mission-driven becomes part of their identity. They are taught not just to "be" but to "do."

Activist education has political consequences. Hong Kong's mandatory liberal studies curriculum, which emphasizes civic engagement, has been cited as a key factor in motivating the waves of anti-Beijing protests since 2019. Pro-Beijing officials quickly denounced the curriculum as a failure; students view it as perhaps the only thing the government has done right since the 1997 handover of the island to mainland China—which is why they continue their defiance against Beijing's 2020 National Security Law that would further curtail their freedoms. A survey in mid-2020 revealed that three-quarters of the island's youth view themselves as Hong Kongers first, followed by "global citizens" and "Asians"—"Chinese" ranked last.

Summarizing the millennial or Gen-Z mindset is not difficult: They

---

* After 9/11, the late political theorist Benjamin Barber launched a movement to declare September 12 "Interdependence Day," a civic movement that even printed its own passports proclaiming principles to advance a global civic order.

want to work to live, not live to work. They want to be happy, do good, and not be poor. It's plausible that the pendulum may swing back to focusing on hard work in pursuit of wealth, but the growing divide between capital and labor suggests that being devoted employees is no guarantee of material or spiritual fulfillment. Corporations are picking up on the shifting tides of employees' interests, offering a wide range of opportunities for personal and professional growth. Credit Suisse has a "Global Citizens" program that allows people with two years of experience in the bank to take two months in the field, volunteering for the Red Cross, microfinance organizations in Africa, education nonprofits in Latin America, or various other charities the company supports. Paid volunteering builds loyalty, character, and camaraderie, while also providing tangible social benefits.

It's unfortunate then that since the 1990s the term "global citizen" has come to be conflated with the untethered capitalist elites derided by the late Harvard professor Samuel Huntington, who coined the term "Davos man." Far more *non*-Westerners identify as "global citizens" than Westerners. Indeed, according to a BBC Globespan survey from 2015, the vast majority of self-proclaimed global citizens come from *developing* countries such as Nigeria, China, India, Kenya, and Pakistan. The archetype of the global citizen is not a hedge fund billionaire in a private jet but the Indian child rights activist and 2014 Nobel Peace Prize winner Kailash Satyarthi, who describes himself as a "global citizen" both because of his universal cause and because his own government has been so derelict. Most people need to look beyond their borders for noble inspiration, and the best global citizens make heroic efforts to act on it.

The next generation of philanthropists aspires to follow in the footsteps of George Soros and Bill Gates, who have turned corporate fortunes into war chests for humanitarian causes. They view being young and rich as an obligation to be a better global citizen, and often wear their dual mission of enterprise and social justice on their sleeve. Each major private bank now has next-gen programs to help guide their clients' philanthropy, while organizations such as Synergos and Nexus cater to youth who have either been successful entrepreneurs or inherited substantial wealth and want to make social impact investments. Whether Western, Asian, Arab, or African, it has become a generational mission to advance the kind of transformation that politics will never achieve on its own.

There are many historical, philosophical, and literary inspirations for would-be global citizens. The German Enlightenment philosopher Immanuel Kant argued that the citizens of any state should be treated in accordance with the natural law of equality. Animated by the spirit of universal humanity, the American revolutionary and founding father Thomas Paine wrote in *The Rights of Man*, "My country is the world." Both Kant and Paine are revered as talismans of cosmopolitanism, the idea that ethical, cultural, and even political communities exist beyond states alone. We have come to exist in what the late London School of Economics political theorist David Held called "overlapping communities of fate." Held argued that a universal human community requires political and legal authority to be relocated above state sovereignty. At the same time, the way to get there is bottom up. More than a utopian idealist, Held was an intellectual activist, what academics call an "ideas entrepreneur." Together with famed sociologist Anthony Giddens, Held crafted the "Third Way" social democratic concepts that guided Tony Blair and Bill Clinton in the 1990s. Their agenda was international as well. Held argued for a "cosmopolitan democracy," insisting that the ideals of democratic government should not stop at the borders of nations but also apply to our global institutions. Only then could we "globalize democracy while at the same time democratize globalization." This remains the agenda that animates most "global citizens" today.

Yet much like "global citizen," the term "cosmopolitan" has also been used as a dismissive epithet. Here again it's all too easy to forget that the original philosopher of cosmopolitanism, the Greek stoic Diogenes, declared himself to be *kosmou polite* ("citizen of the cosmos"), not as a rich man but as a beggar who often slept inside a large ceramic barrel.

Diogenes believed that to be virtuous, one should practice what one preaches. In his wanderings around the ancient Greek isles, he defied the assumption that only the polis into which one was born could be one's primary source of identity. Instead, he argued that there are larger moral obligations beyond oneself and one's immediate family to the shared community of humanity. This is the essence of being a global citizen.

What about "citizen of the world"? At its simplest, this phrase widely connotes someone who has traveled and lived in many places. Like "global citizen," the term also came into vogue in the 1990s to capture the growing ranks of expats and global nomads, whether students, backpackers, executives, entrepreneurs, or others whose international experiences imbued them with a pluralistic sense of identity—a global loyalty that complemented their national one. "Citizens of the world" also wear the moniker with pride as they chase experiences and opportunities wherever they may be. To be a "citizen of the world" is to be rootless by choice. As the meditative traveler Pico Iyer reflects in *This Could Be Home*, "When I was a boy, the first question you'd ask of someone was 'Where do you come from?' Now the more relevant enquiry is, 'Where are you going?'"[9]

Younger millennials and older Gen-Zers are particularly footloose. Ivy League colleges such as Princeton and others encourage and even pay for students to take traveling gap years before enrolling as undergraduates. (The coronavirus all but made this necessary.) Minerva Schools and other colleges have campuses spread across the world among which undergraduates rotate. Lonely Planet does brisk business with books, such as *The Big Trip*, that advise on study abroad, gap years, and sabbaticals. A host of boutique associations (such as Me to We) promote sustainable travel experiences, shifting from the selfie-obsessed "me" to the more collective "we." They are all training today's young citizens of the world.

As with "Davos Man," perhaps nothing did more to elevate the visibility of the term "citizens of the world" than a petty broadside against it. This time it was former British prime minister Theresa May, who in late

2016 declared to her fellow Conservative Party members, "If you believe you are a citizen of the world, you are a citizen of nowhere." The ironies of her speech have been duly picked apart by her countrymen. After all, the UK's globally mobile elite is mostly made up of Conservatives who supported Brexit while shifting their own assets offshore. British expatriation to Spain, Germany, and France surged by more than 500 percent in the wake of Brexit.[10] One is reminded of the author Suketu Mehta's wry comment that "a globalist is a nationalist with a passport."[11]

There are many legitimate ways for individuals, social groups, and societies to construct identity beyond just waving one flag—and many of them overlap. It follows then that inhabiting nations no longer means belonging to them exclusively. The great liberal philosopher Isaiah Berlin cautioned against viewing nationalism as the main mode by which humans identify themselves, given how our individual lives are shaped by the complex interplay of family, ethnicity, business, religion, and other bonds. Loyalty still exists, but it's dividing and multiplying. Identity is plural rather than singular, self-defined rather than only inherited. Identity is alchemy, not dogma.

Theresa May concluded her now infamous "citizen of nowhere" invective with the line "You don't know what citizenship means." Who does? It once stood for a compact between government and society in which people contributed to national well-being through work, taxation, and military service in exchange for legal, political, and social rights. But today's youth have tipped the balance of obligation, claiming their right to environmental sustainability, digital access, universal healthcare, education, and a government that complies with international norms as well. Doha Debates, an independent civic media initiative, asked young people around the world what they thought of when they heard the word "citizenship." The respondents spoke of "protection" and "privilege"—none associated the term with ethnic identity or legal duties. The young are claiming the individual's right to determine what citizenship means—and are willing to fight for it.

## The clash of generations

The modern social contract dictates that the young should care for the old by paying taxes into pensions and staffing social services for the elderly, a process that is supposed to repeat itself generation after generation. Today's youth should appreciate that it was the diligent savings of today's baby boomers that financed the infrastructure they now take for granted. But the elderly also represent a $78 *trillion* debt bomb of pension obligations no young person wants to pay taxes for—at least, nobody who can instead go elsewhere, leaving others behind to pay for it.[12]

This clash of generations is playing out in fiscal debates across the West. Whereas baby boomers benefit from generous retirements, youth demand that the elderly's accumulated savings be spent on affordable housing, broadband Internet, and skills training. At the moment, the old and rich are sitting on overpriced and oversized homes they refuse to sell, while the young gigonomist class can't pay the rent.[13] They assume that once the elderly have perished, developers will rebuild in line with their downsized needs. No wonder one Gen-Z intern in Los Angeles lamented to me, "I can't wait for the boomers to die so that we can afford a place to live." But baby boomer mortality is only predicted to accelerate in the 2030s.

And while boomers are alive and kicking, governments are raising retirement ages from sixty-five to seventy and beyond while benefits shrink, forcing many of them to stay in the job market and compete with youth for Uber fares and IT gigs. In America, two-thirds of AARP members report facing discrimination in the workplace, prompting Congress to pass legislation against ageism in 2020. This is a reminder that many aging Americans are struggling as much or more than youth, but with less time to sort out their future.

As this intergenerational drama unfolds, how many youth will accept a lifetime of higher taxes to pay for a system that will crumble before they're old enough to be rewarded for their sacrifices? Europeans already pay enough taxes in the name of social equity and can't afford a larger burden. In America, 60 percent of millennials don't have sufficient savings to cover their already low taxes (compared to Europe). The fact that Social Security is expected to go broke in 2034 (well before they're due to retire) is yet another reason to fear the future. For the majority of today's American youth, inheritance will be a small reprieve. If and when they inherit a home, the first thing they'll do (especially if siblings get an equal share) is to sell it for a shameful loss and use those proceeds to pay down credit card and student debt.

Meanwhile, the majority of the estimated $30 trillion in global wealth being transferred from boomers to their offspring will remain in the hands of rich Americans, Europeans, and Asians. America's super-rich will invest their windfall in tech stocks, holiday homes, cryptocurrencies, and perhaps offshore assets and foreign citizenship. European wealth is traditionally more rooted in national industries such as automobiles and grocery stores, but with half the world's outstanding pension payouts in Europe, the next generation may just sell off their family businesses and head to Switzerland. Private equity firms are already pushing for layoffs and cost-cutting measures at European firms, clashing with the prevailing pro-labor culture. France's experience with a wealth tax already pushed an estimated fifty thousand millionaires out of the country, something Britain hopes to avoid even though an inheritance tax would raise desperately needed revenue. After all, with little prospect of an economic rebound in the UK, British youth would rather sell off their inheritance than watch it depreciate. France hopes they'll do just that and be lured by schemes launched by its new Ministry of Economic Attractiveness, such as five-year tax holidays for foreign investors. Taxes are a hot button political issue but a much more slippery reality.[14]

In Asia, calls for higher taxes on the wealthy are prompting them to preemptively engineer inheritance windfalls. In 2019, China and India lost the most millionaires of any countries, with Australia and America the largest beneficiaries. Rich young Chinese have fund managers hard at work spreading their inheritance globally to ensure they have an exit hatch in case Xi Jinping's apparatchiks descend on them. In Korea, where inheritance tax can reach 50 percent, toddlers are being granted shares in parents' and grandparents' companies to avoid tax. What can young Koreans do with this money in a country that's aging? Not much, so they're moving it to Singapore or Australia. And so it shall come to this: Aging countries' pension funds will go broke unless they invest their assets in the places where their own youth are going—wherever that may be.

## Youth of the world, unite!

During the summer of 2005, I was on an exciting road trip in a beat-up old Volkswagen, driving from the Baltics through Eastern Europe and the Balkans, and across Turkey through the Caucasus into Central Asia. Turkey exuded an optimistic vibe. It was early in Erdogan's tenure as prime minister, the economy was humming, and per capita income had reached $7,500. Factory towns dubbed the "Anatolian tigers" in Turkey's vast eastern flank were churning out textiles and car parts. Fourteen years later I crossed Anatolia again, but instead of vibrant towns I witnessed a desolate countryside and abandoned playgrounds. Where did all the youth go? To Istanbul, where they took to the streets challenging Erdogan, on his neglect of their provinces, and electing an opposition mayor. Istanbul has been witnessing nearly uninterrupted tension between youth and the government since the Gezi Park protests of 2013, with a wide array of agendas pulling together: anti-corruption, pro-democracy, rural development, better education, women's rights, and anti-gentrification.

Russia, too, has had its chances to elevate its dilapidated hinterlands. But today there are few more apocalyptic sites than Siberian villages that have been hollowed out for more than a decade: jagged roads cracked by winter ice, shattered glass in every wooden house, rust consuming every metallic surface. Like Erdogan, Putin has either ignored the plight of the millions in the country's vast east or assaulted their political dignity by sacking their preferred governors. In 2020, tens of thousands of residents of Khabarovsk defied Moscow edicts to demonstrate against the Kremlin.

Across the world, the middle class protests corruption while the working class protests economic hardship. Together they form a constellation of the *underemployed and overeducated* young men and women who have university degrees and menial work, and the *overworked and underpaid* blue-collar workers who can't make ends meet despite putting in as many working hours as allowed. Inequality surely annoys them, but poverty and lack of opportunity is the more proximate cause of their anger. According to scientist Peter Turchin, modern societies have produced too many overeducated underachievers, a prime cause of today's domestic turf wars.

Chile illustrates the point. In 2019, metro fare hikes in Santiago prompted the first state of emergency since Chile's return to democracy in 1990, and the first domestic deployment of the military since the Pinochet regime. Owing to the prominent role of mining and banking in its economy, Chile not surprisingly has very high income inequality; these industries produce billionaires. But without them, Chile would be as poor as Peru rather than being the richest country (per capita) in South America. At the time the protests broke out, Chile's inequality was actually declining, but ordinary citizens didn't feel it because transport, education, healthcare, and housing were still too expensive for most. The persistent agitation has paid off: In 2020, Chileans overwhelmingly voted to rewrite their constitution.

Youth know rotten governance when they see it. When public transport costs are raised, students riot. When gas and electricity subsidies are cut, mass protests ensue. Wise governments do not repeat one another's mistakes. The same year Chile raised transport fares, Estonia made all public buses free. Iran regularly cuts off Internet access, while Croatia makes sure that it's ubiquitous, fast, and free. But the list of countries where governments are proactively focused on housing, education, and employment is very short. As a result, the global underclass revolt continues.

Even in more deferential Asian societies, youth are making subtle but significant political moves against authority. Analysts of Indonesia (the world's most populous Muslim country) have long feared the rise of Islamism, but the country's most notable new political party, the Indonesian Solidarity Party (PSI), doesn't allow members over forty-five and promotes youth and women's issues.[15] Young Indonesians are far more interested in chasing gigs on the Go-Jek super-app so they can afford homes. In Thailand, members of the youth-led Future Forward Party now openly oppose the country's profligate monarchy, using the three-fingered salute from *The Hunger Games* as their call to solidarity.

Ironically, youth protest most where they enjoy the most freedom and highest living standards: Europe. Over the past decade, movements such as the *indignados* in Spain, and the *nuit debout* (uprising at night) and *gilets jaunes* (yellow vests) in France have brought together Gen-X and millennials against corruption, the lack of jobs, fuel taxes, and other grievances. During the summer of 2011, one act of police brutality sparked riots across London and a dozen other cities, leading to five deaths and more than three thousand arrests. Agitators and looters weren't angry only at the police, but at everything. After the fourteenth century Black Death, the Peasant Revolt in England saw the underclass demand an end to aristocratic serfdom and lower taxes. Don't be surprised if calls to dismantle Europe's opulent monarchies crescendo not only for the unscrupulous behavior of particular royals but simply for their vast land holdings that could easily be repurposed for genuine public benefit. Europe has many Bastilles to storm.

Dispossessed people resent the system that excludes them. For centuries, private home ownership has been considered both an economic right and a check on political tyranny. But home ownership among the young has dropped sharply.[16] Even renting a two-bedroom apartment in a major city is unimaginable on a basic salary.[17] Whereas older homeowners don't want to see their property values fall (further), millennials and Gen-Zers have lower marriage rates, weaker job prospects, and are also more likely to have been arrested than any previous generation.[18] Expecting parents tend to become more law-abiding, but with no kids in sight, we'll see more Bonnies and Clydes.

No two factors better predict civil war than high male youth un-employment and high inequality, and the two in combination with each other—and lots of guns—makes for a tinderbox. Young Arab jihadists, European neo-Nazi militias, Russian mercenaries, Brazilian *favela* street gangs, Mexican drug dealers, African rebel groups—all are made up of millennial and Gen-Z men and boys with nothing better to do. In Amer-ica it's the black or Latino underclass and white boogaloo neo-fascists. After the Iraqi insurgency, the Pentagon began dusting off doctrines for urban guerrilla warfare in anticipation of similar unrest in megacity slums—only to find the streets of its own country exploding in 2020.

Enter Antifa. The Antifa movements of mid-twentieth-century Eu-rope had all but died out until the 2010s, when anti-austerity protests in Europe and the election of Donald Trump brought them back on both sides of the Atlantic. These collectives of communists, socialists, and anarchists oppose strongman governments and white supremacist move-ments, but operate as autonomous cells. Rather than fear their govern-ments, Antifa members set out to evoke the very brutality they oppose. Portland has been America's most active Antifa stronghold—but cells popped up all across the country during the 2020 Black Lives Matter protests—inspired, motivated, and goaded by their peers worldwide on Twitter, Instagram, and WhatsApp. Online tools will continue to evolve amid protestors' cat and mouse with authorities. They'll hack in the name of transparency, encrypt to maintain privacy, and use the blockchain to establish a parallel world of secure identity and transactions. A connected and mobile generation will continue to cause headaches across the world.

Or could it be that millennials and Gen-Z will eventually become conservative adults as was the case with many of America's Woodstock and Europe's '68 generation? That would require them attaining some stability to cling on to. Most of today's youth are still physically sitting on the sidelines, a silent majority occupied with prosaic concerns such as finishing school and looking for work. The longer they have to wait for change, the more likely it becomes that they'll move in search of communities where protesting is not a full-time job, and where people share their understanding of identity and priorities.

## Millennial eco-authoritarianism?

In late 2019, Greta Thunberg expressed dismay that after a year of global activism, there had been no serious action against climate change. At the level of international diplomacy, there may never be. No wonder then that activism has become a full-time job. Having grown up watching democracy dither on climate change and inequality, 85 percent of Americans under thirty unsurprisingly want "fundamental change" in Washington, not just returning things "back to normal" (which 70 percent of those over sixty-five favor). To Gen-Z, "normal" is such a disaster that half of them don't even believe they live in democracies.[19] The millennials' dismissive swipe at their elders, "#okboomer," has become a way of saying "Whatever, your time is up, step aside." They want to have their turn before it's too late.

Though Western youth are empowered by liberalism, they're not averse to a hypothetical ecological authoritarianism. It isn't out of the ordinary to hear youth speak about the need for a "global union," a supranational equivalent to the EU, marrying the universality of the UN with "good power" to compel action on climate change. Since that too is unlikely, millennials are now at the forefront of ecoterrorism. Extinction Rebellion—whose global funding comes from crowdsourcing and billionaires alike—has disrupted flights with drone swarms, attacked oil company headquarters, and sprayed fake blood on government offices.

Anti-pipeline protests have disrupted major railways across Canada, with CEOs demanding the government take a hard line against such "terrorists." Imagine cabals of youth one day occupying pristine habitats to prevent commercial activity, or staging mass suicides to evoke action to combat climate change. What would Greta Thunberg think about that?

## Micro melting pots

Over the past four decades I've been fortunate to immerse myself in several of the world's most cosmopolitan cities—Dubai, New York, Berlin, Geneva, London, and Singapore. All have a high percentage of foreign-born residents and are the better for it. Such urban microcosms of the global village may appear to be self-organizing, but they're anything but. Constant curation is required to create a harmonious multiracial environment in which all can thrive with no fear of others.

London's global demographics stand in sharp contrast to England's more monochrome rural areas, helping explain why the capital's stance on Brexit differed markedly from the heartland's. London in particular is not only the headquarters of such globally concerned organizations as Amnesty International but also has been home to many cosmopolitan writers such as Ian McEwan and Kazuo Ishiguro, whose work explores themes of civility and cross-cultural assimilation. The Turkish novelist Elif Shafak identifies as an Istanbulite and Londoner, but most of all an advocate for open society—the kind of place where one would be proud to be a citizen. London's diversity of people has kept it thriving despite Britain's collective decisions against its own interests. Ironically, though Boris Johnson backed Brexit as prime minister, while mayor of London he advocated for "London visas" to ensure the city maintained its talent pipeline. Now his successor as mayor, Sadiq Khan, is pushing for "fast track" visas so that London can bring in the skilled workers it needs. For its own sake, the rest of the UK should hope he succeeds.

Throughout history, great cities have been open to trade and talent, knowing that their survival depends on it. Singapore evolved over several centuries into a multi-ethnic milieu as Chinese migrated southward and Indians were circulated across the British empire. But since independence in 1965, it has become a melting pot by design as founding father Lee Kuan Yew insisted on ethnically mixed public housing to prevent ghettos. Mandatory national service in which all races share bunks and basic training also gave rise to lifelong friendships across ethnic lines. The result: Singapore has by far the world's highest rate of interracial marriages (about one-third), especially Indo-Chinese couples who become parents of "Chindian" children. As mixed race families become the social norm, pleas for ethnically based politics become weaker and having multiple identities becomes a genetic norm.*

The tension Singapore must manage is between granting every ethnic group its license—official language, national holidays, right to practice their various customs—while also relentlessly promoting a *national* identity that is pan-ethnic and nondenominational. Even though it's a majority Chinese country, this civic identity appeals to common experiences such as postcolonial state building and points to a future of shared prosperity. But the task of nurturing communal stability is never complete. A new wave of mainland Chinese (and to a lesser degree Indian) migrants have set up shop without absorbing the principal features of Singapore's civic identity such as actively embracing diversity and learning English. Belatedly, the government has stepped up assimilation programs to avoid foreign enclaves from taking root.

There is as much to be learned from failure as success. Despite Hong Kong's status as a capitalist mecca attracting talent from around the world,

---

* In 2019, the US-based Appeal of Conscience Foundation recognized Singapore as the world's most religiously tolerant country.

it has failed for decades to build sufficient affordable housing and address massive income inequality. Meanwhile, the influx of more than 1 million mainland Chinese over the past two decades has created an identity crisis. These underlying frustrations combusted violently when China passed a controversial extradition law in 2019 and the even more ominous national security law in 2020. High living costs and political turbulence have not only diminished Hong Kong's allure to foreign professionals, but also ironically pushed droves of Hong Kongers north to Shenzhen, which is now both wealthier than Hong Kong and appears a more orderly model, with huge new blocks of subsidized apartments. Meanwhile, the inflow of mainland Chinese into Hong Kong continues, from tycoons to bureaucrats, import-export salesmen, and military police. China is quickly replacing the "bad fish" with its own "good fish" who will buy into Hong Kong's now devalued real estate and financial markets and act more in the interests of the mainland. The movement of people shapes the allegiance of places.

You only need to be forty years old today to have witnessed firsthand how the UAE's composition has changed drastically from its days as an Arab Bedouin society living off pearling and trade with other Gulf tribes and Iran into one of the world's wealthiest countries, glittering with skyscrapers built by millions of Asian guest workers. The UAE's population has grown *fortyfold* since its founding in 1971, when its population was merely 250,000. Today it is the world's most post-national country by far: Everyone is a minority—even the Emiratis themselves, who make up only 1 million of the country's 10 million population.

Given its nomadic history and central geography, the UAE has been defined by the comings and goings of new settlers, both permanent and temporary. Middle-class expats and bonded migrant laborers move in tandem: The arrival of the former begets more work for the latter. By contrast, when a large number of expats bail out due to financial crises or the pandemic lockdown, there is less need for maids, deliverymen, and security guards. Unless families across the board are made to feel like settled stakeholders, the UAE can't rely on their loyalty.

How will the UAE attract more permanent residents when the vast majority will never become citizens? For decades, Indian professionals—who make up one-third of the entire population—were considered docile temporary workers with no guarantee of residency rights. But in recent years, the UAE has granted ever more foreigners long-term residency, even allowing them to fully own companies without local partners. Whereas once it rejected visas for their elderly relatives, the 2019 "expat law" allows Indians earning a decent income to bring in family members. Rather than viewing the elderly as a financial burden, the UAE is now offering air-conditioned retirement colonies for them, while building its medical tourism industry to attract Europeans and Americans. If India's environment continues to worsen—both ecologically and politically—even more wealthy and upwardly mobile Indians will decamp to the UAE.

Similarly, Indian expat kids who grew up in the UAE but had Indian passports (like me) eventually moved to America or Canada for better work and citizenship. They too thought of themselves as what scholar Deepak Unnikrishnan calls "temporary people." But to retain some of this lost talent, the UAE is starting to offer citizenship to non-Arabs as well—irrespective of their religion. Indian migrants to the UAE have mostly been Muslims (as well as Christians and Hindus), from Kerala or Tamil, and Punjabi Hindus, hence the UAE's tolerance for Christian churches and Hindu temples. On Saadiyat Island in Abu Dhabi, a large interfaith complex is slated to contain a mosque, church, and synagogue adjacent to one another. More broadly, the UAE has changed a suite of civic codes to allow for unmarried couples to live together, foreign laws to govern divorce, and public alcohol consumption.

The country's commercial hub of Dubai is the epitome of such perpetual circulation and overlapping identities. The law enforces stability, while policy seeks to promote harmony through an AI-powered city concierge called "Rashid" who provides guidance on enjoying Dubai life, the awarding of "happiness diplomas" to companies for positive workplace culture, and a "Happy to Pay" app that encourages people to do community service in lieu of paying traffic fines.

Many cities are at risk of allowing migration without promoting assimilation, enabling ghettos that beget more ghettoization as more migrants come in and take the path of least resistance. But it's still not too late to move beyond the anachronistic understanding of "citizenship" so that these legions of noncitizens become loyal stakeholders. A generation ago it would have been difficult to imagine noncitizens being given voting rights, but New Zealand allows all permanent residents to vote in any election, and Toronto has opened municipal elections to all legal residents irrespective of citizenship. New York and Los Angeles have been among the "sanctuary cities" giving out IDs to undocumented migrants to protect them from deportation. The more cities make all residents meaningful participants by virtue of their contributions and obligations, the more loyalty to the city supersedes that to the nation.

Globally connected city-states are the incubators of the new postnational global civilization because they can succeed only through inclusive rather than exclusive policies. They hold themselves together through efforts at inclusive civic pluralism and pride. The Canadian scholar Daniel Bell calls this rising urban pride "civicism," a twenty-first-century rival to nationalism with roots in ancient Athens, where politics was open to all residents.

As people, goods, and data stream in and out of global cities, it becomes more difficult than ever to pin down their identity. Like superpositioned atoms, people exist in multiple states of mind at the same time, belonging to both local and foreign worlds. *Where* we are is just as important to us as *who* we are—and the more people who seize the mobility opportunity to shape their own destiny, the more important the former becomes in defining the latter.

There is no better bulwark against the recklessness of identity politics than melting pot cities. With their multinational companies, postnational workforces, and "third culture" kids, global cities are the breeding ground for young cosmopolitans. Among kids with parents of two different nationalities, the scene has evolved from alternating between their parents' respective national costumes for annual "Uniting Nations Day" festivals to protesting the school for causing an identity crisis. For global youth, identity is cumulative, not substitutive. The more young people congeal in melting pot cities, the more cosmopolitan identities become our common future. To these young people, "finding oneself" is not about "going home" but about feeling "at home." As Pico Iyer elegantly puts it, "Home can be as much a creation of the future as the past."[20]

## Postmodern pilgrimages: Communing as faith

The prevalence of youth loneliness is one of the great paradoxes of our connected age. But youth are also driven toward sites of nomadic communion. For the jet set it's membership in SoHo House or A Small World. In the entertainment space it's festivals such as Burning Man, Coachella, and Ultra. Thematic and exotic retreats are popping up such as the exclusive Secret Solstice gathering on a secluded glacier in Iceland or the cooking- and music-focused Bottlerock Festival in Napa Valley. The mood of these events sometimes treads the fine line between progressive communing and apocalyptic hedonism, like Woodstock in the shadow of climate change.

More than 100 million European youth seem content with the simple life of paying affordable rent, biking to jobs, taking cheap flights or trains on a whim, and planning life no more than six months in advance. As Janan Ganesh of the *Financial Times* writes, pleasure trumps possessions. Well-to-do millennials and Gen-Zers like to blend networking and adventure at conferences such as One Young World and Summit

Series, and brain spas such as TED and its many spin-offs. Beyond that, a good gym (or yoga studio) is as close as they get to a religious experience.

As much as digital detoxes allow youth to commune face-to-face, technological immersion (or obsession) is the opposite extreme of the new spirituality. The annual Consumer Electronics Show (CES) in Las Vegas is a tech fantasist's dream, with nearly two hundred thousand annual attendees. The Web Summit, and Apple and Huawei product launch events, also draw enormous crowds. We once had a millennial nanny whose main priority in every city we traveled to, from Cape Town to Dubai to Seoul, was to visit the Apple Store—the irony being that unlike churches or mosques or temples that have unique local styles, Apple Stores are pretty much the same everywhere.

If there is one nearly universal community of believers, it's football. Soccer has developed into a new kind of religion with many denominations, sects, and partisans. It's a faith with loyal followers who spend time and money at its pilgrimage sites—Wembley, Old Trafford, Camp Nou—worshipping its deities such as Lionel Messi and Cristiano Ronaldo. While some Pentecostal churches have large mass events, the scale of weekly soccer matches in dozens of cities around the world is unparalleled. Far more so than cricket (the global sporting religion of the British postcolonial generation), football is a truly global community of adherents who devote far more time to playing, watching, re-watching, analyzing, and video gaming matches than they could possibly spend reading the Bible, Koran, or other scripture.

Football is also a non-segregated faith, indeed one that thrives on immigration. The import of a foreign talent is not reviled but celebrated, as if a new Messiah has arrived to rescue a struggling local squad. The German national soccer team is half made up of immigrants; two-thirds of the English Premier League players are foreigners. European national and club teams are leading global campaigns, such as "No Room for Racism," "Show Racism the Red Card," and "Kick It Out," that pressure leagues to suspend matches if players are subject to racist behavior. Unlike ancient religions that purport to be egalitarian but conceal deep hierarchies and injustice, the church of football is meritocratic (if commercial) and inclusive, no matter one's race or faith.

## From *homo economics* to *homo faber*

The answer to *what* people will do in the future very much depends on *where* they move to do it. This underscores the reality that our main challenge is not man versus robots but skills versus geography. Even as automation eliminates millions of jobs in retail, logistics, finance, law, and other areas, the demand for human talent to upgrade our infrastructure and social services remains enormous. Hence Michael Chui of McKinsey argues that the solution to mass unemployment is mass *re*deployment.

A mobile civilization requires people with skills, irrespective of whether there is a university degree attached to them. Some of the most crucial areas facing labor shortages, such as construction and healthcare, from building and installing modular homes to providing physical therapy for the elderly, don't even require a high school degree. Higher education is in any case facing a perfect storm. The financial crisis of 2008 and Covid-19 together put dozens of colleges out of business as their cost exceeded their reputation, they failed to go digital, or both. By 2026 and certainly thereafter, hundreds more colleges will go defunct. How do we know? Because exactly eighteen years after the baby bust of 2008, the number of American high school graduates will fall off a cliff. Those who had been planning on attending college nearby may pack up and leave for good, joining college employees who have no reason to stick around, together turning once thriving towns into dust bowls. The southern US will be hit hardest, as it represents nearly 45 percent of American high schoolers as well as the most colleges closing shop. (In Texas, only 56 percent of high school students go to college anyway.) The South will only be able to revive its local economies by attracting people—natives or foreigners—willing to uplift these dilapidated communities.

Mobile professionals can be trained through mobile education as well. Many youth began tracking their learning portfolios from the ninth grade, collecting credits across academic and vocational courses, through in-school and extracurricular activities, and on edX and Coursera. Some have completed the content of an online MBA well before they'd ever have been old enough to apply for one. Most Americans think an internship at Google would be better for their long-term prospects than a Harvard degree.[21] Google's new "career certificates" train in six months the equivalent of a four-year degree and are recognized by major corporations. Lamda Academy, with its nine-month program in data science, full stack web development, UX design, and other areas, places graduates in tech jobs so they can pay back the tuition from their salaries. These entirely remote corporate curricula make no pretense that geography matters: their part-time subscribers will choose places where they can afford to live, work, and study at the same time. A decade from now, far more than the present 4 percent of American youth could be homeschooled to take advantage of these offerings.

Today's youth know they'll need to get retrained and upskilled each place they go. In 2020, the White House Ad Council launched a "Do Something New" campaign to urge Americans to use apprenticeships as a path to well-paying jobs such as aerospace or wind turbine technician, computer hardware maintenance person, or registered nurse. The Royal Institute of Chartered Surveyors (RICS) has an apprenticeship program to get recruits prepared for jobs in land development, property management, analyzing real estate utilization data, and curating experiences in mixed use spaces. Industrial 3D printing operators earn more than the average academic.

The generational project that lies ahead is for Washington, Wall Street,

Silicon Valley, and the Ivy League to forge an ecosystem of credit and technology platforms for entrepreneurs and small businesses. Gen-Z is not lacking for ambition. Money-minded Gen-X used to run investment clubs with Monopoly money and check the stock market performance weekly; now teens trade on Robinhood with real money. Shows such as *Shark Tank* have been wildly popular, turning the word "venture" from a verb into a career. In the wake of the pandemic, new business applications shot up 77 percent from the year prior, indicating that America's appetite for entrepreneurship is enormous.

But neither growth nor innovation is an end in itself. People either build things, sell things, or do things: What higher purpose can these activities serve? Our top priority must be to get off the status quo treadmill and begin engineering the future, from 5G base stations to urban farms. This mission to build sustainable and inclusive habitats will attract youth who are fed up with decrepit infrastructure and want to make things that are useful rather than just consume things that are not. What John Seely Brown calls *homo faber*—man who makes—will take over from *homo economicus*. The hackathon is real.

## Humans have their own capital

The substitution of machines for humans changes what Karl Marx called the "organic composition" of capital. People are no longer the essence of the production process, technology is. Whereas once humans were needed to operate it, now it operates itself with little or no human input. But this doesn't mean that *human capital* is irrelevant. When Nobel laureate Gary Becker developed the concept of human capital, he sought to quantify the value of secondary education in America's post–World War II decades of expansion. Subsequently, economists have tried to boil human capital down to statistics such as labor productivity. But even though ubiquitous technologies such as mobile telephony and cloud data storage make us immensely more efficient, productivity statistics undervalue these benefits because the technologies are effectively free. The more productive technology gets, the more we need to think of human capital as a form of self-worth beyond educational certifications and productivity statistics.

Indeed, human capital has become tantamount to all the life skills one possesses. Aristotle thus becomes a more useful entry point in appreciating human capital than Economics 101. The ancient Greek philosopher argued that *eudaimonia*—human flourishing, well-being, and happiness—was the critical ingredient to a successful society. A wide range of factors contribute to such societal welfare: a national spirit or ethos, social cohesion and equity, education and talent, order and safety. In this sense, human capital boils down to more intangible questions such as: How content are you as a person? How useful are your contributions to society? Like love or other intangibles, one can say of human capital: You know it when you see it.

# CHAPTER 4
# THE NEXT AMERICAN DREAM

## Getting unstuck

In the decade after the subprime mortgage crisis began in 2007, more than 8 million American families were ejected from their foreclosed homes. Many of those worst affected have yet to recover, eking out an existence in "Hoovervilles" or "Trump towns," as they've come to be known. Evictions and homelessness were on the rise even *before* the pandemic exacerbated Americans' ability to meet rent and mortgage payments. Home ownership has been falling steadily from the pre–financial crisis peak of 70 percent. Meanwhile, there are nearly 14 million vacant homes nationwide, especially in metro areas.[1] If all of America's homeless were given free housing, all prisoners released from jail, and immigration restored to 1 million per year—America would still have an excess of vacant housing.

Like countless people all over the world, Americans too are forced into mobility: When firms collapse, financial crises strike, and economies fall into recession, they have to look for new jobs, downsize homes, or move to other cities, states, and counties.* For more than a decade, millions of Americans have been shifting from the rust belt and Northeast to the more affordable South and West, taking new jobs in retail, logistics,

---

* Those who move outside counties often do so related to employment (starting a new job or relocating for one), whereas moves within a county have more to do with housing (seeking better or more affordable).

or tech, leaving overpriced New York, San Francisco, and Los Angeles for Denver, Austin, and Raleigh.

Even though an estimated 20 million Americans moved during 2020, still too few are able to relocate in order to improve their lot in life. From the 1940s to 1960s, about one-fifth of Americans moved every year as the population grew and expanded westward. More recently, however, domestic migration has stalled. Ironically, this is because *under*employment has rendered many youth "stuck in place": They should move to places where housing, healthcare, and education are cheaper, but they can't afford to.[2] As today's hordes of unemployed youth look for work again, they'll have to get moving to find it.

The American Dream needs to be redefined. Instead of owning a home, the new ideal should be *mobility*—enabling every American to go wherever they need to go, to where their skills are needed and they can earn more. Research by Harvard's Raj Chetty shows that over the course of a generation, socioeconomic performance improves once families move to places with greater economic opportunity.[3] Physical mobility, then, is the best pathway to economic mobility.

### Mobile real estate

In the fall of 2018, Kyle Nossaman, an editor at *Gear Junkie* magazine, and his wife locked the door of their upscale apartment in Minneapolis and set off for a year of exploring America. They visited most of the lower forty-eight states and almost all the national parks. They rode mountain bikes and a motorcycle, camped and hiked, visited old friends and made new ones, all the while keeping up their jobs part-time, even saving money along the way. And they did all this without ever getting on a plane—because they were driving and living in their very own converted school bus.[4]

The Covid lockdown was an existential disaster for America's retail sector—unless you happened to be selling mobile homes. Sales of Thor

Industries large camper vans surged after the pandemic lockdown ended, and Mercedes even released its iconic Camper (that sleeps four) in the US after years of popularity in Europe. The RV Industry Association reported a nearly 200 percent jump in sales from the same period of 2019.[5] Trailer homes have emerged as a trendy, cost-effective, and sustainable alternative to traditional home ownership. Movements like #skooliebus on Instagram (featuring school buses retrofitted into mobile homes) and "tiny houses" on Pinterest point to the growing popularity of mobile and minimalist living.

The trailer home is the ultimate symbol of the new American mobility. Twenty-five percent of mobile homes are owned by millennials, and the more they and Gen-Z reach home-buying age, the more mobile home sales go up.[6] In other words, youth are consciously choosing *not* to buy houses (that they can't afford anyway), snapping up motor homes instead. Having witnessed the financial crisis demolish their parents' house value, they can hardly be blamed for having more faith in mobility than property.[7] Are we witnessing the reinvention of the American dream for the quantum age?

Mobile homes are part of American lore, but a surprising feature of America's present and future. An older generation of RV dwellers already roams the country seeking part-time jobs that offer cash and food, often exploited like migrant laborers, as Jessica Bruder documents in her book *Nomadland*, whose film adaptation won the Oscar for best picture in 2021. Trailer home communities have a sense of identity and security that now also draws in young people. Gloria Steinem's memoir *My Life on the Road* fondly recalls the pride of an all-female trailer park in Arizona that had streets named after Gertrude Stein and Eleanor Roosevelt. For women or the LGBTQ community, trailer parks provide the vibe of a gated residential community but without the price tag. With ever fewer school age children in America, there are plenty of school buses available for purchase—though their engines should ideally be switched from diesel to electric.

"Mobile real estate" is becoming an asset class unto itself, a wise investment for a world where flooding could sweep away your home, giant hailstones could smash through its roof, or a sinkhole could emerge at the end of your driveway. You're better off if your home is a giant car. Sea-lander's trailer has an onboard motor that turns it into a boat, perfect for navigating flooded areas. Especially if you don't know where your next job will be, a mobile home means you can move to it on short notice. Moving is the ultimate expression of reinvention, and perhaps the most effective as well.

America's youth should stop chaining themselves to homes they neither need nor can afford—and which aren't located where they need to be. Instead, we should be designing and building for an age of perpetual mobility. The real estate industry continues to pour concrete into McMansions, and even claims there is a nationwide housing shortfall of 2.5 million homes. But does their crystal ball tell them where people will want to live five years from now? Do they know where the jobs will be? Are they sure they're building in climate-resilient areas?

The great demographic deflation means an inevitable crash in real estate prices, and competition from prefab homes will bring those down even further. Freddie Mac (which provides liquidity to the housing market) has launched a slew of programs to encourage first-time home buyers to invest in far cheaper prefab homes—even if it leaves municipalities and banks sitting on trillions of dollars of stranded housing. No wonder then that an investor such as Warren Buffett has quietly become one of the largest owners of "pre-fabulous" home manufacturers such as Clayton Homes. Even in cheaper states, a manufactured home costs less than half the cost of a two-bedroom apartment, and renting a prefab as little as one-third as much.[8]

The best part of the prefab housing revolution? They can be delivered on the back of a truck—and moved as well. The era of 3D-printed micro housing is at hand. Amazon sells do-it-yourself homemaking kits that cost as little as $20,000 and can be solar-powered or connected to local energy grids. Mighty Buildings' 3D-printed "casitas" or "granny flats" can be deposited in backyards to cater to the millions of aging low-income renters or youth on tight budgets. Companies such as Boxabl and Ten Fold make homes that expand to triple their container size in minutes. Millions of discarded shipping containers themselves are easily retrofitted into (mobile) homes. One Estonian startup builds trailer-delivered prefab units that can be homes, offices, shops, storage units, cafes, community areas, or serve many other purposes. All that is required is a flat space for them to be set down on.

Which countries will make the land available, subsidize the cost, and enable or even require public service delivery to 3D home encampments? The Netherlands and France have become leaders in this progressive social policy, while Swedish furniture maker IKEA and construction company Skanska have teamed up to launch BoKlok (Live Smart), a firm that has built more than ten thousand homes in Scandinavia already. In their UK pilot, new occupants pay BoKlok whatever they can afford. Rather than cluttering homes with IKEA stuff, you can just buy your entire home from IKEA.

Movable homes are rolling off assembly lines through an entirely new production process that combines 3D printing, recycled materials, and robotic efficiency. For overpopulated countries in precarious geographies, SoftBank-funded Katerra does turnkey home design and construction for entire towns on short notice, while Icon has already 3D-printed entire villages in Mexico and sturdy units for those living in tents around Austin. But there is a reason why these homes are made to be disaster-resistant: One might have to move again. Self-sufficient, solar-powered container homes can be wheeled to adjust to rising tides, with portable loos that use microbes rather than water to turn human waste into odorless fertilizer. (These are even being deployed on Mount Everest.) This makes great sense for a world of seasonal migrations in which climate change and natural disasters as much as professional preference dictate where we live. For those choosing wheeled residences as a lifestyle choice, architects are designing stylish micro homes with woodstoves; solar power; rooftop water collection; compost toilets; separate kitchen, bedroom, and living areas; and large windows. Their owners can Instagram every new vista.

## Great mobility makes great nations

The extent to which mobility is essential to daily life is lost within its own predictability: the commute to work or walk to school. Yet even within a single place, mobility is decisive to our well-being. Most prosperous cities have dense networks of mass transit such as trains and buses and peer-to-peer ride-sharing platforms, all functioning simultaneously as an urban mobility system. By contrast, mobility is agony in cities with clogged roads and poor public transport that drag down both individual and national (economic) health.

Commuting to and from key urban centers is the day-to-day lifeblood for hundreds of millions of people and entire national economies. New York and Los Angeles are America's two most significant demographic and economic hubs, both dependent on the daily movement of millions of workers between homes and offices, and in and out of suburbs. On any given day in small countries such as Lebanon, Georgia, and the UAE, half or more of the entire national population commutes in and out of the capital or largest commercial city, earning money by day to bring home to poorer areas at night.

Great mobility makes greater nations. America's interstate highway system paved the way for millions more Americans to settle the West and take pride in the country's continental vastness. The German Autobahn is not just a network of highways for carefree speeding; it embodies the arteries fueling the country's miraculous postwar economic miracle, known as the *Wirtschaftswunder*, and its current role as Europe's economic motor. And China's high-speed rail network is now even more dense than Europe's, enabling Chinese to circulate around their imperial domain.

## The great climate resorting

As remote work policies kicked in during the pandemic, Manhattan's financial jet set wasted little time in snapping up beachfront real estate in tax-free Florida, ensuring they spent as little time as possible in their New York high-rises. Florida's "Follow the Sun" campaign was a resounding success—but how long before these mobile elites have to abandon their coastal mansions?

Natural disasters are forcing more and more Americans to move. With sea-level rise punishing the Atlantic and Pacific seaboards, coastal living is shifting from rite of passage to reckless luxury. America's four most populous states—California, Texas, Florida, and New York—all face climate reckoning. Among all global coastal cities ranked by asset value at risk, New York and Miami rank first and second. New York has yet to prepare itself for the next Hurricane Sandy–like superstorm that could bring even more coastal and inland flooding of its subways and streets, nor has it upgraded its electricity grid that suffered major outages during the 2019 heat wave (that also led to the cancellation of its major triathlon). Miami's South Beach, downtown, and even the new tunnel from its port have been flooded; the Florida Keys will be sunk as there are too few homes to merit spending on raising roads. The psychological and economic impact may be far greater: With each story of climate disaster emanating from Florida, fewer people plan to buy property or even visit.

Florida could, however, be home to ever more of the Caribbean's climate refugees, much as it took in victims of Haiti's massive 2010 earthquake. Within one year of the devastation wrought by Hurricane Maria in 2017, more than two hundred thousand Puerto Ricans had fled to the mainland US, most if not all for good. Despite the Bahamas' high income from tourism and offshore finance, the island of Grand Bahama was declared "dead" after Hurricane Dorian in 2019. Thousands of the country's four hundred thousand residents have already resettled in Florida and other states—and perhaps eventually they all will.

More than a century ago, millions of liberated black sharecroppers embodied the Great Migration as they shifted northward to the Midwest. In 2005, Hurricane Katrina pushed nearly one hundred thousand poor black residents of Louisiana out of the state—and perhaps many more will leave after the state's poor handling of the coronavirus. Already cities such as Atlanta, Dallas, Charlotte, and Austin are gaining climate migrants from elsewhere in the southern US.[9] The next great migration is accelerating.

Each time an American family loses everything, they become that much more likely to move. Vast swaths of American real estate are no longer deserving of their price—and certainly won't be a decade or so from now. As sea levels rise, towns on the "new coast" from Connecticut to Louisiana will have to raise taxes to fund sea barriers—and they'll have to pay for the barriers themselves since catastrophe insurance is drying up. The EPA currently ranks Alabama, Mississippi, Florida, Georgia, and the Carolinas as the states least prepared for climate hazards, with hurricanes reaching deep inland from America's Atlantic and Gulf coasts. But inland flooding from the Missouri and Mississippi Rivers also torments more than two dozen states, wiping out roads and bridges, wrecking countless homes, and even threatening nuclear reactors. According to BlackRock, most of American real estate west of the Mississippi is in water-stressed areas. The Great Plains states, such as the Dakotas, Nebraska, and Oklahoma, are America's breadbasket, making the region among the leading producers of corn, soybeans, cotton, and alfalfa, as well as livestock (cows, pigs, sheep, chickens). But while they're safe from the sea, they suffer from the combination of floods, which alter planting seasons, and oppressive summer heat waves. Together, these climate risks have made property in-surance either unaffordable or unavailable. Property owners and workers have crunched the numbers themselves: It's much cheaper (and smarter) to just move.

The federal government is finally taking a pragmatic stand. After $500 billion in disaster-related expenditures since 2005, adaptation is no longer a worthwhile expense. A coalition of agencies such as FEMA, HUD, and the Army Corps of Engineers (ACE) is pushing an agenda of "large-scale migration or relocation" packages for threatened coastal areas, especially along the Atlantic and Gulf coasts. Next they'll exert eminent domain, destroy at-risk homes, and provide buyouts for occupants to move.[10]

The more the financial industry quantifies climate risk, the more it will motivate migration decisions. Already baby boomers are reconsider-ing where to retire, both for their own sake and to avoid handing down depreciating (or nonexistent) assets to their children. Older Americans tend to want to pick one place to live and stay put—but this is not as easy as it seems. Retirement used to mean heading for the seafront, but increasingly it implies moving inland or into the mountains.

A map of the population density of the US and Canada reminds us how much space we have to spread into in search of livable geographies to cultivate. As in most industrialized countries, two-thirds of the Ameri-can population lives in cities, which represent just 3 percent of the land area. Half the American population lives in just nine states—but they won't be the same ones in 2030, 2040, and 2050. Which American states bring together the combination of climate resilience, job creation, and progressive politics young Americans are looking for?

As much as California has led the way in liberal governance and even (ironically) emissions regulations, the state is ill equipped for the climate challenge. America's West is two decades into a mega-drought in which hotter air absorbs more water from the ground while rainfall diminishes, turning California and its southern neighbors Nevada and Arizona into tinderboxes. Each year brings hotter temperatures and more severe wildfires, meaning California faces water, energy, and housing crises all at the same time. From the Bay Area to Los Angeles, thousands of homes of both the rich and poor have been charred, with insurance companies decades behind and billions short on payouts. California's utility PG&E has preemptively shut down power supply to prevent wildfires spreading through burnt power lines, but also blocked homeowners from switching to off-grid solar power, so the utility can continue collecting fees, effectively leaving even some of the richest Americans without power for days. Meanwhile, Los Angeles County continues to approve new home construction in fire-prone areas, but the more Hollywood studios and film sets get disrupted by climate change or coronavirus, the more the entertainment elite may decamp to European countries that offer tax breaks and healthier lifestyles.

California is becoming like its counterparts on the Atlantic and Gulf coasts: a survival society, an economy built around rebuilding itself. It has been pumping ever more from underground aquifers for agriculture, to cope with declining snowmelt and rainfall in the Sierra Nevada Mountains. But unless it can solve its water crisis by replenishing Lake Mead and Lake Powell and ramping up desalination, living there will become more liability than asset. For many, it makes more economic sense to just leave and start over someplace cheaper. California had long been America's promised land—until it wasn't.

Many Californians have already pushed into the inland West, but from Glacier National Park in Montana to Yosemite in California, the major parks they seek to be near have closed for months at a stretch due to wildfires. Authorities across the region will need more funds to absorb new migrants from the coast—and prevent their new homes from burning as their old ones in California already have. Duke University researchers have modeled the complexity of each American habitat zone to forecast the interactions of human, local animal species, soil and flora, tree cover, emissions, and other elements of our ecosystems, showing how easy it is for the delicate balance that we consider "normal" to be upset by increasing the temperature, the number of people, or other factors.[11] As we move, we bring risk.

In the cottage industry of climate gentrification, the Rocky Mountain region appears ascendant. Colorado has the altitude, water supply, and progressive politics that attract ever more millennials. Denver has expanded its airport, built a light-rail network downtown, and launched a World Trade Center business campus. The state's ski season is getting shorter, but it's attractive year-round for hiking and cultural festivals. Boulder has rejected high-rise buildings, adding to its aura as "America's happiest town."[12] But as temperatures rise, Colorado also faces winter rains and rapid snowmelt, drier summers and a diminishing Colorado River that sustains 40 million people across the southwestern US. Snow can only last as the state's most important source of water so long as there actually is snow.

In the Midwest, breadbasket states such as Nebraska, Kansas, and Oklahoma also face rapidly depleting groundwater. Particularly the southern US and Mexico rank among the most water-stressed regions of the world. But there are exceptions. Houston, America's busiest port city and oil capital, is gaining about a hundred thousand people per year, but its drainage system dates to a time when it barely received any rain. No wonder many areas are still recovering from Hurricane Harvey in 2017 and Tropical Storm Imelda in 2019, which brought five feet of flooding.

The complexity of climate change means that we can't be too confident in any one place guaranteeing safety from extreme climate events. For example, a 2012 report by the Nature Conservancy identified the long-derelict Appalachian region as a "natural stronghold" against climate change. Back then, one might have assumed that the hiking season would be longer and the ski season shorter, but otherwise no major downside effects in the medium term. More recent studies, however, suggest that the central Appalachians will actually experience significant temperature rise, biodiversity loss, and increased incidence of forest fires.

A roughly rectangular or diamond-shaped box around the Great

Lakes region, from Minneapolis down to Kansas City in the west, east-ward to Pittsburgh, and angling northeast to Poughkeepsie, with Canada's powerhouse provinces of Quebec and Ontario to the north—enjoys an abundance of freshwater and is set for milder winters. This greater rust belt region has been losing population since the financial crisis but will regain it due to climate migration. Illinois today is a fiscal basket case and Chicago ranks as America's most bankrupt large city—none of which will matter once Americans surge toward the region seeking a more sta-ble climate. Duluth, Minnesota, has earned the "climate refuge" moniker and is branding itself accordingly to boost its population of just under a hundred thousand people.[13] Well aware of their propitious geography, residents of Toledo, Ohio, have been pressing for a "Lake Erie Bill of Rights" to allow them to sue polluters. Bringing more residents there without strengthening environmental protections first would be a grave mistake even if it were not a crime.

Other climate-resilient zones are retrofitting themselves for their fu-ture as neo-industrial hubs. Minneapolis and Kansas City are recruit-ing startups, while Dayton is revitalizing its historic downtown district, known as the Arcade, that had been shuttered for several decades. Aban-doned company towns such as Buffalo are attracting Arab asylum seekers, Puerto Rican climate refugees, and fresh-off-the-boat Indian families. University towns such as Rochester (New York State's third biggest city) and Pittsburgh (home to more than three dozen higher education insti-tutions, including Carnegie Mellon) are doubling down on innovation districts and upgrading their water pipes and sewage treatment to prepare for future populations. Ann Arbor, Michigan, whose university represents more than one-third of its population of 120,000, needs to do all this as well since these college towns are well suited to absorb both academic and climate refugees from the south. Grand Rapids, Michigan, has nearly 1 million people in its metropolitan area (up from 750,000 in 2000) and is building an ecosystem of multipurpose technicians for the automotive and biomedical sectors.

There is an irony to how difficult it has been for retirees to sell their homes in the Hudson River Valley, from northern Westchester to Albany. While it's understandable that young families don't have the financial security to invest in large homes beyond the commuting range of New York City (especially since companies from IBM to Pepsi have shrunk their headquarters), few geographies offer the combination of elevation, freshwater, tree cover, safety, and other virtues. Climate change and Covid herald a regeneration for such climatically livable areas, as the new telecommuting class seeks out leafy and spacious suburbs. Even before Covid, clever states such as Vermont launched tax break schemes to attract remote workers. Tulsa, Oklahoma, is giving $10,000 to each new arrival. Other states with low living costs, such as Alaska, Tennessee, Idaho, Wyoming, and North Dakota, could easily do the same.

People will also move to places whose administrations take the reins after climate crises rather than bumbling along. Boston expects to have thirty days of high-tide flooding annually by 2030, and Logan Airport to be among the first in America to sink under the sea.[14] The city's authorities are now planning to buy and rezone land to build a new airport despite local political obstacles. By contrast, it's wise to avoid states losing people and facing a wave of municipal bankruptcies; they'll play chicken with Washington and lose, their decrepit public services eroding further. From North Carolina to Texas, the trash is no longer being collected in some small towns as the state abandons them and big cities finance only their own roads and sanitation.

Could there be an upside to America's staggeringly underfunded infrastructure renewal? America is littered with hundreds of thousands of derelict bridges, dams, and power lines. The country gets barely 10 percent of its energy from renewable sources such as wind and solar, and with three separate grids (East, West, and Texas), a Green New Deal seems a long way off. But new infrastructure plans could incorporate climate assessments and prioritize renewable power, with roads and residential zones located in areas from South Dakota to Missouri to Pennsylvania that are most likely to gain in population. Putting their overhaul first could bring America's future geographies into better alignment.

## New social distances

What will happen to America's major cities as a weak economy collides with listless youth and pandemic paranoia? Well before Covid, rising housing costs, bad immigration policy, and a global digital workforce were enough reasons for tech entrepreneur Balaji Srinivasan to prophesize a Silicon "exit." This "tech-sodus" has been underway for years as companies raise money in the Valley but spread their manpower globally. Numerous tech executives relocated their firms to Vancouver, referring to British Columbia as the "new California." Covid-19 then pushed the biggest tech companies to switch to (permanent) remote work, prompting a spike in Silicon Valley home sales. To keep struggling talent in the Valley and loyal to their companies, major tech firms have offered income share agreements and loans to help employees pay off their student debt and save to buy homes.[15] Google, Facebook, Apple, and others have also committed $4 billion to build homes in the Bay Area, but two hundred times that amount is needed. In any case, youth loathe corporate slavery and psychological burnout. They value urbanity and community, but it doesn't follow that they need to remain on the margins of others' lives to attain it.

New York City and Los Angeles are in a similar boat but at a far larger scale. In recent years, the outflow from coastal giants New York and Los Angeles has been backfilled by a new crop of ambitious, adventurous, or rich youth. But large corporate headquarters are downsizing in favor of smaller satellite offices and remote work—the triumph of digitization over agglomeration. Before the pandemic, only 4 percent of the American workforce were telecommuters. That figure could increase fourfold or more in the years ahead. Many companies would rather pay salaries or offer consultant contracts to remote workers who have quality connectivity at home rather than spend on expensive commercial real estate.

So what kind of places will youth prefer as their hub, the place they sleep, make friends, and spend free time? The US has more than two dozen major urban regions, each of which is competing to guard or upgrade its niche to remain viable and attract new residents. Millennials and Gen-Z are getting clever about calculating their post-tax cost of living before deciding where to take a job.[16] They have been snapping up houses in New Hampshire, Missouri, and Idaho, and fueling the percolating tech scenes in Salt Lake City, Atlanta, Indianapolis, and Phoenix.[17] Another winning formula is that of so-called "18-hour cities"—such as Denver, Charlotte, Nashville, Portland, San Antonio, Atlanta, and San Diego—that have a lively after-work culture in their downtown areas.[18] Las Vegas also lured young thrill seekers with full-service lifestyle hubs like AREA 15, with its pop-up retail and futuristic entertainment. Minneapolis has unveiled a 2040 plan to reduce housing inequality by eliminating the zoning bias toward single-family homes and building more affordable units. Such cities could become a nationwide model attuned to future demographics.

When Americans move within the country, they bring a greater density of businesses and investment. New York and California are home to almost half of America's small and medium-size businesses, but these are being lured to low-tax "sunbelt" markets such as Texas, Florida, North Carolina, Colorado, and Georgia. And instead of the West Coast and Boston hogging all the VC investment and tech jobs, Austin, Pittsburgh, Nashville, and Charlotte are expanding as living labs for blue chip corporations such as Amazon.[19] They'll also draw tech incubators such as Plug & Play or 500 Startups. AOL founder Steve Case's Revolution is devoted to boosting tech ecosystems in neglected cities nationwide.

States today are divided between low tax and low regulation (as in Texas) or high tax and high regulation (as in California), but the states that may win the future are low tax and high regulation, such as Washington. Seattle has the fastest growing population among America's fifty biggest cities but has kept traffic down through huge investments in railways, buses, and bike lanes. Giant Seattle-based companies such as Boeing, Microsoft, Amazon, and Starbucks, and the thousands of smaller firms in their ecosystems, have become a world unto themselves, propelling the city into the top ten of America's metro-regional heavyweights.

Rising city costs, the Covid lockdown, and the explosion in telecommuting are also likely to bring about a substantial suburban revival. As large cities lose residents, suburbs could regenerate as the full-time oasis for well-paid telecommuting executives. Covid-19 witnessed an exodus of the nearly five hundred thousand wealthy from urban centers to second homes in the Hamptons and Catskills outside New York, Napa Valley north of San Francisco, and the Atlantic or Mediterranean coasts for Europeans. Over the course of the summer, thousands of residents of New York's major boroughs bought homes in Upstate New York, Long Island, and New Jersey with plans to permanently relocate out of the city. What once were holiday or country homes are now being retrofitted (especially with fiber broadband) as primary residences far from urban lockdowns and protests. Big-city dwellers used to gloat to their rural relatives about their superior quality of life; now it could be the reverse. Or maybe not: Some who fled San Francisco for Napa Valley in the summer of 2020 had to be re-evacuated *back* to San Francisco because of wildfires. The next superstorm that hits the Northeast may not spare the Hamptons either.

In the meantime, even a 10 percent shift from cities to suburbia would have a significant (and opposite) impact on both in America's $27 trillion real estate market. If suburbs become spacious, full-service enclaves with greater density of activity, the new suburbanites will treat cities as pay-per-use and spend their tax dollars on strengthening local communities and schools in their counties. Youth are looking for charismatic communities, and the ideals of small-town America hold growing appeal as they become alienated from big-city life.

In any case, the main destination for many millennials since the financial crisis has been their childhood bedrooms in their parents' homes. Now they've been joined by their Gen-Z siblings: As of September 2020, 52 percent of America's young adults live with their parents. For those who can't afford to move out, remote work may provide sufficient incentive to stay and live rent free, though perhaps supporting their parents' mortgage payments. American homes have been getting bigger while families have been getting smaller, but maybe the suburban family home will make a comeback as an affordable multigenerational hive. Many youth will wind up as suburban service workers—cooking, cleaning, babysitting, fitness training, and performing other tasks for the new settled class. Tinder-like apps will match young people to jobs in every zip code. Youth have little choice but to follow the money.

## America's next Americans

There are many reasons to be awed by America—its size, wealth, and freedom. But culture shock shouldn't be one of them. After all, America has the world's largest migrant stock, more than 50 million people representing every corner of the planet. No matter where you're from, you've got a community like you somewhere (or in many places) in America.

It's a convenient myth, then, that reducing immigration would allow America to focus on improving race relations and restoring high employment. Fortunately, even where the view from the top dictates immigration retrenchment, the bottom-up reality has been continuously expanding immigration. Consider how the 1882 Exclusion Act barred Chinese immigration for generations, yet Chinese represent the largest Asian population in the country today, and Asians overall are the fastest growing demographic of new immigrants. Asian-Americans have been targets of racist attacks from the nineteenth century cholera outbreak to the 2020 coronavirus pandemic, yet their numbers have continued to swell to more than 20 million.

White nationalism may be a potent force in American politics, but it doesn't change the fact that only 29 percent of young Americans are white and Christian, and that by 2045, blacks and Hispanics together are expected to make up half or more of the total US population. While only 18 percent of boomers are nonwhite, 48 percent of Gen-Z is non-white (especially black, Latino, or Asian). White nationalists and freedom militias such as the Proud Boys (who famously protested the coronavirus lockdown by brandishing their weapons at state capitols) tell themselves that they have become America's outcasts, and turn to websites such as Infowars, American Renaissance, and Stormfront to find allegiance among the disgruntled. But they are a dying breed (often at their own hand). The Base, a fledgling neo-Nazi group, has resorted to plugging into Gen-Z social media platforms such as iFunny to attempt to recruit curious members. Whether restricting immigration only to white people or replacing the federal government with an Aryan Nation, white nationalism's goals are about as realistic as ISIS becoming a new global caliphate.

A society with a robust consensus about its national identity has the collective confidence to absorb more migrants. But if a country can't agree (any more) about what its identity is, then its debates over immigration are bound to be convulsive. But youth certainly aren't the ones who blame immigrants for crime or globalization for job losses. A 2020 Gallup poll in America showed the highest level of support ever registered—77 percent—for greater immigration.[20] This shouldn't come as a surprise since it's precisely because of decades of expansive immigration that youth have grown up in a country far more racially diverse than what their elders remember; youth simply don't view nationality in purely racial terms. In 2020, a record three hundred black, Latin, Asian, Arab, and Latin Americans ran for congressional offices.

The evidence that divisive identity politics is backfiring lies in historically "red" states such as Colorado, Arizona, Georgia, Florida, and even Texas tilting ever more "blue" as educated and diverse youth file into their cities. The question for Texas isn't how white natives and immigrants in general get along, but how Mexicans and Indians get along—and the answer in San Antonio appears to be: just fine. The greater problem is white nationalism: Texas has the most shootings of any state. Immigrants have streamed into Oregon and Washington for the placid scenery only to encounter violent standoffs between right-wing militias and Antifa groups (as well as gun-toting ranchers and police). America's shambolic handling of the coronavirus and the social fuse lit by the George Floyd protests led many immigrants to second-guess their decision to come to America in the first place.

Overall, however, Latin and Asian immigrants have the zeal of the born-again Americans that they are. According to a CATO Institute survey, three-quarters of naturalized immigrants say they're "very proud" of being American, a higher share than the native-born population.[21] Indian immigrants have become patriotic Americans to such a degree that India's far right RSS Hindu movement considers many of them to be traitors. They also reinforce "American values" since they're more likely to remain married, in two-income households, and go to college. Any non-racist view of "American identity" should fully support how immigration renews America's essence.

On the present course of diminished migration, it's likely that rich America (urban whites and Asians) will continue to decouple from the rest of the country. A high-tech manufacturing renaissance automates most industrial production, but takes away most of the basic retail and logistics jobs on which many lower-income African-Americans, Latinos, and whites depend. The marginalization of African-Americans in major cities ensures (another) lost generation of black youth unable to thrive outside of their ghettos. Intermarriage accelerates as whites and minorities mingle, but so does white flight as white families shift out of neighborhoods increasingly populated by blacks, Latinos, and Asians (feared for their academic rigor).[22] America thus becomes both more mongrelized and ghettoized at the same time. Low-skilled immigrants are admitted to care for the elderly, but 100 million or more Americans require a government crutch to get basic medical care and housing. The population resorts to neo-medieval enclaves of privileged versus disenfranchised—federalized not just politically but in every facet of life. This America would be larger, but not richer.

Things may continue to get worse before they get better. But what does "better" look like? An America that is greater than the sum of its parts would regenerate itself through large-scale investments in infrastructure, skills, and mobility, turning wealth into opportunity for all. And it would embrace demographic renewal. For more than two centuries, immigration has made each generation of Americans more diverse, and the nation's identity ever more textured. In America today, you can't easily tell who is and who is not an "American." Perhaps only when it becomes too late will the country realize that it's best to let people come and become American rather than deciding in advance that foreigners are not American enough. Nations are "imagined communities," in the words of scholar Benedict Anderson—and each generation is entitled to imagine a new one.

## Go north, young man!

While the US convulses over immigration policy, its spacious neighbor to the north has far fewer qualms. Canada has entered the immigration big leagues, taking in almost 350,000 migrants annually to add to its 30 million population—a far higher annual percentage than the US. Canada's "Century Initiative" openly aspires to grow the population to 100 million—at which point its population will likely surpass that of Russia. Is Canada the migration magnet of the twenty-first century?

In the 1970s, Canada's main internal cultural fissure revolved around the semi-autonomous French-speaking province of Quebec. The government of Pierre Trudeau pushed for Canadian identity to encompass not just the Anglo-French dualism but all minorities, such as the indigenous Inuit and growing number of South Asians. Since then, generations of Canadians have grown up in an officially multicultural nation. Multiculturalism *is* Canadian identity. Citizenship ceremonies for newly minted Canadians are sometimes held in hockey stadiums (the closest thing in Canada to a mass church) with fans cheering to welcome their new compatriots. Canadians know that their current migrant intake constitutes social engineering on a grand scale. For the experiment to succeed, national political and societal support will have to buck the populism that animates American and European politics. The country will also need a strategic demographic plan that transcends the vision and charm of the Trudeau family—both *pere* and *fils*.

Canada embodies the reality that immigration policy is economic policy. Its aging population requires caregivers; its eastern and maritime provinces need to be rejuvenated with new industries, from IT to hydropower; its thawing frontiers require hearty workers to cultivate the bounty, and connecting its oil patch and farmlands to global markets requires new pipelines and a vast freight rail network. There aren't nearly enough Canadians to do it all. One-fifth of Canada's current population is immigrants, who account for most—and soon all—of its population growth, especially South Asians and Chinese. If Canada continues this high immigration trajectory, by 2036 half the country's population will be foreign-born or have at least one immigrant parent. Canadians foresee a future that is "as brown as white."

The greater Toronto area city of Brampton is already far more brown than white. But rather than setting up self-governing enclaves, Brampton's Punjabis are running for office and asking for greater representation in public sector jobs. The fact that 15 percent of seats in the House of Commons are occupied by parliamentarians with immigrant backgrounds demonstrates how Canada has crossed the point of no return toward a mongrelized future.

Canada is far more comfortable than the US with becoming a majority nonwhite country. It may pull ahead in the next wave of the immigration-innovation nexus as well. Canada is on the hunt for talent as it seeks to diversify its economy, and Indians are an easy target to poach. The number of annual Indian immigrants to Canada more than doubled between 2016 and 2019, to nearly ninety thousand, more than migrated to the US. Critics of Trump's 2020 executive order suspending the H1-B visa program dubbed the order the "Canadian job creation act." Next Canada could pluck from the five hundred thousand Indian-origin residents of Silicon Valley alone. American nationalists shouldn't separate the innovation emerging within their borders from the diverse nationalities of the brains that produced them. Without the latter, much less would happen in the former.

Americans themselves in growing numbers have awakened to the Canadian model. After all, the "Canadian Dream" is much more attainable than the American Dream. Canada is not only a case study in systematic mass migration and assimilation, but also a policy lab for experiments in reducing inequality. Canada ranks far higher than the US in social mobility: Almost 20 percent of Americans are born below the poverty line, a figure that's less than 8 percent in Canada—where homeless people are given homes, as well as jobs feeding hungry people. America, meanwhile, is going through its second eviction crisis within a decade, worsening both poverty and hunger.

Americans and Canadians have been moving with relative ease across their long interoceanic border for two centuries. The expansion of large-scale farming just over one hundred years ago lured 750,000 Americans to Canada's prairie provinces of Alberta, Manitoba, and Saskatchewan. Today as many as 2 million Americans live north of the border, and their numbers are rising. After 2016, it was Trump's election that drove a new wave north of the border. In 2020, at the height of the coronavirus, Americans jammed Canadian real estate websites, buying properties unseen. Canadians joke they'll need to build a wall along their border to keep Americans out. At least they wisely banned assault weapons in 2020, keeping out the most odious American trait.

European numbers may well expand alongside American. Like America, Canada has a large Eastern European diaspora, and as those homelands continue to depopulate while unemployment remains high, many of the jobless could skip across the Atlantic to join their relatives. Remember that with its parliamentary form of government and welfare system, Canada is much more like continental Europe than the US or UK, which partially explains why its politics since the financial crisis has stuck to the centrist path of the Netherlands, France, and Germany rather than the virulent populist nationalism of America and Britain.

There is one other major reason for youth to favor Canada: The vast majority of new jobs created are full-time rather than just temp work. Indeed, Canada's immigrant surge coincides with oil's collapse, meaning the country is betting on a more diversified economy focused on manu- facturing and services as well. To cope with its growing population and to prevent an anti-immigration backlash, Canada needs to build far more residential communities, schools, and hospitals. Most migrants to Canada concentrate in the major cities, near the US border, such as Toronto, Montreal, and Vancouver, but even as Vancouver is one of the world's hottest property markets, rising sea levels and forest fires threaten its mild climate and pricey real estate.

Canadians old and new are therefore likely to become more dis- persed—farther and farther north. Towns in Canada's inland provinces of Ontario and Manitoba—such as Churchill, Manitoba—are becoming much more desirable as the climate warms and Hudson Bay becomes a grand Arctic gateway. Most Canadians are unfamiliar with their northern provinces of the Yukon, Northwest Territories, and Nunavut—thinking of them as a vast emptiness—yet they're incredibly rich in energy and minerals, and home to vast boreal forests (*taiga* in Russian) of coniferous pine and spruce trees. Canadians will become much more aware of their bounty in the years ahead. As Canada warms, its agricultural output has swelled, with organic farming and crop rotation across millions of hec- tares producing ever greater yields of wheat, legumes, millets, flax, and oats. The acreage of protein-rich soy growth has also accelerated all across Canada. A single drone made by Flash Forest can plant one hundred thousand trees each month, meaning billions more trees sprouting by 2030. Canada's energy, agriculture, and technology sectors are expanding in lockstep with its population.

But Canada is not without climate risk. Sea levels are rising along the Atlantic coast province of Newfoundland, the incidence of forest fires is increasing, and if the US diverts Great Lakes water (in violation of a 2008 compact), Canada may have to draw from its freshwater basins in the north as well as its Rocky Mountain glaciers. The current agro-boom, while promising, has a patchy road ahead. Temperatures are rising at twice the global average: Today's farms could turn to dust tomorrow, and new agricultural belts will be stable for shorter periods.

This is why some suggest that Canada choose the path of "zero growth": keep the population low, stabilize emissions, and focus on domestic social concerns. Growth would decline for a period but eventually stabilize, while living standards for the existing population should eventually improve by upgrading technology rather than importing people. Of course, Canada could also reduce its carbon footprint simply by deploying existing technologies to green the extraction from its noxious oil sands. This could be done without returning to the boring low-immigration society it used to be—or abandoning the path of the high-immigrant society the world needs it to be.

# CHAPTER 5
# THE EUROPEAN COMMONWEALTH

### The European way

Sometimes it takes awhile to get used to a new flag. The twelve-starred European flag was adopted in the mid-1980s, but only hoisted in front of buildings across the Union after the 1992 Maastricht Treaty. Shortly thereafter, I remember the euphoric atmosphere at "Euro 2020" conferences in which we boisterously simulated the EU's diplomatic rituals, pushing Model UN to the side. Yet because young Europeans can't remember a time before the EU, they also came to take it for granted.[1] Only after Europe's recent moves toward greater fiscal solidarity—and perhaps a glance across the Atlantic—has the EU's popularity recovered. According to a Pew survey, from 2012 to 2019, the EU gained 26 percentage points in favorability in generally Euro-skeptic Greece, reaching 53 percent. In Germany, Spain, Sweden, and the Netherlands, the EU's standing is nearly 70 percent; in Poland, it's 80 percent. Four years after Brexit, the EU's popularity in Britain was ironically higher than ever.[2]

The EU today has a population approximately twice the size of America's, including about double the number (180 million) of teens and young adults. While America and Europe have diverged in fundamental ways—Americans scorn Europe's geopolitical weakness while Europeans mock America's crass inequality—they observe each other closely enough for ideas to spill over. Alexandria Ocasio-Cortez's push for "democratic socialism" is nothing other than a repackaging of the social democratic welfare state hundreds of millions of Europeans have enjoyed for decades. Meanwhile, from Occupy Wall Street and Black Lives Matter to Google, Europeans are inspired by America's unbounded social energy and entrepreneurialism.

But Europe has built-in advantages over America when it comes to reflecting the preferences of youth. Most obviously, while the US has minimum ages to be a member of the House (twenty-five), Senate (thirty), and to be elected President (thirty-five), Europeans face no such restrictions. Far more young people have become mayors, parliamentarians, or even prime ministers than is conceivable in America. Europe also has multi-party political systems rather than America's rigid duopoly, meaning compromise within coalitions is essential to avoid gridlock. This also means that whereas America's young politicians are forced into party discipline, Europeans can start new parties such as the Pirate Party, which has been successful across northern and eastern Europe. All of this helps to explain the recent surge of green parties in France and across Europe. In a number of German provinces and in Austria, there are now "black-green" coalitions of conservatives and greens, forcing these seeming extremes to work together on issues such as raising the retirement age, supporting more flexible worker insurance, and promoting clean energy.

These political differences stem from divergent philosophical foundations and lead to very different outcomes for ordinary people. Whereas the American Bill of Rights and Constitution enumerate individuals' protections *from* the federal government and states' purview, European constitutions delineate people's right *to* voice and welfare as well as protections *from* abuse of power. The average European country spends nearly 30 percent of GDP on social services, far higher than America's 15 percent. Europeans thus enjoy free education and healthcare, while at the same time banks can't rip them off, tech companies can't steal their data, and energy companies can't pollute their soil and water. During the Covid-19 lockdown, European governments ensured that the unemployed received a majority of their wages without having to wait for a meager check in the mail as Americans did. Many firms switched to what Germans call *Kurzarbeit*, in which all employees work reduced hours to avoid anyone getting fired. Europeans won't give up on their progressive regulations in the name of higher "competitiveness."

For Americans, Europe's social scaffolding must seem utopian: universal medical care, basic income, subsidized college tuition, and savings accounts. European nations also fare much better in education levels, affordable housing, and public transportation, all crucial factors in enabling social mobility.* The Global Peace Index finds that almost all of the top twenty-five safest countries are in Europe (supplemented by Japan, New Zealand, Singapore, and Bhutan).

What Europeans are not accustomed to, however, is working in the gigonomy. As a result, like their American counterparts, most have either no savings or barely enough for three months of expenses. But unlike Americans, most Europeans don't possess credit cards by which to pile on debt. They're frugal with their debit cards and use mobile banking services such as Revolut or Klarna to slice up and defer payments. Also, more Europeans continue to live at home with their parents, providing a higher degree of basic stability. European millennial life is civilized, but full of ennui.

Europeans have been so accustomed to free tuition, stable employment, and universal benefits that curbs to benefits are met with mass street protests by unions and students. But Europe is also where genuine experiments in lifelong social stability are being rolled out, such as Finland's life account system that doesn't tax savings, and Dutch portable pensions managed by the state but funded by employers. European countries not only have shock absorbers for individual workers' wages, but also provide stronger backing for SMEs rather than large corporations. Even though Europeans pay on average between 40 to 60 percent of their incomes in

---

* Since 1980, the bottom 50 percent of Americans have seen incomes rise a mere 3 percent, whereas the lower half of Europeans have had a 40 percent gain in incomes. According to a study published by Georgetown University in 2019, America is a country where it's far better to be born rich than smart. See: Abigail Hess, "Georgetown Study: 'To Succeed in America, It's Better to Be Born Rich Than Smart,'" CNBC, May 29, 2019.

taxes, their nations occupy the entire top tier in Wharton's ranking of the best countries in which to run your own business.

Europe doesn't have innovative tech giants, but it deploys innovations for public benefit. For example, the high-performance and open-source operating system Linux was invented in Finland. Unlike America or China, where corporations or the state control data, Europe is most progressive in personal data protection, allowing pro-citizen data marketplaces to thrive. Coworking too is far older than WeWork. The Belgian coworking pioneer IWG (formerly Regus) began in 1989 in Belgium and is far more widespread than the flashier unicorn WeWork, without the financial chicanery. Europe's post-Covid recovery plan includes billions of dollars to grow clean energy, IT, and other European champions to assert Europe's autonomy from both America and China. It's ironic that Washingtonians speak about a world of two models when the model most of the world wants to emulate is the European one.

One should never bet against America, but one can get very impatient with it. That's certainly the view of the throngs of Americans who have moved to Europe over the past decade, abandoning America's excessively creative destruction and the politics of outrage in favor of regulated capitalism and liberty with sensible constraints. Many Americans no longer want to wait for America to become a European-style welfare system—they're just moving to Europe to get it. Rather than amassing six figures of debt, a rising number of American students are going straight to Europe after high school and doing their full undergraduate degree in English-language programs. And with teacher salaries higher in Europe, ever more English teachers are being lured across the Atlantic as well.

The number of Americans moving to Europe annually has jumped, bringing the total to more than 1 million today. The UK is home to the most American expats, but Germany and France are gaining popularity.* Ump-

---

* An estimated 800,000 Americans reside in Europe, with 216,000 in the UK, 127,000 in Germany, and roughly 50,000 each in France, Italy, and Spain, with a further 50,000 spread across Eastern Europe. United Nations, "International Migrant Stock by Origin and Destination," Department of Economic and Social Affairs, Population Division, 2019.

teen websites and blogs have cropped up with self-congratulatory stories of Americans moving on one-way tickets to Ireland, the Netherlands, Italy, and a half-dozen other countries, extolling the virtues of European public safety, affordable healthcare, consumer-friendly regulations, and family-friendly employment policies—and providing step-by-step guidance on how to follow in their footsteps. During the nineteenth century, European migrants gave American industry and society a seismic boost in manpower. Could Americans do the same for Europe during the twenty-first?

### The rise of Asian-Europeans

Over the past thirty years, there has been a soft competition among Western European nations to attract the best and the brightest from the exodus out of the former Soviet Union (particularly Russia), with Germany and Britain (together with the US and Israel) being the clear winners. But when it comes to Asians, America has garnered the largest share of Japanese, Korean, Chinese, and Indian talent. There are more than twice as many Asian-Americans (just over 20 million) as there are "Asian-Europeans"—which is why that term doesn't really exist. But the coming years will witness the Asian-European population surge, making it not only a category in its own right but perhaps one that eclipses Asian-Americans in number.

As Eastern Europeans have uprooted themselves en masse to head for Western Europe, their homelands have become fertile ground for migrants from farther east who are also moving west. Keeping the land fertile, however, will require some work: During 2020, droughts forced Poland and Romania to ban grain exports. They and other countries in the region will need to invest much more in new hydro-engineering projects to remain breadbaskets for both east and west. But with funds from the west faltering, more will come from the east—and more farmers and other migrants too.

Romania is becoming a test case of what this might look like. The country has branded itself as a low-cost tech hub with wages as modest as those of India's IT industry. In fact, the town of Cluj invited Indian software executives and engineers to coach it on how to become a Romanian version of Bangalore. Romania still faces a shortage of about *1 million* skilled and unskilled workers—hence its plan to lure that many from India, Pakistan, Sri Lanka, and Vietnam to work in construction, medicine, tech, and agriculture.[3] How many will ever return to Asia?

The Czech Republic is already one of the hottest relocation destinations in Europe, with foreigners making up 10 percent of the country's workforce. The majority of new arrivals are Russians, Ukrainians, or Americans, who have cemented Prague's status as a hot study-abroad hub. Already one-quarter of the country's entire student population are foreigners. As the Czech education system pivots to English, ever more students will come from around the world for an affordable and scenic degree. Furthermore, as with other European societies, Czech fertility levels are abysmally low. While government funding for up to three IVF cycles has had a negligible impact on Czech fertility, it has given rise to a thriving IVF industry catering to cost-conscious would-be parents.

This influx of students and young families helps small and insular European states gain comfort in their openness while filling their labor shortages. It also gives foreigners a toehold in societies far more stable than where they come from.

Given Europe's low birth rates, it's ironic that almost all of the top-ranked countries in the world for raising children (based on variables such as female empowerment and child nutrition) are in Europe. With such a large idle housing stock and quality infrastructure, it would be a pity for future generations not to enjoy the benefits of the life Europe has built. Indeed, the only way for European nations to maintain their generous welfare states—even for themselves—is to import new taxpayers who pay into the pot from which they collect.

Only Poland has managed to stabilize its population, mostly by attracting an estimated two hundred thousand neighboring Ukrainians. To reverse brain drain, it has also scrapped its income tax for young workers. Poland and Croatia have become home to some of the hottest e-learning startups, while Ukraine (and until its present unrest, Belarus) has attracted Estonian and Russian investment as a low-cost tech back office. The Belt and Road Initiative has made China one of the largest investors in many Eastern European countries, opening the door to a long-term Asian merchant population as well.

And so begins the soft competition among Eastern European states not to ward off talented foreigners but to attract them. But even as young Russians continue to seek a more liberal life to the west, there aren't enough Slavic youth left to repopulate Europe—either eastern or western. But farther east lie many hundreds of millions of highly and semi-skilled Asians eager to become Asian-Europeans.

### Southern Europe for sale

In January 1968, an earthquake struck Italy's treasured island of Sicily, claiming more than two hundred lives and leaving more than one hundred thousand homeless. Some towns, such as Poggioreale, were so decimated that Rome commissioned famous architects to design entirely new ones to which survivors were resettled. The mayor of nearby Salemi had another idea: He could attract citizens to come and rebuild his town by effectively giving away homes. Forty years later, in 2008, his successor updated the policy and, in keeping with the country's new currency, officially launched a scheme to sell abandoned homes for exactly 1 euro.

What started out as a local gimmick has become a nationwide arms race among villages, towns, and mid-size cities to lure new residents—or risk disappearing off the national map. Some offer tax abatements and even 25,000 euros to anyone willing to start a business. Many such measures were rolled out first to the national population—with tepid results. Southern Italy won't survive as an inhabited region without convincing far more *foreigners* to make its vacant provinces their new home. With a number of towns in Calabria and Abruzzi Provinces unscathed by Covid, campaigns such as "Operation Beauty," in the town in Cinquefrondi, have gained momentum as a wide range of Europeans seek safety in emptiness. The Italians want not just individuals and couples but people who will bring yet more relatives and friends in tow: You could recreate your entire social circle in an abandoned Italian town.

Even populous and wealthy regions such as Spain's Catalonia have taken the cue and launched their own versions of Italy's schemes. There you can buy an entire village of eighty hectares, with fourteen homes, for 280,000 euros—and become the mayor by default. You own the place, after all. Since hosting the 1992 Summer Olympics, Barcelona has undergone a major renaissance, which combined with its worldly history has made it Spain's most cosmopolitan city. More recently, however, its overregulated property market—construction costs are too high and tenancy rights too lenient—has scared Spanish developers away. As a result, even prime neighborhoods such as the Barceloneta district, by the city's scenic port, are in tatters, with aging (or even deceased) owners hoarding decrepit buildings. Why not build affordable and sustainable housing for young workers and talented entrepreneurs?

This wouldn't be the first time Spain has needed to import hardworking immigrants to fill labor shortages. In the 1990s and 2000s, many young Pakistanis entered the country on temporary permits, over time gravitating toward the seaside climate of Barcelona, where they settled down, started families, and learned to speak both Spanish and some Catalan. Now they diligently run electronics shops and pharmacies, living comfortable working-class lives. During a recent visit, I had only one *non*-Pakistani taxi driver over the course of an entire week. Barcelona's Raval neighborhood (just off the famed Las Ramblas boulevard) has become a Gothic Lahore.

Spain continues its haphazard efforts to cobble together its next generation. There are about 2.5 million Latinos in Spain, but it could easily attract more Mexicans or Colombians. As in Germany and Italy, birthright policies are being revised to more easily grant citizenship to those who share the country's heritage. Citizenship can be acquired after residing in Spain for ten years, and in 2015, a law was passed awarding citizenship to Sephardic Jews (who were expelled from the country in the fifteenth century) on the basis of cultural and historical ties.

Portugal is with good reason one of the more popular destinations for Europeans and others seeking long-term stability. Climate change is expected to have less impact on its freshwater resources, which are abundant in the north around Porto and in the southern region of Algarve. Portugal's socialist-leaning government has reversed its post-crisis economic decline, boosting public investment in trains and subways and raising wages. It's also seeking to lure back more than 2 million overseas Portuguese. In the 2000s, down-and-out Portuguese sought work in their thriving former colony of Brazil—now it's the reverse. During the pandemic lockdown, Portugal gave full rights to all migrants and asylum seekers already in the country, so they could get Covid tests. Others could learn from this brand of progressive socialism.

Europe faces a choice between assimilating migrants or falling off a demographic cliff. As in America, Europe needs unskilled migrants to fix infrastructure, collect trash, care for the elderly, help integrate other foreigners, and countless other functions. Europe depends on Polish plumbers, Romanian farmers, and African sanitation workers. Despite rising unemployment in the UK and a seventy-thousand-worker shortage picking crops, only one hundred Britons showed up in response to a government call to step into farming roles during the Covid lockdown. Societies that don't accept the necessary number and range of migrants to plug their labor shortages wind up poorer.

Even southern EU members such as Greece, Italy, and Spain have shortages of farmers, kitchen staff, and street cleaners. Rather than firing with machine guns at boats loaded with Syrian asylum seekers, they should figure out how to make the most of them. Refugees from as far as Afghanistan and Nigeria have squatted in empty buildings in Athens, but just as they began looking for work, the Greek government evicted them and corralled them into tent camps where they sit and do nothing. Instead, they should allocate migrants to different provinces and cities based on an assessment of local needs, employment levels, and housing capacity, balancing the load not only to spread the benefits of immigrants but also to avoid listless ghettos.

From Spain to Italy to Bulgaria, southern Europe is a squatter's paradise, a finders-keepers world of abandoned towns and villages. Its vast tracts of fertile land and fixable housing are practically crying out to be occupied by tens of millions of migrants, who in exchange for a stable new life could revitalize ailing economies. Ultimately, this would give these lands a higher purpose than to be sentimental graveyards. Egyptian billionaire Naguib Sawiris offered Italy or Greece $100 million for a depopulated island to repurpose for sheltering Arab refugees. Should an uninhabited island's sovereignty matter more than its utility?

### An assimilation emergency

In the past decade, more than 1 million Arabs from countries such as Syria and Libya and 1 million Africans (mostly from the Congo, Eritrea, Somalia, and Sudan) have made it into Europe, mostly via Turkey or across the Mediterranean. But while Europe has generally been welcoming toward Slavic and Balkan peoples, it has had much more difficulty absorbing Arabs, Africans, and Muslims in general. Indeed, the bargain holding Europe's internal borders open is that the Mediterranean routes must be shut.

But Europe has to grapple with the millions of migrants already in its midst, the young Arabs loitering in city centers and the Africans who often stay on the move, sharing through the grapevine which towns are becoming more tolerant versus abusive. Drug dealing, burglary, and other crimes have shot up drastically. Barcelona has earned a reputation as a "smart city" for its mixed-use urban design and data sensors to facilitate traffic, but as many travel websites already forewarn, it's also the "pick-pocket capital of the world." Thus far, Spanish authorities have resisted taking the more intrusive approaches to "smart-ness" found in New York and Beijing: ubiquitous police cameras. Yet the downside of Barcelona's magnetic status may be the need for more muscular governance to maintain law and order.

Though the UK has already become something of a surveillance society, crime has been rising there as well, with forty thousand knife attacks in 2018 alone, mostly perpetrated by young black or Muslim males. Acid attacks are also on the rise, with the main perpetrators and victims being white, Afro-Caribbean, or Pakistani. Clearly, the fact that many immigrants have fled illiberal countries doesn't mean they don't harbor their own intolerant tendencies, or adopt those attitudes once they have resettled.

In Britain, an older generation of Pakistanis and Arabs have set up their own parallel social world of arranged marriages imposed on their effectively Western children. From suburban turf wars to underage prostitution among so-called "grooming gangs," the Pakistani Muslim community in the UK has many members who seem unaware that they live in a country that prides itself on human rights and the rule of law. In boroughs of east London, Pakistani radicals from Muslims Against the Crusades push for Shariah self-policing, effectively calling for their own Islamic emirate that forbids drinking, gambling, and music, and in which adultery is punished with stoning, and stealing with cutting off hands. All of this helps explain how three of the four perpetrators of the July 7, 2005, bombings in London that killed fifty-two people were British born and raised Pakistanis who attended radical mosques.

Wherever migrants have come from, the challenge of assimilation is a generational one—and unfortunately addressed a generation later than it should have been. As with Latinos in the United States, Arab and African migrants in Europe tend to stay longer than expected and have higher birth rates than indigenous populations. The cities with the largest Muslim populations—Brussels, Birmingham, Antwerp, Amsterdam, Marseilles, and Malmö—have entire neighborhoods consisting only of migrants. Islamophobic terror is on the rise, with anti-immigrant groups torching mosques, shisha bars, and other places Muslims convene. Meanwhile, there are tensions between migrant groups themselves. In 2019, a viral video taken on a crowded London double-decker bus showed a Somali woman in a hijab ranting against an Indian man, denouncing his smell and imploring him to go home. They may well both have been British citizens. Nationality is no guarantor of civility.

As Syrians and Turks, Indians and Pakistanis, Chinese and Vietnamese all settle in Europe, they don't leave their countries' rivalries behind. Instead, their animosities become domestic disputes that play out on European streets. In the 1990s, Kurds and Turks bombed each other's shops and gas stations; today the Kurds take to the streets protesting Turkey's incursion into Syria. Turks in Europe are themselves divided over President Erdogan, with football players of Turkish descent publicly shamed for saluting him while European governments heavily criticize his authoritarianism. On an otherwise calm day in the shadow of the Acropolis, it's no longer a strange sight to see a column of traditionally clad Pakistani men marching behind a van with a loudspeaker blaring praise for Allah and denunciations of India's actions in Kashmir—all in Urdu, which nobody else in Athens understands.

Who is to blame for what sometimes feels like a clash of civilizations playing out on European city streets? The fault lies both with unassimilated parents as well as a nativist chauvinism that doesn't accept as equals people from former colonies—or quite frankly from anywhere. Either way, one solution to better integrate the millions of migrants in their midst is for law enforcement agencies to hire more men and women with ethnic backgrounds who understand the cultural nuances of those they're protecting from one another. The other obvious and overdue measure would be to subsidize a mass program of intensive language training so they can prepare to become functionally self-sufficient and employable.

Europe doesn't have a migration problem. It has an assimilation problem, one that can be solved by smart socioeconomic policies. Between demographic decline and assimilation challenges, the latter ought to be the preferable choice. Migration will continue—the only question is whether cultural assimilation will succeed.

## The new Germans

Between 2015 and 2016, Germany accepted more than 1 million Arab asylum seekers, a stunning demonstration of the country's *Willkommens—kultur* that was lauded across the world. With its famous logistical prowess, migrants were allocated to and embraced in cities and towns across the country, with Berlin's Cold War–era Tempelhof Airport serving as a temporary refuge as well. But as the spotlight faded, the task of processing hundreds of thousands of indefinite new residents did not. What will it take to assimilate millions of migrants in a country once synonymous with race-based identity?

Turks in Germany represent one of the most settled diasporas, albeit one that has never been fully at ease psychologically. A first generation of postwar *Gastarbeiter* worked hard to gain acceptance in German society, and were responsible for the greater official recognition of Turkish language and culture. This led to a bicultural Gen-X cohort that in-

cluded respected actors, athletes, and politicians but on the whole still be-
longed to a parallel Turkish community. An even larger crop of millennial
Turkish-Germans aren't sure whether they should perhaps be referred
to as German-Turks instead. They hold German citizenship by birth and
wouldn't dare give it up for the Turkish equivalent, and speak German
more fluently than Turkish.

Turks now represent 5 percent of the German population, a significant diaspora over which the Erdogan government has sought to wield
influence by directing Turkish consulates and associations to aggressively
promote Turkish and Koran classes among Turkish youth. To counter
Turkey's clout, many German public schools have begun teaching Turkish as well—except they face a shortage of Turkish teachers capable of
strengthening Turkish youth's "native language" skills. Given Erdogan's
current assault on the Turkish liberal establishment, however, there are
plenty of teachers in Turkey willing to emigrate—meaning yet more
Turks residing in Germany and a continuation of Turks' dual identity
there.

German politics is a reminder that immigration debates are really
about economics as much as culture. While other capital cities in Europe are also national economic engines (think London or Paris), Berlin
is poor and riddled with anti-capitalist populism. Hipster youth chased
away Google even though it would have brought thousands of new jobs.
They claimed victory for "community," but their main achievement was
to perpetuate their own dependency on the city's indebted government.
Berlin residents pursued an initiative in 2019 to nationalize the largest
private property owner in the city (Deutsche Wohnen) because rents
were too high, and in 2020, a five-year moratorium on rental increases
passed the local legislature. While this nominally gives the city some time
to convert vast unused land tracts into affordable housing, the city still
needs to attract more residents for developers to justify building it. Slow
politics and bad economics are the problem; investing to absorb migrants
is the solution.

More than any other city in continental Europe, Berlin has proven itself as a cosmopolitan urban milieu. In the thirty years since the fall of the Berlin Wall, the city has steadily attracted waves of Turks and Eastern Europeans, West Germans and Western European yuppies, Asian students, and now Arab migrants and refugees. While Germany's overall fertility rate is low, Berlin boasts the highest birth rate of any city in Europe, evident in the continuous opening of new *kitas* (daycare centers) in the millennial-populated neighborhoods of East Berlin. The city's population today has finally caught up to what it was one hundred years ago. While some politicians vocally resent not hearing German spoken on many streets, many residents have simply made English their common denominator. For Berlin youth, the half-English sentences of "Denglish" are German.

Contrast Berlin with its environs. Surrounding the city is the former East Germany, where the combination of low fertility and demographic exodus has meant dozens of abandoned towns few Germans would ever voluntarily move (back) to. Trillions of dollars have been spent since re-unification to elevate the former eastern states' economic prospects, but as the workforce shrinks, the government is losing interest in spending more. Meanwhile, many of the hardworking migrants that do come are scared away by the right-wing Alternative fuer Deutschland (AfD) party.

The AfD is an important case study in why not to ascribe to populist parties a coherence that doesn't exist. While its rise has been troublesome, most of its supporters—like those who backed Brexit or Trump—are aging and reside in less populous areas, such as the state of Sachsen, whose largest cities are Leipzig and Dresden. When I visited friends in Dresden in the late 1990s, it was a thriving university town with lively squares and packed evening cabaret shows (the equivalent of *Saturday Night Live*). But Dresden, along with the rest of the former East Germany, has been experiencing demographic collapse. Rather than make greater efforts to lure new residents, Dresden officials were forced to declare a "*Nazinotstand*" ("Nazi emergency") in 2019 due to the growing prominence of far right parties. The AfD's anti-immigrant sentiment is now being rewarded in a manner befitting its agenda: Nobody is moving to Dresden, but anyone finding opportunity elsewhere leaves. As Dresden withers, the AfD has turned quasi-socialist, promising its xenophobic voters that it will keep swimming pools and libraries open even though there are few users left. The AfD started out as anti-euro and anti-immigrant; now it's also anti-wind power.

Both demographic and political Darwinism will eventually deliver the AfD the fate it deserves. And perhaps not long after these xenophobes have passed away, their abandoned towns will become home to a million or more migrants. Already tens of thousands of Afghan and Syrian asylum seekers are being housed in vacant apartment blocks in cities such as Magdeburg. If they were granted asylum and allowed to work, they could fix Germany's degenerating infrastructure—and perhaps raise political and financial support to rebuild their own countries as well. The other scenario is that middle-aged xenophobes and young neo-Nazi extremists corral themselves in East German enclaves where they can feel pure—and once they're old, they'll grow to appreciate the immigrants taking care of them.

Far right parties barely register in populous German cities that have accepted large numbers of migrants, such as Berlin and Hamburg, nor do they make a political dent in the southwestern industrial powerhouse of Baden-Württemberg around Stuttgart, where tens of thousands of refugees and migrants have received professional training in building cars and locomotives, contributing directly to the province's most vital exports. It's thanks to these cities—and the immigrants that have flocked to them—that Germany's workforce actually expanded in 2018 for the first time in thirty years.

Germany's financial capital of Frankfurt also presents a compelling tale of immigrant-led rejuvenation. The city has long had glitzy office towers but lacked cultural dynamism. Now the combination of Brexit exiles, fintech startups, and droves of Asian and Arab migrants has put a premium on international schools, restaurants, nightlife, and artistic events. The headquarters of SAP, Europe's largest software company, already feels like that of Cisco in Silicon Valley: a glassy and industrial Little India. Particularly over the past ten years, young Indian knowledge workers have settled down comfortably in Germany's medieval academic center of Heidelberg, their children attending local schools. With Germany offering a nearly unlimited supply of "blue cards" to Asian tech talent—and by extension giving them access to the rest of the EU as well—a new micro-generation of Asians is planting roots in Europe at a much higher rung on the ladder than the South Asian shopkeepers of London's Southall. One slogan of the anti-immigration movement in Germany used to be "*Kinder statt Inder*" ("Babies, not Indians"), but today Germany is doing a much better job at recruiting the latter than producing the former.

Germany and France have anti-immigrant movements, but these countries are far more defined by the fact that they have *already become* immigrant societies over several generations. The reason there is backlash to immigration is because it's already too late. Remember that France's ban on headscarves, Germany's immigrant vocational matchmaking programs, and Dutch language requirements are hardly expulsion strategies—they're assimilation policies. And to a large degree, they have worked.

Germans generally appreciate the contributions of immigrants who have risen to become ministers and heads of political parties, and made up half the 2014 men's football World Cup championship team. From Algerian Zinedine Zidane's 1998 French World Cup–winning team to the 2018 repeat victory led by Cameroonian Kylian Mbappé, the French national football team is also thoroughly multiracial and evidently that much better for it. Today's German music charts are topped by rappers with backgrounds from Turkey, China, and Eritrea. In reality, the tribal definition of the national "self" is no longer the norm against which multiculturalism is pushing but rather the reverse.

Germany is already home to millions of Turks and Persians who have had German passports since birth even though they don't conform to the historical archetype of German-ness. Twenty percent of Germany's population is of immigrant origin, whether from EU neighbors, the Balkans, Russia, or the Middle East, and one in ten people is a foreign citizen (half from other EU countries, and half from the rest of the world). The estimated 1 million people of African descent in Germany have achieved sufficient weight that in 2020 they demanded an official black census.

Now Indians, Arabs, and Vietnamese are also joining the journey toward becoming "*die neuen Deutschen*" ("the new Germans"). Every society has a historical path from noun to adjective: America to American, Germany to German, Canada to Canadian, and so forth. But after decades of demographic dilution, today that identity is a moving target. Rather than assume everyone must conform to antiquated ethnic ideals, Germany is now engaged in a serious conversation about what German-ness actually means. What is the threshold for being considered German, or at least German enough? Must "German" mean white, Christian, and Germanic? Or is it enough to enjoy football, cars, and sausages? Or something in between? It's common to hear that too much immigration can be an affront to a country's values, but far less common to hear a clear statement of what those values actually are.

There is no doubt that culture clashes abound as migration intensifies. In recent years, there have been dozens of honor killings among Muslims in Germany, for example. Yet over time, it appears that once Muslims get to Europe, they effectively abandon Islam in ever larger numbers. While there are still some Salafist-funded mosques active in Europe, governments in the Netherlands and Germany are actively patrolling them and supporting more moderate competitors. In Berlin, Turkish-German feminist Seyran Ateş is the first female imam of a mosque named *both* for medieval Islamic philosopher Ibn Rushd *and* German poet Johann Wolfgang von Goethe. It welcomes homosexuals and has mixed gender prayer. Germany now wants all new imams to speak German.

When migrants can't speak the national language, they can neither contribute to society nor stand up for themselves—while resentment against them grows for the same reason. Angela Merkel championed immigration but also confessed that German multiculturalism was failing due to foreigners not learning German fast enough to properly integrate. Chinese artist Ai Weiwei, who took refuge in Berlin in 2016, declared in 2019 that he found German society intolerant, citing difficult experiences such as unfriendly taxi drivers. But there's little doubt that he'd have had more pleasant interactions if he could have communicated with the legions of Bosnian, Turkish, Persian, and Arab taxi drivers in their common German vernacular. Frankfurt Airport is never anyone's favorite for transit, but in recent years whenever I pass through, I can't help but smile when I overhear the airport staff—new Germans from Nigeria to Iran—sharing their life stories with one another, in German.

## Alpine oases

Climate models predict that Europe's temperate latitudes will experience compressed rainy seasons in which they receive less rain or short deluges—both followed by longer, hotter dry spells. Yet despite continental Europe's summer heat waves, the Alps come as close as the world can offer to the ideal combination of latitude and attitude—with the added benefit of altitude.

The countries of the Alps—Switzerland, Austria, Germany, France, and Italy—benefit from the world's cleanest water supply. (Not surprisingly, they're also the world's top sources of bottled water.) And more water will be coming down the mountain as Alpine glacier melt accelerates—eventually taking their ski industry with it. Even the perverse trend of flying in snow on planes, as some resorts have done, has its limits.

Among the world's mountainous regions with glacial water—the Andes, Alps, and Himalayas—only the Alpine countries have the engineering prowess *and* track record of cross-border cooperation to harness glacier melt into reservoirs (especially underground ones so that water doesn't evaporate) and pipes to serve the regional population—which will undoubtedly grow in the years to come. With oil pipelines increasingly redundant in Europe, water pipelines will be necessary to channel water from the Alps and Pyrenees to the parched geographies of southern Spain and Italy.

But Switzerland and Austria are also fortress nations. Because of its small size and diversified economy, Switzerland already has among the highest foreign-born populations in Europe, but strict immigration policies have broad political support. Only the talented or rich need apply. Each of Switzerland's more than two dozen political districts, known as cantons, sells the right to spend up to a year in it for up to 300,000 francs—with no residency rights included. Unless you are hired by a company to work in Switzerland, you'd have to invest similar amounts per year just to support yourself as an individual investor migrant.

Perhaps Switzerland will even consider a more accessible investor residency program, such as that of Slovenia. Located at the eastern fringe of the Alpine range, Slovenia was the first of the former Yugoslav republics to enter the EU and has propelled itself to the status of one of the world's most equitable and sustainable countries. For 7,500 euros, Slovenia offers investors residency, and after five years they can apply for citizenship. Some of the first takers have been Italian companies capitalizing on the country's lower corporate tax rate. It remains for Northern Italy to become an Alpine melting pot as well.

## Welcome to Padania

On an early morning jog through Bologna, I watched young African boys take up their positions on designated corners, where they stood to watch and wait. Bologna is home to one of the world's oldest universities and has a youthful bustle, but the Nigerian mafia is on the lookout for apartments to occupy once they've been vacated by the dying elderly. As day turns to dusk, the boys pass on any useful details to their bosses and to the fellow teens who take up the night shift—exactly as they do in Lagos.

Well before this latest wave of Arab and African migrants, Italy had grave difficulties assimilating foreigners. Consider how about two hundred thousand Roma (Gypsies) have lived for decades in segregated shantytowns, even though half have Italian nationality (and the other half hail from Balkan countries). They can't be legally expelled, so the government does nothing for them. In fact, instead of integrated social housing, the government has initiated a "Nomad Plan" to forcibly evict Roma from their informal settlements near major cities and place them in rural camps.

Italian citizenship laws remain notoriously strict, even for those born in the country: Citizenship by descent (*jus sanguinis*) carries far greater weight than citizenship by birth (*jus soli*). As of 2018, laws have been tightened to reduce the number of immigrants or their children who can apply for citizenship at all. But once a first generation of migrants plants local roots and acquires residency, their children become more accustomed to their new home than to their ancestral one. Northern Italy, for example, is already home to a long-standing community of Sikhs from India's Punjab. Drawn to the flat and fertile landscape of the Po Valley, Sikh families have been milking cows and making cheese there since the 1980s, and now produce 60 percent of all of Italy's Parmesan exports. As a reward, the Sikh community of the town of Novellara has been allowed to build a *gurdwara* temple. As the mayor herself said, "It would be impossible to think of this industry without the support of people from India."[4]

Whether or not these migrants are ever granted Italian citizenship, they're an important reason why this northern "Padania" region—the Po River valley stretching across the main provinces of Northern Italy—has re-emerged as the country's beating heart. But with an immigration strategy so at odds with the federal government, the provinces of Padania act more like an autonomous city-state. Padania did, after all, symbolically declare independence from Italy in 1996.

If Padania had a capital, it would of course be Milan, a city that was in decline in the 1990s and written off by the 2000s, but has surged back with improved public transportation and expanded bike lanes, new event venues, and modern, affordable housing. With a favorable climate, freshwater from the Alps, major industrial companies, and improved roads and railways to France and Switzerland, Milan is already far more important to Italy's future than Rome. Not surprisingly, Milan has absorbed far more migrants (especially aged eighteen to thirty-five) than any other city in Italy.

The Saturday morning flea markets in Milan and other regional towns are emblematic of the new global demographic of Northern Italy. Side by side, Italian, African, and Arab husband-and-wife teams sell nylon blouses, plastic sandals, and household wares to cost-conscious elderly, students, and one another. Nearby, the Bengali grocer opens his shop for the day, next door to the Chinese dry cleaner. Though neighbors by day, at night they return to neighborhoods increasingly populated by their ethnic groups. Milan's Chinatown has an estimated thirty thousand residents, and there are even more Filipinos in the city and a growing number of Sri Lankans. As Italians pass away or move north, they're being backfilled by Africans and Asians from the south and east. This heartland of medieval Europe has become the archetype of a new Middle Ages, with fluid populations and demographic tides linking the Mediterranean to the South China Sea.

The younger generation of Italians is already quite attuned to multicultural urban life. The recent arthouse film *Bangla* about a second-generation Bangladeshi-Italian boy's romance with a spunky Italian girl nicely captures how mainstream and Italian many immigrants have already become—like Indians in America, with their own cultural baggage that clashes but ultimately reconciles with local customs. Most importantly, the youngest inhabitants of this new ethnoscape—the toddlers in

Milan's kindergartens whose parents hail from Italy, Africa, Venezuela, and South Asia—will scarcely be aware that there ever was an Italy populated exclusively by Italians. They'll think of the pre-multicultural Italy as what digital natives think life before the Internet was: irrelevant.

Today's educated Italian kids will grow up to be doctors and engineers, teachers and journalists, politicians and bureaucrats, military officers and athletes, architects and fashion designers. But they already rely on immigrants to be their trash collectors and hair designers, taxi drivers and handymen. Just outside of Milan in the town of Bergamo, an "Academy of Integration" takes in migrants from Nigeria to Pakistan and puts them through a boot camp in which they learn Italian and basic skills, from ironing clothes to waiting tables to operating garbage trucks, and places them into jobs so they can gain the financial independence necessary to apply for residency. Then, in the next generation, it will be their children who will be the country's doctors and athletes.

## Can Britain be great again?

The 2016 Brexit referendum continues to roil British politics, yet its impact on the composition of the British population may ultimately be insignificant. Nearly three hundred thousand migrants entered the UK in 2018, placing it just behind the US and Canada in annual inflow. Based on current trends, the country's population is expected to reach some 80 million people by 2050 (from 66 million today).[5] If Brexit was about controlling borders and immigration, has it brought Britain any closer to its goal?

The late Oxford philosopher Michael Dummett believed that a state should be able to refuse entry only to criminals, or to limit mass immigration that would lead to overpopulation or submerge its culture. Dummett thought this would rarely be the case, but the logic tacitly became cover for Brexiteers' anti-immigrant paranoia. Yet with its industrial base in tatters, Britain will have to repurpose its economy to focus even more on services—and will need more people to do it. The acute shortages already apparent in the UK's labor force, from healthcare to utilities, suggest that Britain can't afford to lose eighty thousand or more of its own citizens each year due to Brexit unless it brings in that many and more in number, wealth, and talent.

One reason Britain should want more migrants is to take advantage of central England's climate opportunity. London and its southern England environs face long spells of dry heat and freshwater shortages, even as about 20 percent of London's residences are at risk from tidal surges in the Thames estuary. London will need to spread the wealth. Prior to Brexit and the pandemic, the "rest" of the UK was in the early stages of a recovery from decades of infrastructural neglect and brain drain, with young and educated Brits lured to Manchester, Liverpool, and Birmingham, to which engineering and tech companies also shifted to save costs. Now the UK will have to make do with even less foreign investment, other than the French who are recultivating English farmland into vineyards as their own climate becomes hostile for wine growing.

It would be wise for Britain to move ahead with long-standing plans for a better integrated "Northern Corridor" from Leeds to Liverpool, especially given that British youth's desire to live in a big city has shrunk to just over 20 percent. Instead, the Covid lockdown sparked a surge of interest in rural properties. Britain may be going back to its roots. No doubt the UK's most economically deprived counties, near the Scottish border, would benefit from more workers in agriculture and light industry.

Scotland itself senses a climate opportunity given its oil wealth and water resources. Already blessed with thirty thousand freshwater lakes (or *lochs*, none inhabited by monsters), the country has seen rainfall rise substantially. It's also planting more than 20 million trees per year. Edinburgh is a cosmopolitan center of free thinking, historical monuments, and international cuisine attracting top students and academics from around the world. Scots are now actively developing an Arctic strategy to link their ports to those in Canada and Scandinavia. If Britain doesn't cater to Scotland's interests, the separatist movement will once again gain steam. Meanwhile, Northern Ireland may choose to reunite with its more pragmatic kin. Britain has left the EU, but may soon be surrounded by EU members on all sides. Brexit will remain more in name than reality.

## Nordic by nature

Even by European standards, northern Europeans have a good life. Owing to their wealth and solidarity, Nordic states such as Norway, Denmark, Iceland, Finland, and Sweden perennially rank as the world's "happiest" countries. There is much to be admired in their egalitarian social policies that make locals swell with pride and foreigners glad they came. Sweden allows private sector workers a six-month sabbatical to try their hand at entrepreneurship, with no penalty for returning to work later. Finland gives the homeless a permanent home and helps them find jobs. Denmark counters loneliness and depression by taking citizens out to concerts. Generous pensions and universal affordable healthcare are the norm across the region—a right rather than a privilege—even though their rising costs require fiscal reforms. Scandinavians understand the basic economics that a dwindling tax base requires either cutting benefits or importing taxpayers. They continue to wisely choose the latter.

Nordic countries are relatively large in size, but each has very few people. Despite their homogenous societies, they have been quite open to increased immigration, even given the glaring culture clashes. But will their commitment to a liberal social contract sustain itself amid aging pensioners, low growth, high debt, and rising ethnic diversity?

Young Danes, like Berliners and Milanese, have grown up with immigrants as a part of their society and are fond of foreign foods and musicians as an element of daily life. Rather than oppose immigration, they insist on serious efforts at assimilation, even if it means banning headscarves for Muslim women. To maintain support for open borders, Danes feel they must enforce their cherished liberalism.

Far larger Sweden has twice Denmark's population, and has also managed to lift its birthrate to the highest in Europe. Sweden has been taking in Arab migrants for decades, with prominent actors, musicians, and athletes of Arab descent in the mainstream. Nonetheless, its acceptance of 160,000 asylum seekers in 2015 (the highest in Europe per capita) from countries such as Syria, Iraq, and Afghanistan raised alarm bells. Violence has risen within migrant communities, as have hate crimes such as attacks on asylum centers. In August 2020, riots broke out in Malmö after a right-wing group burned a Koran. Far right parties captured nearly a quarter of the vote in the country's 2018 elections. Sweden has also stepped up repatriating asylum seekers to their home countries once those countries are deemed safe.

Sweden and Norway are also home to tens of thousands of Indians and Pakistanis, with approximately one thousand Indians applying for citizenship in each of those countries annually. In Norway, Pakistanis are the third largest immigrant group after Poles and Swedes, and well ahead of Indians. From the early Punjabis who came in the 1960s to the extended families who joined them in subsequent decades, multiple generations have become assimilated Norwegians and even risen to high levels of politics. Two out of every three taxi drivers you'll encounter in Oslo or Stockholm is South Asian. My kids used to think speaking Hindi and Urdu was only useful in India, Pakistan, Dubai, and Singapore—until we went on holiday across Scandinavia.

Finland is roughly the same size as Sweden and Norway, but has barely 5 million people. Due to its history of military mobilizations and evacuations from the Russian border, it has built a superb national infrastructure network that allows it to control natural disasters (such as forest fires) better than neighboring Sweden. It also has plans to extend its railways into northern Norway to connect to the port of Kirkenes and accelerate exports to Asia. With an aging population, however, all of this will require far more migrants. Prior to the Arab refugee crisis, a mere four thousand Somalis constituted Finland's largest non-European minority, yet still conservative governments took a hard line on immigration. At the same time, even Finland's most prized and global industries need more foreign labor. For example, mobile technology pioneer Nokia not only has an Indian CEO, but will need legions of Indian IT workers and manpower to compete with Huawei in installing global 5G networks.

As northern Europe gets thrust into the spotlight as an attractive year-round destination that's neither too cold in the winter nor too hot in the summer, their tourist economies are flourishing. Southern Europeans seeking respite from the sweltering Mediterranean and continental heat have begun to establish a greater presence in the north, much as Scandinavians used to do in reverse. Winter sports will shift from the Alps to the northern regions of Norway, Sweden, and Finland, while summer outdoor activities will expand as well. Arctic cruises, camping, and survivalist boot camps get tens of thousands of new tourists each year. The pristine Karelia region on the Finland-Russia border boasts sixty thousand lakes and offers weeklong dogsledding expeditions in the winter as well as camping and fishing in the summer. Fortunately, wealthy Nordic countries can afford to maintain sustainable habitats even with the new tourist influx.

Traveling around the Nordics from Kirkenes in northern Norway to Denmark's capital, Copenhagen, reveals how even the most homogenous corner of the world is becoming a thriving multinational commune. This process will snowball if Scandinavia proves as welcoming to climate refugees as it has been to political and economic ones. Scandinavians such as Greta Thunberg have become global icons in urging action against climate change, but given how much milder the climate effect will be on their region, the real test of Scandinavian solidarity with the world will be how many climate migrants they're willing to absorb. The combined population of the Nordic countries is under 30 million. Are they willing to quintuple it?

If Scandinavia does become home to many millions of new migrants, its nations would need to devise a post-national identity the way Canada has. Since English is widely spoken already, they may well become multilingual melting pots with English as the common denominator. These may turn out to be the most straightforward aspects of the northward migration. Indeed, a large-scale shift to the Nordics will be much more complicated than drawing a straight line to the region's beautiful capital cities. For one thing, Copenhagen, Stockholm, and Helsinki are at risk from rising sea levels despite their own ambitious plans to go carbon-neutral. It could well be that these cities' success in localizing food supply and deploying renewable power will ultimately be most useful much farther north and inland from the Baltic Sea. Indeed, Sweden's northernmost county of Norrbotten is already entirely hydrogen- and wind-powered. And with strong rule of law, Scandinavian countries won't allow foreign land grabs. In fact, Sweden has declared that large landholders can't prohibit people from crossing their property to enjoy nature. Livable space is becoming a precious public good, as is the right to move freely on it.

# CHAPTER 6
# BRIDGING REGIONS

### *Keeping cool in the Caucasus*

In the remote highlands of eastern Turkey lie the lakes that for millennia served as the lifeblood of Mesopotamian civilization. Just as Americans have been ditching California for the Rockies, Turkish entrepreneurs have been flocking to this misty region of dense oak and pine forests, renovating towns such as Erzurum, which has become the Aspen of Anatolia, a mountain ski hub buzzing with year-round athletic activity.

But while the headwaters of the Tigris and Euphrates Rivers continue to nourish eastern Anatolia's rich landscapes, the lands downstream no longer resemble anything like the "fertile crescent" where settled farming first appeared. It was droughts that brought down the Akkadian empire four thousand years ago, and today again the region is occupied by severely water-stressed countries such as Syria, Iraq, Iran, and Pakistan. With economic deprivation and civil unrest wracking Turkey's entire southern frontier while temperatures cross seventy degrees Celsius in parts of Iraq and Iran, can one not imagine Arab and Persian refugees prying their way upland and resettling in this Anatolian oasis?

Eastward along the Black Sea, Anatolia transitions into the Caucasus, once a collection of Ottoman protectorates and more recently three quite homogenous Soviet republics: Georgia, Armenia, and Azerbaijan. Georgia spent much of the 1990s and 2000s pretending its Christian heritage made it superior to its Turkic neighbors, while in reality it acted much like a tinpot failed state. But few countries have made such a dramatic turnaround in the past decade. There is still plenty of political bickering, antigovernment demonstrations, and constitutional confusion in the capital Tbilisi, all while Russia still occupies 20 percent of its territory. Yet Georgia has managed to strengthen its road network, become a major rail transit corridor between Turkey and Azerbaijan, and establish productive manufacturing zones. The country has hosted as many as twenty European-style cultural festivals in a single year, and is knocking hard on the EU's door to revive membership negotiations.

Tbilisi today oozes with both ancient charm and modern chic. Its skilled masons have recruited German developers to upgrade turn-of-the-century buildings into boutique apartments and hotels. Like a breezy East Berlin, it has become a low-cost English-speaking hub for Western youth. And with its river network fed by the more than twenty glaciers of Mount Elbrus—Europe's highest mountain located just over the border in Russia—much of Georgia is well placed to weather climate change. Today Georgia is the "it" country for backpackers; tomorrow it might be their home—especially given the attractive "nomad visa" program the country recently launched.

Azerbaijan presents an even more interesting case of how economic and environmental trends may drive large numbers of migrants to a forgotten corner of the world. Azerbaijan has about four times as many people as Georgia, and oil wealth has made Azeris four times wealthier per capita than their Georgian neighbors. Spanning the snowy Caucasus Mountains to the deserts outside its capital of Baku, Azerbaijan is home to the full planetary array of micro-climates, including dense forests and wetlands. To ward off the encroachment of its deserts, it launched a tree planting binge and pipes cool water down from the Caucasus for irrigation and urban cooling.

It's appropriate that Baku's lavish redevelopment has earned it the moniker "Dubai on the Caspian," for a large number of Emiratis (and Saudis and Qataris) have been buying up fancy properties there as a refuge from the Gulf heat (not to mention to take advantage of Azerbaijan's

more liberal liquor laws). And given that Azeris are ethnically and lin-
guistically Turkic but religiously Shiite, with close ties to Iran, Azerbaijan
has become an important—if roundabout—portal for Gulf Arabs to do
business with Iran.

Iranians may also come to see Azerbaijan as a safe haven from their
country's warped politics and searing climate. Already there are more
Azeris in Iran than in Azerbaijan itself, largely located in the northern
Iranian border provinces. Iranians who used to seek Western visas at embassies in Damascus before Syria's civil war now attempt the same in
Baku, which has branded itself as the Caspian region's diplomatic hub.
It would not be the first time. The oil boom of the 1870s brought large
numbers of Europeans to Baku, giving its Caspian corniche a glittering
Victorian facade that has been impeccably refurbished to cater to today's
delegations of Arab and Turkic, French and German, Indian and Chinese
traders and contractors. Listening to them all mingle and bicker in Baku's
medieval old city is a reminder that the Caucasus are once again claiming
their role as a corridor of both the east-west and north-south silk roads—
though in the nineteenth century these various nationals all spoke one
another's languages with far greater felicity.

The poorest of the three Caucasus countries, mountainous and land-
locked Armenia, features an arid climate that will become more so in
the years ahead. Given its hostile relations with more powerful neighbors
Turkey and Azerbaijan (including the loss of strategic territory to the
latter in 2020), Armenia continues to depend on Russia as a military
and economic lifeline. Indeed, Russia is already home to almost as many
Armenians as Armenia itself. Besides plans to double the amount of its
land covered by forests, the best climate resilience strategy for Armenia's
current 3 million population is likely to move to Russia. Armenia's other
strategy is to follow in Estonia's footsteps and digitize itself. The president,
Armen Sarkissian, is a theoretical physicist and computer scientist who
wants the country's dispersed diaspora to remain unified in the cloud. His
term for this next step in nationhood: "quantum country."

## *The next Russian revolution*

The world's largest country also wants to revitalize its Black Sea underbelly. In 2014, Russia hosted the Winter Olympics at the Black Sea resort of Sochi, and more recently it completed the twisting Volgograd bypass and bridges over the Volga River to handle the enormous cargo volumes between Moscow and the eastern regions bordering China. Despite Russia's demographic decline and feeble economy, it still occupies one-tenth of the world's land area and presides over vast oil and gas reserves that are crucial to European and especially Chinese industrial output. Even in an eventual post-oil world, not only will Russia's petrochemicals still be essential for the production of plastics, rubber, fibers, and other materials, but it also has a huge share of the world's uranium, which is critical for nuclear reactors. Russia is not a traditional superpower anymore, but in terms of functional geography, few countries are remotely as important.

Russia is set to become even more fascinating a story than it was in the twentieth century, especially as the Arctic takes on greater prominence. In geopolitical parlance, Russia is a Eurasian "heartland" power (lacking year-round access to ice-free seas), but within ten years, its flotilla of nuclear-powered ice-breakers will need some other purpose as there may no longer be any ice to break. After centuries of maneuvering to gain access to seas farther south, climate change is handing Russia the status of a "rimland" (maritime) power without firing a shot.

From the Murmansk oblast on the Norwegian border to the Chukotka federal district across the Bering Strait from Alaska, Russia is militarizing its thousands of kilometers of Arctic coastline with new battalions, upgrading its northern naval fleet, and deploying floating nuclear power stations that will provide steady electricity to the nearly 2 million Russians who are seasonally cut off from roads farther south. The mineral deposits of the Arctic generate 20 percent of Russia's GDP, and as the permafrost melts, much more could be discovered and extracted. Russia's ecological landscape potential is surging—and Russia wants to put its land to work.

What it lacks, however, are the people to do it. While its population is presently three times larger than Canada's, aging, alcoholism, and exodus are all driving its demographics downward at an alarming rate. And whereas Canada seeks to become an immigration superpower, Russian president Vladimir Putin has described immigration as a poison; his regressive ethnonationalism makes Russia, in many ways, the anti-Canada. But beneath the icy political veneer lies a country desperate to remain relevant as a bridge between the 700 million people of Europe and the 4 billion people of Asia. To fulfill its new Eurasian ambitions, Russia too will have to recruit migrants, most likely Turkic, Chinese, Arab, and Indian laborers who are more than willing to leave their corrupt or polluted lands to develop Russia's resources and industries. What seems politically impossible today could be common sense tomorrow: Russia needs to become the Eurasian Canada.

If you moved to the central Siberian city of Yakutsk today, however, you'd find that it's still unbearably cold in the winter, sinking in the spring, and suffering from torrid heat waves and uncontrolled wildfires in the summer (that deplete and release ever more carbon from the soil). Permafrost is thawing so fast that residents are extending the height of the stilts their homes are built on, while elsewhere the bog simply gives way, draining entire lakes and revealing giant sinkholes. As millions of square kilometers of once sturdy ground turn into mushy swamps, the land can no longer support the weight of the roads and machinery that are needed to extract the vast natural gas deposits beneath them. Oil spills and toxic chemical leaks are poisoning once pristine terrain, with no public services within hundreds of kilometers to clean it up.

Over the next several decades, however, NASA estimates suggest that up to 85 percent of Siberia could be fully habitable and fertile, producing not only wheat but also apples, grapes, corn, and peas. Russia already ranks among the top geographies gaining in vegetation area, and its vast forests (representing 20 percent of the world's total versus 30 percent in Canada) are vital carbon sinks. All manner of seeds can be planted and fertilized to expand Arctic agriculture, potentially supplied by Dutch scientists and traders and Canadian agribusiness companies with experience at similar latitude. The world's food supply needs Russia as much as it needs Canada.

After decades of neglect, Russia is finally taking advantage of both Chinese infrastructure investments and resource potential to rethink its spatial organization and demographic needs. The Trans-Siberian Railway is being upgraded, and new Chinese-funded rail lines will make Eurasian commerce more efficient. In southern Russian cities near the borders of Kazakhstan and Mongolia, such as Novosibirsk, Krasnoyarsk, and Irkutsk, officials have laid out plans for highways, railroads, and river ports, and turning secretive Soviet-era nuclear facilities into "science cities." As the climate improves, desirable jobs for young talent are appearing in places their parents once abandoned. Both Novosibirsk and Krasnoyarsk have universities that rank in the top ten largest in Russia, full of students who want to use data science to diversify their economy. (They also use the ample energy supply to mine Bitcoin and other cryptocurrencies.) As I've seen across the former Soviet Union, young technocrats are inheriting the mandates to manage infrastructure, telecom, urban planning, financial regulation, and other important areas. They don't want to live in a depopulated failed state.

If there is one thing Russia has in abundance, it's resource-rich terrain with almost no people. Western Russia has water-rich republics lying between the Volga River and the Ural Mountains, such as Tatarstan and Bashkortostan (famous for its diverse flora and wild honey). Farther east lies the Altai region, the truly remote four-corner zone where Russia, China, Mongolia, and Kazakhstan meet. Russia's Altai Republic (governed as part of Siberia) has only two hundred thousand people, making it one of the least populous in all of Russia. Yet the Altai is a spectacular region of glacial mountains, the Katun and Biya Rivers (which merge to form the Ob River flowing north to the Arctic), and huge freshwater lakes, not to mention gold, silver, and lithium deposits. Given its long winters and population that's nearly 50 percent from the Turkic Altai tribe, the region has remained under the radar. Today, however, its beauty and resources have attracted commodities brokers and real estate developers, as well as more frequent visits by Russia's nouveau riche. As connectivity and climate change make the republic more habitable, soon it could become home to ten times more people.

Russia's Far East is similarly depopulated today but could become a far more dense and textured demographic milieu. Port cities such as Magadan have lost half their population since the Soviet collapse, but as frigid winters shorten to just two to three months, youth are needed to harness the region's vast mineral deposits. Russia has unveiled its own version of America's 1862 Homestead Act that gave 160 acres to Western settlers and transferred title ownership to them if they made productive use of the land within five years. Another plus recently: Social distancing is easy in these sparsely populated areas. But how many Russians will take the offer?

It's far more likely that Russia's Far East will absorb large numbers of Chinese and other Asians facing water shortages and food stress. They'll spend much of the year on Russian soil but travel home for the winter. China is prepared to send millions of underemployed young and middle-aged men across the Amur River to help Russia rebuild itself and fulfill its growing mandate to feed and shelter Asia's masses. Russia has the world's second largest supply of freshwater (behind Brazil), but whereas Brazilian water can't easily be shifted to another continent, Russian rivers can potentially be diverted to eastern China's rivers and canal projects.

Russia is wary of its giant southern neighbor for good reason. The steady growth of Chinese in eastern Siberia is reminiscent of the Mongol Yuan dynasty. Eight centuries later, Chinese climate nationalism could justify a new irredentism. The German geographer Friedrich Ratzel's response to the Malthus conundrum—that population size would outstrip resources—was not only population control but also expanding *Lebensraum* (living space), an argument that in the 1930s became prominent in the Nazi lexicon to justify its expansionism.

Will future maps of the Russian Far East label it "Sino-Siberia"? On the shores of fabled Lake Baikal, Chinese have built illegal hotels and bilked authorities on taxes. As with many of its border agreements, China considers the 1858 treaty that ceded territory to Russia unfair—it still refers to Lake Baikal as the "North Sea." China has not yet conducted any land grabs in Russia, but it has over-harvested timber and leaked toxic industrial waste into the Sungari River, which flows into the countries' shared Amur River border.

Russia can't maintain its sovereign equality vis-à-vis China without support from other major powers—perhaps eventually even the US. For now, it's luring more investment from Japan, and in 2019, Vladimir Putin featured India's Narendra Modi as the chief guest at the Far East Forum in Vladivostok, the region's capital. Indian businesses have been busily upgrading steel mills, setting up pharmaceutical plants, and modernizing farms and food distribution centers across numerous Far East states. Russia has tried to recruit farmers from as far as South Africa, but it's India that has long been a Russian friend: Its farmers consider Russians the "Punjabis of the north." Indians in Siberia may even serve as a trip wire against Chinese control.

Over the next several generations, a wide range of nationalities will mingle and multiply the stock of Asiatic hybrid peoples across this vast Siberian frontier. It wouldn't be the first time: More than thirty thousand years ago, this is where Western Eurasian and East Asian peoples fused into a common race. Fourteen-thousand-year-old tooth fossils found near Lake Baikal show that these ancient Asiatics were the first to cross the Bering Strait land bridge to Alaska and are related to Native Americans.[1] Russia's Far East could once again become a common Asian frontier. The rugged, volcanic Kamchatka Peninsula will soon be home to a massive year-round ski and hiking resort, a precursor perhaps to an influx of inhabitants taking advantage of its rainy climate and fertile soil. Vladivostok's Asian gentrification may make it a mirror image of Vancouver across the Pacific.

Russia doesn't appear keen on mass migration, but when it wants to, it lures workers with a wave of the pen. Two million Ukrainians live in Russia, with an estimated three hundred thousand moving east each year. To punish the new government of Uzbekistan for not submitting to Russia's plans for a customs union, Putin offered Russian *passports* to all Uzbeks who wanted to move to Russia. In 2020, Russia passed a dual citizenship law to convince more people to take Russian nationality without having to give up their own. (American whistleblower Edward Snowden was an early taker.) Russia too is engaged in the war for talent, both from its former satellite republics and beyond.

The next Russian Revolution won't be about who rules Russia but who occupies it. Unlike the fast-moving Bolshevik takeover of a century ago, the current revolution is a slow-motion epic as Russia turns gray demographically, green topographically, and brown and yellow ethnically.

## Would you consider Mongolia?

Sandwiched uncomfortably between Russia and China, Mongolia has grudgingly accepted its destiny as a new Silk Road passageway. Northern Mongolia has reindeer farmers and may well fuse climatologically with southern Siberia, while southern Mongolia's Gobi desert region will wind up much like China's province of Inner Mongolia—either desertified or reforested through initiatives like China's Great Green Wall. Mongolia too has launched a major tree planting drive to grow back forests that have shrunk down to just 7 percent of its territory. With a small population of only 3 million people—and 66 million livestock—roaming the steppe, Mongolia today faces a major trade-off between groundwater depleted for its mining industry versus the potential revival of its pastoral traditions and cottage industries such as luxurious cashmere wool. If it can balance those interests amid rising temperatures that will temper its extreme winters, it may well attract a human population as large as its herds of cattle.

### Stepping up to Central Asia

Central Asia is an ancient space occupied by very young nations. The vast area of steppe and desert stretching between the Caspian Sea to the west and Russia to the north, China in the east, and Indus civilizations to the south has for millennia been as much crossroads as settlement. The nomadic Sogdians were the original Silk Road scribes, translating between Persian, Turkish, Chinese, and even ancient Greek upon Alexander the Great's arrival in the fourth century BC. Islam arrived in the seventh and eighth centuries from Arabia, after which the *caravanserai* of Khiva, Bukhara, and Samarqand (in today's Uzbekistan) became rest stops for merchants traveling out of everywhere from Turkey to Mongolia—from which Genghis Khan's marauding hordes descended in the thirteenth century. After the Turko-Persian general Tamerlane reclaimed the region from the Mongols, his great-grandson Babur founded what became the Mughal empire, establishing itself in Delhi and ruling from Afghanistan through most of India. Even after more than a century under Russian dominance, the region's multi-ethnic patchwork is more revealing about Central Asia's essence than any of its borders.

Kazakhstan, the largest of Central Asia's republics, is nearly the size of Australia, with a similarly sparse population and a commodities-driven economy that has propelled it ahead of its neighbors in wealth and prestige. As the key bridge to the oil-rich Caspian Sea, Kazakhstan has quickly become a major trans-Eurasian logistics gateway, with high-speed freight trains crossing from China to Europe. Its capital, Nursaltan (formerly

Astana), is a fast-growing hub for regional finance as well as home to new universities and dazzling architectural sites such as the World Expo 2017 pavilions.

After twenty-five years of sending its professionals and workers abroad, mostly to Russia, Kazakhstan is itself the region's main magnet. With Russia's economy cooling, more than 3 million Central Asians have found work in the country's booming construction industry and other sectors. Kazakhs born in neighboring Russia and China have also returned to the new Kazakhstan. The recent population influx is a sign of things to come, for Kazakhstan could be one of the world's true climate oases. Today Kazakhstan has only 20 million people. Is it ready for another 200 million?

Nestled at the base of the Tian Shan mountains, the country's commercial hub of Almaty has benefited from a succession of mayors (dating to its time as a Russian military garrison) who mandated constant tree planting and enforced curbs on tall buildings. Today the city's 2 million residents enjoy continuous beautification: new playgrounds, pedestrian streets, bike lanes, and cool mist-sprayers.

Kazakhs' rising confidence is on display not only in the country's relatively high birth rate but at posh car dealerships, chic shopping malls, trendy nightclubs, and angular apartment complexes. Zhibek Zholy Street resembles Belgrade's Knez Mihailova with its musicians, break-dancers, street artists, and cafes offering an eclectic array of cuisines. Ubiquitous money changers, on every corner, quickly trade all regional currencies for the growing numbers of business travelers and tourists. This is fertile ground for an Alpine Asian cosmopolitanism.

On a typical summer day in Almaty, it's hard not to notice the throngs of Indian tourists escaping South Asia's searing heat while exploring their own heritage. The cultural affinity between Central Asians and Indians runs deep, from Mughal legacies to Bollywood classics that became popular during the Soviet period. I've only watched one Kazakh soap opera, but every line of the city-meets-village clash-of-dialects plot could have been written in Mumbai. Not far away in Uzbekistan's capital of Tashkent, I've met more than a few shopkeepers who speak impressive Hindi. Uzbekistan allows visa-free entry for Indians, and there appears to be quite an appetite among middle-aged Indian men to fly in for a weekend of sex tourism.

Are we heading for a reversal of the Mughal empire, a steady south-to-north migration of Indian pioneers settling the lands of their ancestors? Enterprising Indian doctors have already set up private clinics in Almaty and Tashkent. Indian chefs lead the kitchens at hotels most frequented by Indian travelers. And with English international schools the new vogue, demand is rising for qualified teachers from India as well. The more unlivable India becomes, the more Indians will find themselves heading north in search of temperate climate and entrepreneurial opportunity—reversing their ancestors' footsteps in the process.

Kazakhstan and Uzbekistan provide ample evidence of how Central Asia's cultural syncretism could draw many new residents from the region's Turkic tribes but potentially millions more from its cultural catchment area spanning today's Iran, Pakistan, and China. Consider the 20 million Uighur Muslims of Xinjiang who have been suffering the torture and humiliation of Chinese re-education camps. Thousands have fled across the border and resettled in Kazakhstan, and millions more may follow. In the 1990s and 2000s, there was considerable fear that Islamist movements would gain traction in the region, especially given Afghanistan's insecurity. But for the combined 50 million people of Kazakhstan and Uzbekistan, Islam appears more a cultural characteristic than a religious yoke. Students visit mosques and madrassas much the way tourists do: to learn history.

This is surely comforting for Iranians as well, who have been stifled both by their Shia Islamic theocracy and the country's environmental crisis. Iranians have traditionally fled to North America or Europe, but they share the closest ethnic and linguistic kinship with Tajikistan—the countries have been described as "one spirit with two bodies." Iran has built power plants and tunnels in Tajikistan, and progress continues on the "Dari belt" corridor through the swath of northern Afghanistan separating them. Its aim was trade, but it may well become a migration route for Persians seeking a high-altitude refuge, given Tajikistan's abundant glaciers. Iran and China have signed a twenty-five-year strategic partnership focused on commercial deals in Iran, but as the clock ticks on Iran's climate, they might conspire to channel Pamir mountain range glacier melt into the Panj River and hydrate a de facto Iran-Afghan-Tajik "Farsi-stan" state.

Thus far, Central Asia's rising migration has occurred more by accident than by design. Kazakhstan's government has granted amnesty to hundreds of thousands of previously undocumented illegal migrants and recruited regionally for students, but there has not been an active dialogue among citizens as to the profound implications of the demographic encounters that lie ahead. Except, that is, when it comes to the Chinese. The influx of Chinese workers and property investors has led to anti-Chinese protests and project strikes in both Kazakhstan and Kyrgyzstan, with all sides scrambling to save face and find equitable solutions to labor and contract disputes.

But the more visitors and residents Central Asia attracts, the more its governments will see migration as part of their business model and road map to economic diversification. Foreign labor will be essential to broaden roads, construct railways, build housing colonies, expand irrigation channels, and build massive solar power plants, projects for which Kazakhstan is issuing green bonds and drawing in investment.

If Central Asia's population grows from 50 million to five or six times more, it will need to find ways to feed everyone as well. The region is at last recovering from decades of disastrous Soviet-mandated cotton production that caused the near total disappearance of the Aral Sea. Kazakhstan is planting hundreds of millions of drought-resistant seeds in the Aral area to restore its once vibrant agriculture. Uzbekistan (which is 80 percent scrubby desert) now offers tax breaks to investors who have the capacity to tap underground aquifers, build new water canals, and install efficient drip irrigation. Greenhouses are popping up to expand production of watermelons, cucumbers, tomatoes, pomegranates, cherries, and other fruits and vegetables, while the food processing industry is getting upgraded to extend the shelf life and market reach of the country's agriculture. The long rows of prefab houses with solar-paneled roofs sprouting along the Amu Darya River are a sign that Uzbeks have sufficient energy, water, and food to survive the hot decades ahead.

The so-called continental climate of Central Asia features seasonal extremes from summers as hot as fifty-five degrees Celsius to winters when temperatures drop to minus twenty degrees. As average temperatures rise, the region can expect not-as-chilly winters but hotter summers. During the summer of 2019, the Uzbek government issued its first public service announcements alerting people to stay indoors from 12 p.m. to 4 p.m. (Personally, I'd suggest 11 a.m. to 5 p.m.) In my experience of consistent daily exposure to forty degree Celsius, dryness makes the heat tolerable so long as one stays in the shade, while such heat in humid conditions is unbearable. Evenings in the region are pleasant; the streets come alive after dusk.

With its higher latitude and more varied elevations, Kazakhstan ultimately stands a much better chance of adapting to climate change. The country is now one of the world's largest wheat exporters, and also grows barley, sunflowers, flax, and rice. New agribusiness and cooperative subsidies help farmers get better fodder, fertilizers, and equipment and produce more milk and crops. But with longer dry seasons ahead, Kazakhstan will need to invest much more in expanding irrigation channels from the Tian Shan mountains, and capturing more glacier melt into reservoirs.

Kazakhstan's immense size also makes it a sensible candidate for atmospheric sulphur treatment to reduce the sun's glare, cloud seeding to boost rainfall, and the planting of billions of trees. Kazakhstan's steppe forest—a region the size of England—is growing even larger thanks to government subsidies for afforestation programs. A sustainable approach to improving the dilapidated infrastructure of this forested belt could create a vital ecological refuge.

Though Central Asia is blessed with the Pamir and Tian Shan mountain ranges, the fabled "water towers of Asia," elevation alone isn't enough to ensure livability when dealing with countries as corrupt as Kyrgyzstan. Despite its moniker as the "Switzerland of Central Asia," Kyrgyzstan is failing to protect pristine environments such as Lake Issyk-Kul. A salty, high-altitude version of the Dead Sea, Issyk-Kul saw a cottage industry of curative sanatoria develop around it during the Soviet era. But overfishing and pollution indicate a country unable to enforce environmental laws, a dangerous sign, given China and Russia's proximity and influence. Kyrgyzstan's promise lies in its latitude and altitude, but its attitude still has much room for improvement.

Collectively, if Central Asia's population climbs from 60 million today toward 200 million or more, its nations' very names would become misnomers: The suffix "-stan" means "land of," but these countries would no longer be demographically dominated by the Turkic tribes whose names identify them. Instead, their demographic ratios of nationals to foreigners would resemble that of the UAE, where barely one-tenth of the population is Emirati while 90 percent is migrants. Much as Emiratis are a small tribe hosting a melting pot, so too would Kazakhstan become a nomadic people hosting global nomads.

If Russia and Kazakhstan both open to robust population growth, Kazakhstan would become even more a transit country from south to north than it already is. The nearly seven-thousand-kilometer border with Russia—the second longest in the world—could return to its nineteenth- and twentieth-century fluidity, though strictly managed by muscular gatekeeper Russia. The grave responsibilities climate change is foisting upon the region's regimes will surely be ample justification for them to continue in their heavy-handed ways. At the same time, Kazakhstan already works with the International Organization for Migration (IOM) to promote migrant rights; next it may appeal to international agencies to assist it in co-governing foreign-populated zones.

Kazakhstan and the livable parts of its neighboring countries meet the conditions for potentially absorbing much larger populations than they're presently home to: They have abundant space, need human labor to modernize their economies, could sustainably survive the next decades of climate change, and offer a high likelihood of managed political stability. For now, their investments in roads and railways, agriculture and food processing, housing and medical care appear sufficient. But for the future, they aren't nearly enough.

# CHAPTER 7
# NORTHISM

## *Continental cousins*

More than three-quarters of the world population live in the northern hemisphere, with just over 500 million in North America and just over 5 billion in Eurasia. The North is also home to all the powerful states in the world, those with size and resources as well as the capacity to harness them and absorb more people. The North American and Eurasian continents are therefore both the historical and future seats of demographics and geopolitics. In the nineteenth and twentieth centuries, European technology and emigrants helped North America catch up in wealth, with the US alone representing half the world economy at the end of World War II. But with both the European and Asian ends of Eurasia far larger than North America in population, while achieving parity in wealth and technology, North America's share of the global economy has dropped to 15 percent.

North America's advantage nonetheless lies in its strategic stability and manageable population size. Though its three major countries have tensions over industrial policies and immigration, the US trades more with both Canada and Mexico than it does with China, and the US is also by far the largest investor in both countries. The continent's two major borders are symbolically potent, but the countries' deep complementarities in energy, agriculture, and industry are far more significant. The American regions most resilient to climate change, such as the Rockies, the Great Plains, and the Great Lakes, are all geographical and topological zones the US shares with Canada—further underscoring the inevitability of a more integrated North American Union.

America's demographic blending with Mexico also belies the notion of an impenetrable border fence. There are already 37 million Mexican-Americans, and dual citizens comprise an ever larger binational community populating towns across California, Arizona, New Mexico, and Texas. El Paso and Juárez are joined by a bridge across the border, with thousands moving north daily for school, shopping, or to give birth, or south to visit family or for cheap medical care. With retirees and younger Americans alike seeking a cheaper lifestyle, the number of "American-Mexicans" living in Mexico has ballooned from just two hundred thousand twenty years ago to 1.5 million today.[1] In the decades ahead, climate migrants from Central America may become a northward swell that dwarfs anything seen to date.[2]

Leading geography scholar Alec Murphy of the University of Oregon argues that the movement of people over time alters the grand narrative we associate with each region of the world. In this way, human geography allows us to investigate deep questions such as: What role will North America and its population play in a complex planetary society amid accelerating climate change?

We must explore the future of Eurasia with the same weighty agenda. Eurasia's rediscovery of the medieval Silk Roads has been accelerating over the past three decades, since the collapse of the Soviet Union. In the 1990s I began taking European trains south into the Balkans and watching the EU expand eastward toward Russia, and its influence reach the Caucasus countries by the Caspian Sea. In the 2000s, I followed Chinese roads and pipelines from the other direction, across Kazakhstan until they reached the Caspian as well. And in the past decade, Europe, Russia, and China have actively collaborated (and competed) to promote high-speed freight railways connecting London to Shanghai.

In the decades ahead, trans-Eurasian infrastructure investment will modernize economies, promote urbanization, and facilitate the circulation of industrious workers. Long dormant cities such as Samarqand may thrive again, with merchants from far and wide setting up shops and selling their wares. Cryptocurrencies will flourish across borders, making money accessible anywhere. Soybeans, vegetables, and rice will be planted in far more diverse geographies, with logistics improved to ensure supply meets demand. In addition to gas pipelines and railways, high-voltage electricity cables transmitting solar power, as well as water canals linking major rivers, will form a new infrastructure network spanning the area from Russia to India. The next Silk Roads will be multidirectional, multifunctional, and green.

## The Geography of Food

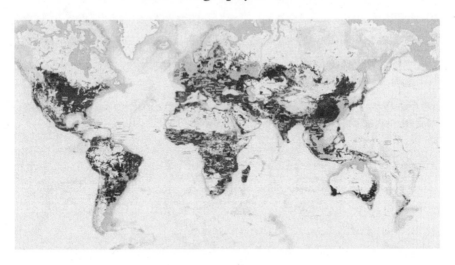

Global agriculture today largely overlaps with our population distribution. With the exception of the Arab world, food production is concentrated in geographies with the largest populations, such as China, India, the United States, and Brazil. But rising temperatures and changing rainfall patterns are changing the optimal geographies for agricultural production.

## *Terraforming the Arctic*

More humans are clustered along the 27th parallel than any other single latitude. More broadly, over the past six thousand years, we've grown accustomed to the 25- to 45-degree north latitudes being the most fertile and comfortable for human habitation. As climate change pushes us out of this optimal band, would we be better off farther north in latitudes with lower temperatures and population density? In his book *Evolution and Freedom*, Duke University mathematician Adrian Bejan explains how populations, like crowds, flow from narrow points to wide areas. Today we are densely concentrated in the equatorial and tropical latitudes; next we may disperse into the vast northern expanses. Our human geography is destined to evolve from equatorial origins toward a northern future.

Nearly five hundred years ago, the Little Ice Age spurred the explorations of the Spanish, Portuguese, Dutch, and British, making maritime Europe the cockpit of global power. Today, however, these former global empires are in economic retreat. Meanwhile, Germany, Scandinavia, and Russia—which suffered most during the Little Ice Age—are now warming and absorbing new populations. North America and Eurasia's largest states—Canada and Russia—bestride vast geographical expanses and are well positioned to sell massive quantities of freshwater from their broad rivers and melting permafrost to their thirsty neighbors to the south: America and China. What Canada and Russia also have in common is that they dominate a region that has never before played such a central role in global geopolitics and demographics: the Arctic.

Sci-fi culture and extraterrestrial missions have long inspired visions of terraforming other planets, engineering them for human habitation. Long before those dreams are even attempted, we must prepare rugged and sparsely inhabited parts of our own planet for large-scale settlement. The biosphere facility in Arizona was conceived three decades ago to simulate the kind of ecological community humans might construct on the moon. Now it has been repurposed to test how we can adapt to harsh environmental conditions such as droughts and heat waves.

It's tempting to claim that the solution to global warming is simply to move toward the Arctic Circle. The Arctic is warming at twice the rate of other latitudes, and food production (especially wheat) is rising. Forests are expanding farther north into the tundra. With only about 5 million residents across a geography the size of Africa, the Arctic's potential to host a billion or more residents seems plausible. Arctic towns are growing quickly, as I've witnessed during both summer and winter visits to northern Norwegian towns such as Tromso and Kirkenes. Norway even has a wine industry.

But remember that while Arctic summers may be balmy, you'll need to bring your eyeshades for the twenty-four-hour daylight, and although winters may no longer be as insufferably cold, they'll still be perpetually dark and thus inhospitable for those suffering from Vitamin D deficiency. Deaths from the cold are falling but heat-related mortality is rising. Forest fires have broken out from Alaska to the Nordic countries, but there are few fire stations (or other basic infrastructure) to cope with them. In Norway, torrential flooding is sinking small towns, while summer droughts are starving cattle. Even idyllic islands are in for trouble: Stunning Svalbard is experiencing thawing permafrost and avalanches; Iceland's melting glaciers mean rivers are drying up.

We also can't fully escape the pollution we generate elsewhere on the planet: Pristine snowfall in the farthest northern reaches now contains microplastics. Even worse: Beneath the permafrost and ice lie long dormant bacteria and diseases, such as the plague that killed millions of people and animals in centuries past, that are defrosting and infecting again. Thawing permafrost not only releases greenhouse gases such as highly flammable methane, but also mercury, a dangerous neurotoxin. Meanwhile, any road we build would be frozen for months and then consumed by peat bogs that act like quicksand. So terraforming the Arctic involves roads that will turn to mush and chemicals that can kill you.

## Moving to the Arctic?

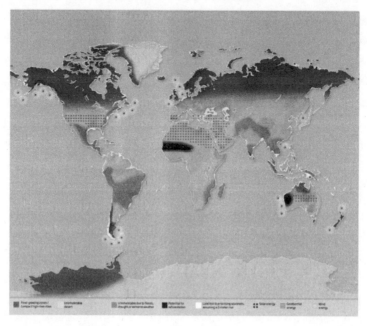

If temperatures rise by four degrees Celsius, Canada, northern Europe, and Russia would be the only regions of the planet suitable for year-round human habitation. Today's most populous countries, such as China, India, and the US, would be unsuitable due to droughts and other environmental hazards, though the US and other parts of the world could still be producers of solar, wind, and other renewable power sources.

And yet we will try. America's only partially Arctic state, Alaska, has been flagged in the EPA's Climate Resilience Screening Index (CSRI) as having the highest number of counties prepared for climate hazards. With its low population density, it also had the lowest Covid infection rate of any American state. But currently, Alaska is actually losing people annually to better jobs in the lower forty-eight states. No doubt it will attract rugged Americans seeking a low tax escape to start a new life and enjoy less scorching weather. But even in Alaska, dozens of coastal towns are being engulfed by rising Pacific tides, while heat waves have been killing salmon in rivers before they can spawn. Farther inland, oil drilling and timber logging threaten the state's nature preserves. A fresh start may well mean building new towns altogether. There and across Canada one will find an archipelago of new Arctic melting pots.

In Europe, the gold rush for Arctic real estate has already begun, driven not least by massive gusts of hot Saharan desert blasting north from Africa. Before the long heat spell of 2019 arrived, a Spanish meteorologist announced, "Hell is coming." A longer dry season in Germany's Brandenburg region has caused wildfires and ashen haze in Berlin, with similarly black-red skies during heat waves in Moscow as well. Scandinavian property developers keenly offer summer *dachas* to Europeans from farther south. The first company that announces it's building an Arctic outpost to relocate its staff during the summer will need AI to scan through all the CVs flooding its inbox. After all, with twenty plus hours of daylight in the summer, there will be plenty of time for both work and play.

Arctic territories will take on a new purpose. To be *there* will be the reason to be there: to build something for humanity where before there was only nature. Like the Amish or Mennonite communities who pioneered westward in nineteenth-century America, small communes will strive to live off-grid, harnessing local water supplies and agriculture to reduce dependence on the unruly world beyond their horizon. The Arctic will also be tempting for scientists, engineers, environmentalists, and financiers seeking to establish research settlements. They're already coding their community in the digital sphere through simulating architecture in VR and transacting in cashless blockchain contracts. Next they'll raise funds from investors and negotiate with governments to grant them land to colonize in exchange for investment and access to the benefits from these new businesses. It will be, in the words of Balaji Srinivasan, "Cloud first, land last."

A more populous Arctic region may come to resemble the resource-rich continent of South America, where indigenous people, Iberian colonists, African slaves, Europeans and Asians escaping hunger, and Arabs fleeing civil war have all layered over the centuries into a unique milieu. Over time, one should expect to see in the Arctic not only Europeans, Russians, and North Americans, but Syrian and Indian farmers, Chinese and Turkish industrial engineers, and dozens of other nationalities planting trees, building settlements, and harvesting resources. What better geography to promote a new orientation for human identity than the barren far north, which for centuries was stateless terrain?

At the same time, the land grab for resource extraction, agro-industry, and real estate development will accelerate. The Inuit and Sami people already subsist precariously off the land and sea as the ice melts. A new commercial influx may further force them onto reservations, as was the case with Native Americans in the US and aboriginals in Australia. This would be a reversal for Canada given the significant autonomy the First Nations gained in recent decades. Mining companies, billionaire environmentalists, and indigenous peoples may battle in courts and on the ground over sovereignty.

Arctic geopolitics may also further heat up the already warming northern cone. New shipping routes allow North Americans, Europeans, and Asians to evade traditional bottlenecks such as the Suez Canal or Strait of Malacca. At the same time, Russia is deploying armored icebreakers and nuclear submarines to assert its territorial claims as mineral deposits are discovered. Where once Arctic states disputed claims on the ice sheet, now they'll do so on the ocean floor. Given the lucrative resources and trade routes the Arctic represents, perhaps piracy will migrate north too.

China too has taken a growing interest in the Arctic, declaring it a "polar Silk Road." Chinese investors have sought to buy strategic tracts of land in Iceland and Norway, but Nordic democracies have rebuffed offers that don't involve full local control and democratic scrutiny.

A scenario amalgamating these trends points to the rise of a network of northern hemispheric trading hubs across which hundreds of millions of people may eventually circulate. This revival of the early medieval Hanseatic League—with members spanning beyond Hamburg and Tallinn to include St. Petersburg, Reykjavik, Kirkenes, Aberdeen, Nuuk,

Churchill, and other like-minded entrepôts—signals a future in which once again city states and their chambers of commerce drive vital global relations among pragmatic trading powers.

Can we pre-design our movements into the Arctic latitudes in such a way that we tread lightly, gradually preparing the terrain to absorb populations without destroying the resources on which we depend? Or will we bring rapacious extraction, pestilence, and geopolitical troubles as we have elsewhere in the past? If we don't get the Arctic right, there won't be any other options left.

## When Greenland lives up to its name

Because the Arctic is dominated by powerful states such as the US, Canada, and Russia, as well as wealthy Scandinavian ones, its infrastructure of roads, airports, housing, and power plants could ramp up very quickly. Greenland is a case in point. A Danish colony since the early nineteenth century, its residents already enjoy a fairly high standard of development despite its rugged and remote location.

There is a pernicious irony to Greenland turning from white to green. Greenland's ice sheet (second only in size to that of Antarctica) melt is putting at risk the very existence of tropical islands near the equator (where sea levels rise the fastest). But for Greenland, this process signals rebirth—perhaps independently from Denmark as its Inuit population's confidence in self-governance grows. While Pacific islands will have to be abandoned, this giant Arctic island's population could mushroom from sixty thousand to 6 million or 60 million.

Like Iceland, Greenland has abundant hydro, geothermal, and wind power potential. One year of its ice melt could provide sufficient water for one-third of the world population. Global warming has allowed for the rapid expansion of summer vegetation on the island (and there have already been wildfires during summer heat waves).

The greener it gets, the more Greenland becomes an object of geopolitical interest. The US has been trying to buy Greenland from Denmark for more than a century, but Copenhagen scoffs: "It's not for sale." Though the US operates a radar station at Qaanaaq (Thule), the island's leadership is already playing off multiple suitors, from military allies to mining companies, to gain maximum value from their strategic geography. Land speculators shouldn't bother: Private property ownership is forbidden, and the municipalities have been too clever to let foreign real estate dealers rip them off.

Greenland's development will inexorably bring it closer to Canada and farther from Denmark. Greenland and Canada share Inuit populations and customs, and the logistics of Arctic industrialization and habitation will much more heavily require day-to-day Canadian cooperation. Ultimately, Greenland's fate is not to be a Danish colony but to be a member of an emerging North American Union.

## Tomorrow's Climate Oases?

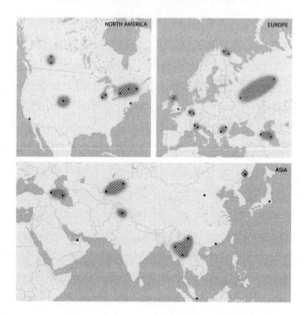

Today's most populous, wealthy, and stable urban clusters include London, New York, Tokyo, and Shanghai. Which geographies could become ever-larger population clusters in the coming decades? These new zones and corridors are among those likely to emerge as population shifts accelerate.

# NORTHISM

## *Cities for all seasons*

About one hour before the devastating 2004 tsunami swallowed the shores of Sri Lanka, elephant herds briskly retreated from the coastline and stomped up-country. Their sixth sense warned them that something was amiss in the earth's vibrations. The caretakers who marched with them also survived the surging oceanic wall. Meanwhile, thousands of unaware beachgoers were crushed to death and swept out to sea.

Immersed in modern technology, humans have lost their ability to *feel* the planet. But when it comes to climate change, we should no longer be taken by surprise. We have both fair notice and scientific models telling us what comes next. We may have lost our sixth sense, but we can use our technologically assisted autoimmune fight-or-flight instinct to run inland and upland from nature's wrath. In the decades ahead, we'll need our ancestors' combination of survival instinct and pioneer spirit if we're to inhabit new frontiers while rolling with nature's punches.

If the earliest proto-humans time traveled to the present, they'd have good reason to believe they were on another planet. In their times, they wandered the Earth seeking only seasonal stability. Today, by contrast, we've built at will on top of nature, modifying it to suit our needs. But our indifference to nature will only have been a two-century-long blip of history. Now nature is fighting back, forcing us to revert from sedentary to nomadic ways.

Climate sensitivity has already forced whales, polar bears, sea turtles, and butterflies to alter their migration patterns. Two particular species of birds have maintained large populations by changing their seasonal destinations: the Arctic tern (*Sterna paradisaea*), which migrates from pole to pole (Greenland to Antarctica), and the short-tailed shearwater (*Ardenna tenuirostris*), which migrates from Australia's Tasmania Island to Russia's Kamchatka Peninsula, then to Alaska's Aleutian Islands and back. At a time when all species are threatened, they continue to survive because they move. Humans too are quite accustomed to seasonal migrations, whether farmers working in the US and Mexico, ski instructors shuttling between the Rockies and the Alps, Mongolians shifting their yurts from the high plains into the capital, or the wealthy who rotate between urban penthouses, suburban villas, and holiday properties.

What do habitats look like in a world of quantum people? The answer is not traditional real estate projects that take a decade to complete using designs that are out of date by the time of occupancy. We already have the technologies—heating and cooling, water purification, and energy storage—to make any terrain—desert, mountain, forest, or tundra—habitable. We are going to need them to cope with life on the move. Why should we continue to erect redundant high-rises and steel towers carrying exposed electricity cables when we can instead deploy modular 3D-printed multipurpose mobile tenements and portable concentrated solar power generators?

Consider the climate migrants of Bangladesh. The vast majority of the country lies barely above sea level, and cyclones and flooding regularly displace more than one-third of its nearly 170 million people. President Sheikh Hasina says, "A sense of hopelessness is gripping the population." And so they move—with solar panels, mobile phones, water filtration systems, and their children and clothing.

But large population movements into relatively unspoiled geographies bring the potential for yet more human-inflicted damage. The solution is to build sustainably—and take our infrastructure with us wherever we go. Rather than impose a heavy urban footprint, we can *pre*-design portable and self-contained settlements that don't anchor into the ground but shift according to soil conditions. The research network AudaCities has launched a "Movable Village" prototype in which water purification, hydroponic food equipment, and other essentials are built into mobile homes and other facilities. Self-contained towns could have water towers that store water from rain, desalination, and atmospheric generators; solar power centers and battery swap-out stations for homes; and food composting, sewage treatment, and materials recycling centers. Helping to restore both wetlands and agriculture, Europe has dismantled thousands of dams that were essential in their day but have fallen into disrepair. The faster the US transitions to solar, nuclear, and wind power, the faster it can do the same.

For locations that are only seasonally viable, there can be pop-up cities. The Zaatar refugee camp in Jordan is an off-grid village of multi-family-size tents, medical clinics, solar power stations, water desalination facilities, schools, job placement centers, and other services for eighty thousand mostly Syrian refugees. Is it a "camp" or a semi-permanent city? Another example is India's Kumbh Mela, the Hindu religious festival taking place every twelve years that rotates among four holy cities. More than 7 *million* people reside on the festival grounds, with more than *100* million visiting over the course of the season. Materials such as bamboo, plastics, light metals, and fabrics are used to assemble—and completely disassemble—the full suite of infrastructures, from electricity and security cameras to water supply and sewage. This Manhattan-size site is an "ephemeral mega-city" in the words of Harvard Design School professor Rahul Mehrotra—yet it has more functionality than many Indian cities. Urbanism should be thought of as an "elastic condition," assembled as and where needed, rather than the decaying permanence of abandoned shopping malls and stadiums. As Mehrotra says, "Why be obsessed with permanence when change is the only constant?"[3]

Mehrotra's insights are just as valid for the rich world as the poor. Ironically, even though we've massively overestimated the future world population, we've *under*estimated our demand for infrastructure, whether electricity or housing. The 1950s through 2000s witnessed a continuous infrastructure boom across devastated postwar Western Europe, superpower America (think of the interstate highway system), and surging Asia (first Japan and the "Tiger" economies, followed by China and India). Well over $100 *trillion* dollars have been spent on highways and railways, pipelines and electricity grids, airports and offices, schools and hospitals—all the hallmarks of modern civilization. At the same time, most developing countries never had adequate infrastructure, especially as their populations *tripled* from the heady postcolonial 1950s through the 2000s. Either way, for most of the world, it hasn't been enough, because wherever we build anything, there is a constant need to repair and upgrade, deploy new technologies like Internet cables, and accommodate growing populations.

Yet from beachfront real estate to short-circuited power grids, so much of our infrastructure is being rendered worthless due to climate change, alternative energy, and population shifts. These "stranded assets" now represent trillions in debt held by governments and zombie companies alike. Much as civilizations of the past abandoned their towering monuments due to drought or other calamity, the detritus of our current civilizational model includes skyscrapers that embody the national ego. But these are not the infrastructures mankind needs in a future oriented around mobility. Arab Gulf states can no longer afford them; China has banned buildings taller than five hundred meters.

Instead of architectural phalluses pointing at the heavens, we must build structures that can adapt to nature's whims. There is good precedent for constantly reusing existing infrastructure: the construction cranes we use to erect buildings in the first place. At the peak of global construction a decade ago, an estimated one hundred thousand cranes crowded the horizon of Shanghai, Riyadh, Sydney, and other cities. Seattle has been more active in new construction than either New York or Los Angeles. One of my daughter's first musings as a mid-2010s child spending time in Singapore, Dubai, and Berlin was "Construction is taking over the wooorrlldd!!" But once a city is built up, the cranes are dismantled, put on flatbed trucks, and shipped to other cities around the world where they're needed. We should now plan to do the same with buildings themselves. As Google's "moonshot" captain Astro Teller has put it, "We might need self-driving buildings as well as self-driving cars."

As much as any breakthrough in software or artificial intelligence, it's mankind's impressive capacity for topographical engineering that is most needed today. Small coastal countries such as the Netherlands have the slimmest margin for error in planning for extreme scenarios. Since the Great Flood of 1953, the Dutch have built a vast network of sea barriers,

pump stations, levees, and other adjustable infrastructures to manage flooding from the North Sea and the Rhine. While extensive land reclamation
has expanded the country's size, it has also designated entire zones as flood
basins to save Amsterdam, Rotterdam, and The Hague. Other countries
have designated parks to serve as wetlands during flooding, and are deploying permeable asphalt to redirect water swells into aquifers. Copenhagen
plans to build a residential island called Lynette Holmen with hills that
block coastal surges, tackling climate change and housing shortages at the
same time. But we can never be too certain of our schemes: Even though
we may not *see* the ocean rising, its encroachment pushes underground
freshwater up through our soil and streets: inundation from below. Perhaps
that's why Danish architect Bjarke Ingels has proposed constructing a set of
interlinked floating city-islands that rise with the sea.*

More than 90 percent of the Earth's territorial surface has no inhabitants. Can we disperse from the vulnerable coastal megacities in
which so much of the global population has concentrated? When I
first searched for cases of de-urbanization, I found very few and at
very limited scale. But now that we can inhabit smaller and more self-
sufficient communities without sacrificing global connectivity, it's far
more plausible a scenario. As we begin to plan to resettle populations,
we should locate them farther inland and at higher elevations, and ideally near agriculture to avoid dependence on far-flung food supplies.
The outskirts of Zurich, for example, feature numerous towns where
agriculture, woodwork, 3D-printed precision machinery, computer
modeling, and other both high- and low-tech industries thrive side by
side amid clean air, freshwater, and low noise pollution—all connected
by railways to major cities in Switzerland and beyond. For large populations, we would install long-distance water canals or pipes, and nuclear-
powered desalination plants and wastewater treatment facilities. Even

---

* Let us hope they're more eco-friendly than cruise ships, which emit more carbon per passenger
than cars or planes, while dumping countless tons of waste into the oceans.

cities of 3–5 million people can leverage their surrounding ecoregions without destroying them.

## "Plan B" for billionaires

A chorus of philanthropists and celebrities have pledged their wealth to finance carbon capture, reforestation, alternative energy, and other climate interventions. At the same time, boomers and Gen-Xers with unlimited means have already begun preparing for the worst. Their "apocalypse insurance" includes buying up tracts of remote Hawaiian islands or vast ranches in Kansas with impenetrable bunkers, off-grid power, freshwater tanks, weapons caches, motorcycles, and helicopters. Switzerland's private bunkers are not only impregnable fortresses but ensure digital resilience so you have access to your Bitcoin. Yacht owners are outfitting their vessels to last for months if not years on the high seas, and investing in a new class of super-yachts that are both ships and submarines. Others are scheming to build floating private islands that make their own laws and dock only in friendly jurisdictions. Given New Zealand's safe distance from turbulent shores and its trustworthy government, rich agriculture, and abundant freshwater supplies, it's no surprise that it has become a desirable end-of-the-world destination for those who are allowed to buy property and citizenship. But New Zealand's population is only 5 million, and it has little interest in raising it much further—unless you're a billionaire.

# CHAPTER 8
# WILL "THE SOUTH" SURVIVE?

## Decaying states, departing people

The first time I consciously noticed the depravity of idle youth was when I was about twelve years old visiting relatives in Uttar Pradesh (widely known as "UP"), India's most populous province. Everywhere we scootered around—Lucknow (UP's capital), Kanpur (my hyper-polluted birthplace), and Varanasi (Hinduism's holy city)—kids loitered on the roadside, in front of shops, in their alleyways, or on the banks of the Ganges River. It was as if they were waiting for something meaningful to come to them. It still hasn't. With more than 200 million people, UP today has twice as many people as China's most populous province of Guangdong (in southern China). However, while the per capita income of Guangdong is roughly $5,500, UP's residents earn about $900 per year, less than half of India's national average.

Many Arab youth have not fared much better. In the 1990s, European countries promised to invest and outsource more work to the Arab societies of North Africa. In the immediate post-9/11 landscape, no shortage of experts drew attention to the despair facing Arab citizens suffering under arbitrary dictatorships; more money was spent on publishing reports about the Arab "youth bulge" than doing anything about it. The US went on to spend trillions of dollars invading Iraq and Afghanistan, while also launching PR campaigns irrelevant to Arab life.

It was in the mid-2000s that I began traveling extensively around the

Arab world to research my first book, from Morocco and Libya to Syria and Iraq. I talked to hundreds of people my own age, twenty-somethings who had little professional opportunity. Those old enough to drive a car would hustle various odd jobs; younger kids often just sat around sniffing glue. The "Arab Spring" revolts of 2011 seemed inevitable.

Two decades on from the "youth bulge" reports, many Arab countries are in worse shape than they were then—while the youth have grown up with neither useful education nor jobs. Meanwhile, Europeans can have robots do their menial work and focus on exporting to Asia—and blocking any boats or rafts of Arabs from making it safely across the Mediterranean. Arabs are on their own. The vast majority of respondents in the Arab Youth Survey still rank jobs and the cost of living as their top concerns. Arab youth unemployment stands at 30 percent, the highest in the world, including university graduates.[1] Youth marginalization is not an episode but a permanent condition—as is their desire to emigrate.

Arabs largely share language and religion, and have spent most of the past thousand years under shared caliphates and the Ottoman empire. Despite their modern division into bordered nations, their descent from postcolonial nationalism into chaotic implosion has been nearly borderless. During my time advising US Special Operations Forces in Iraq, we watched daily as Tunisians, Jordanians, and other disaffected young men streamed in from across the region. The radicalized "ISIS generation" that emerged out of the Iraqi insurgency and Syrian civil war was originally composed of disaffected Iraqi Baathists and Saudi Wahhabi-backed Islamists, but economic deprivation made thousands more vulnerable to seduction by radicals who promised sex slaves in lands liberated from infidel (American) occupation and virgins in the afterlife. Now those conscripts have become the "jihad diaspora" of disgruntled fighters conducting attacks worldwide.

The best hope for the Arab region's failed states is to follow the model of Morocco, which has kept youth gainfully employed by investing in solar power for villages, high-speed railways, water desalination plants, agricultural revitalization, and tree planting. Since most Arab youth won't make it across the Mediterranean, they ought to be deployed toward this kind of nation-building that the past two generations mostly ignored. Otherwise, they'll just head to the Gulf—especially the UAE. There has long been a fluid Arab talent arbitrage whereby one country's demise enables another's rise. The Lebanese civil war that lasted from 1975 to 1990 led to an exodus of savvy multilingual professionals; today there are twice as many Lebanese in the diaspora as in Lebanon. When you walk into a government meeting in the UAE, most likely a Lebanese banker will be in the room as well.

Lebanese, Egyptians, and other down-and-out Arabs have also wound up in the oil-rich Gulf kingdom that has financially propped up their nations: Saudi Arabia. But oil prices are collapsing and the need for their services is limited, for now. The millennial Crown Prince Mohammed bin Salman has launched grand schemes to reinvent Riyadh and erect multibillion-dollar resorts and entertainment complexes on the Red Sea coast. Catering to the 80 percent of the population that's under the age of forty, he has also pushed social reforms, including greater women's rights, to drive, travel, and divorce. If his plans succeed, then another generation of Jordanians, Egyptians, and Lebanese will pour into the hospitality industry. They may even rebuild lost connections such as the Ottoman-era Hejaz Railway that linked Istanbul through the Levant to Islam's holiest sites of Mecca and Medina. This is the optimistic scenario for an Arab renaissance.

But if the Gulf countries fail to reinvent themselves, the rich Saudis and Emiratis will head to Europe while the poorer Arabs will go back (or stay at) home—and take to the streets. In the simmering revolts from Algiers to Beirut to Baghdad, youth have wisely learned to abandon sectarian divides and take on the corrupt ruling class as a united generation. In fact, across the Arab region—including Saudi Arabia—a rising number of young Muslims are abandoning Islam and becoming non-religious and even atheist.[2] Like most young Christians in the West, they're religious more in name than deed. Young Arabs have also dramatically lost faith in religious leaders and Islamist parties. A 2019 *Arab News* survey showed that most Iraqis and Lebanese resent the outsize role of religion in their politics and favor governments that focus on economic policy. They see religion as a personal preference rather than a political prison. They don't want to wait until the afterlife for dignity.

Arab governments have responded to resistance with the reflex they know best: repression. One lesson regimes clearly did not learn between the Arab Spring of 2011 and its reprisal in 2019: Don't tamper with the Internet. In 2011, it took only three weeks from when Mubarak's regime cut off Internet access to the masses flooding Tahrir Square and when his three decades of iron-fisted rule were brought to an end. In late 2019, the Lebanese government proposed a tax on digital messaging services. As soon as word of the "WhatsApp tax" spread, Lebanese youth parked couches in downtown Beirut and ground the city to a halt. They even formed a 170-kilometer human chain stretching the length of the country from Tripoli to Tyre. The tax never came into effect. Instead, ministers were forced to take a big salary cut.

No Arab country faces more dire circumstances than Yemen, whose civil war has become the world's worst humanitarian disaster, all while its 30 million people run out of water. Yemenis will soon flood into their tormentor Saudi Arabia, and have already begun to flee on rafts across the Red Sea to Africa, toward Sudan and Egypt. But Egypt is a political, economic, and environmental time bomb all at once, a civilization on the precipice of collapse. The Nile River itself is the best metaphor for the state of Egyptian society: By the time the country's agricultural lifeblood reaches the Mediterranean delta, it's a swamp. Egypt has gone from cotton titan to having such severe water shortages that its prized industry is disappearing. Soon the Suez Canal will lose relevance as ships take the cooler and faster Arctic route between Europe and Asia and freight trains crisscross Eurasia. Already the country's marriage rate is falling (because men can't afford it) while the divorce rate is rising.

Men are encouraged to get alimony insurance before marriage since in the event of divorce, they'll have to pay 40 percent of their incomes to their ex-wives. Needless to say, this diminishes their prospects for a second marriage.

Egypt has long considered itself the true guardian of the Nile, but in fact almost 90 percent of the water it and Sudan (another military-controlled state of nearly 50 million) receive from the Nile originates in Ethiopia, which is constructing a grand hydropower dam on the upper Nile to boost electricity generation for its fast-growing economy of nearly 110 million people. A lot of things have to go right in the coming years for Egypt, Sudan, and Ethiopia to survive: cross-border power and water sharing, efficient irrigation and desalination, the curbing of corruption and the creation of jobs for tens of millions of listless youth. Since hope is not a strategy, it's a safer bet that many of this restless generation will disperse out of Africa, becoming everyone's problem.

Like Egypt, Iran represents a teeming young society with no meaningful strategy for the future. For forty years since the Islamic revolution, talented Iranians have been ditching home for Dubai, London, and Los Angeles, with most never returning, even to visit family, due to the risk of arbitrary arrest. In this fifth decade of self-defeating isolation, Iran faces not only tighter sanctions and low oil prices, but an overwhelmingly young population stifled by the country's corrupt theocracy and stagnant economy. Uprisings have been sporadic but sizable since the 2009 "Green Movement." After a week scootering around Tehran and meeting dozens of Iranian movers and shakers in 2014, I crowned them the "Just Do It" generation for their brave pluckiness and knack for getting gadgets imported and fixed despite all obstacles. Now they're calling for "*madaniyya*," a civic rebirth, taking the root word *meydan* that means public square. Ukraine's 2004 "Orange Revolution" centered on the *meydan* (parks) in Kiev, and after the Iranian regime shot down a Ukrainian Air flight bound for

Kiev in early 2020, Iran's youth have imported the spirit of Kiev to the streets of Tehran. But each time they return home from another futile protest, ever more plot their escape.

## Ramadan lifestyles and underground living

At the stroke of noon, the power goes out. It's the same thing almost every day in Pakistan—and Egypt, Lebanon, Iraq, Nigeria, and many other countries. The taps often run dry too—even as temperatures soar. Such is life for hundreds of millions of people across north and central Africa, the Middle East, and southern Asia. With water tables falling and electricity grids frying, can daily life be made more livable for people trapped in the scorching subtropical latitudes? As the world heats up, people of all faiths may have to learn to follow a Ramadan-like routine: Waking up early to eat, staying indoors in air-conditioned buildings or resting through the hot daytime hours, and coming back out only after sundown. Maybe we should also dress like Gulf Arabs, in simple white, flowing cotton gowns that reflect light and keep us a bit cooler.

Heat waves and water shortages may also return us to communal practices abandoned long ago in the West but still thriving in the Middle East. For example, more people may take comfort in the bathhouse (*hammam*) culture that was the norm for many centuries. To avoid baking at home without air-conditioning, Europeans will congregate in climate-controlled public arenas or coworking spaces cooled by water from underground aquifers piped in through district cooling systems. This may well reinforce some of the social cohesion that has been fading as neighbors have become strangers.

Many bathhouses are subterranean, constructed to provide access to natural thermal springs or cool streams. Perhaps entire settlements will be built underground. Decades ago, some cities accustomed to frigid winters developed extensive underground shopping arcades, eateries, and even cinemas. Moscow is famed for its artistically decorated underground metro, and Kiev for its subterranean bazaars. Montreal's underground walkways stretch for thirty-two kilometers of pedestrian zones, even linking residential buildings. Similar plans have been developed in Helsinki, Toronto, Beijing, and Singapore—though none include actual housing. Humans still prefer to live aboveground rather than subject themselves to claustrophobia. But imagine searing heat, devastating storms, and other natural disasters befalling us on a regular—or unpredictable—basis. The same cities that built underground passages as a refuge from the cold might use them to provide a respite from the turbulence ahead.

## Africans trapped on the go

Africa is the continent that the Club of Rome's 1972 message did not reach. It embodies how a growing population can be a great thing—until it's the worst thing. Its population size has expanded well beyond economic necessity and pushed it deep into ungovernability and ecological crisis. Africa needs more productivity, not more people it can't afford. The question now is: What to do with the 60 percent of the continent's population that's aged twenty-four or younger?

Over the past thirty years, Africa's food and mineral resources have become much more connected to the global economy, leading many to predict that the twenty-first century could belong to Africa. But none of the trends that elevated Africa has guaranteed longevity. China and India are diversifying their commodities imports, making Africa less relevant as a supplier—yet as oil and mineral prices sink, African nations may fail to make debt payments and be forced to give up their oil fields and mines as collateral. From Djibouti to Niger, the countries most indebted to China may be in civil war when China comes calling. The European migrant crisis is partially made in China, whose projects are displacing communities and altering river systems to grow food for export, driving Africans northward. But European investment—despite various iterations of a grand African support strategy—is stagnating even as Europe closes itself off to future migrants.

But the migrants have tried their best to come anyway. Hundreds of millions of African youth live in poverty,[3] and especially those from central African states such as Congo and Niger have fled northward to Libya, where the same militias that plague the country profit from allowing thugs and pirates to extort and starve those seeking to cross the Mediterranean. Many never make it: Far more Africans (nearly twenty thousand since 2014) have drowned in the Mediterranean Sea than Latinos perishing from heat exhaustion crossing the Mexican desert to reach the Rio Grande. The continent's rampant population growth and environmental stress have led to ethical pleas for more open migration to Europe, but the northern hemisphere's reply has been: Stay home and have fewer children.

Africa's most populous country, Nigeria, is the linchpin of forecasts of Africa's continuing population explosion and economic rise. But Nigeria is as much or more a story of resource stress and decay, and more likely to become a civil war zone than a bustling market of 300 million. It's a country often described as being on the brink of imploding, rather than stating more plainly that its implosion is accelerating. Lagos, Africa's largest city, is also at risk from rising sea levels; slums such as Makoko are built on swamps soon to be engulfed by the encroaching Atlantic Ocean. Nigeria is home to one of the world's deadliest terrorist groups, Boko Haram, and numerous other militias that campaign against Christians and other minorities. When Nigeria criminalized people trafficking, young Nigerian smugglers lost their livelihood and now make the journey themselves, adding to the exodus from equatorial Africa.

If any people were born to move, it's the Eritreans. Severe poverty, decades of drought, and a late 1990s war with far larger Ethiopia forced about 1 million Eritreans to flee into neighboring Sudan. Two decades later, the number of Eritrean refugees, asylum seekers, and migrants still stands at more than 750,000, about one-quarter of the total population. Some cross Sudan to Libya followed by rafts to Europe. Others make it to Uganda, from which a haphazard series of flights lands them in Uruguay, where they set off to walk or hitchhike all the way through Brazil, the Andean nations, and Central America until they reach the US and settle in California. As crossing to the Mediterranean and Atlantic becomes more perilous, they can opt to cross Sudan into Egypt, or take rafts across the Red Sea to Saudi Arabia. With an overwhelmingly young population, most Eritreans have grown up seeing those older than them leave the country as soon as possible. Migration is their life—and they have no idea where it will take them next.

Africans are clamoring to get to Europe, but most will have to content themselves with frequent internal migrations instead. Even that has proven more difficult due to the devastating impact of the coronavirus on public health systems. Nonetheless, Africans circulating within Africa already represent one of the largest migrant groups in the world, and the continent's ill-defined borders are transit zones for people, goods, food, minerals, drugs, and weapons. African governments have all agreed to a continent-wide free trade and mobility area by 2025—a move that both ratifies the obvious and also represents a noble effort to untangle Africa's arbitrary colonial borders. With a $2 phone coming into their hands and mobile payments spreading to every country, Africa has an opportunity to use mobility in all its forms as a springboard to reinvent itself.

It may seem obvious that the path forward for Africa's development lies in manufacturing and trade, services and skills, urbanization and digitization. The bustle of Nairobi, Kenya's capital, gives off this positive vibe. But most African youth don't enjoy even that minimal level of entrepreneurial bustle. Does Africa need more people stuck in traffic jams, or selling Chinese toys and Nestlé chocolates?

The African Development Bank has a better idea: It wants to turn agricultural areas into major job-creating zones for more efficient food production, powered by renewable energy. Africa has almost half the world's uncultivated arable farmland, and is the largest exporter of phosphate fertilizers, yet tens of millions face acute food shortages. Smart countries such as Ghana have launched programs to professionally train more farmers and get them better equipment. Rather than grow flowers for Europe, Africa should grow more food for itself.

To do so, Africa will need to conserve its water. Already the drying of Lake Chad has exacerbated tribal tensions across Chad, Cameroon, Nigeria, and Niger, driving nearly 3 million people from their homes. Droughts have also reduced the flows of the Zambezi River, and hence the once majestic Victoria Falls at the border of Zambia and Zimbabwe may gradually be reduced to a mere spout. This means less farming, less tourism, and less electricity from hydropower. Africa also exports water when countries such as Sudan sell farmland to Saudi Arabia and other Gulf states buying up the upper Nile, leaving Sudan to borrow money to import wheat from other countries. Eventually, as East African countries dry out, their people may flee south to Kenya, north to Egypt, or east across the Red Sea to Saudi Arabia's coastal cities with their desalinated water. It's as if the African mega-drought of a hundred thousand years ago is repeating itself.

Some parts of Africa have the potential for medium-term livability, such as Gabon, which is 80 percent rain forest, as well as coastal Congo and Botswana, each representing natural ecosystems still in balance. These are the places where Africans can build sustainable new enclaves along the lines of those imagined for Wakanda in the futuristic film *Black Panther*.[4] And if they do, African youth will surely move there.

## Scenarios for the South

The fact that most people may never leave the country, region, or continent in which they were born is particularly damning for 1.2 billion Africans and 450 million South Americans, who are less likely to be able—or allowed—to leave. This is a tragic irony, for Africa and South

America are projected to have the largest number of people displaced by climate change. Recent decades of economic growth in developing countries brought about a slight reduction in the stubborn North-South divide, but climate change and the coronavirus will widen it again with a vengeance. One UN official has stated, "We risk a 'climate apartheid' where the wealthy pay to escape overheating, hunger, and conflict while the rest of the world is left to suffer."[5]

There are wildly divergent scenarios for the fate of the global "South." If south-to-north migration remains heavily restricted, then South America and Africa will continue to be victims of climate change (mostly the North's fault) and political decay (mostly their own fault). They could invest in infrastructure, industry, agriculture, education, clean energy, and healthcare, building greater self-sufficiency in making things for themselves while exporting to the world—or they could suffer an accelerated combination of ecocide and fratricide, fighting over scarce water and food resources while many millions perish each year.

Either way, the North will still want to have its cake and eat it too: extracting minerals, negotiating access to its food supplies, and siphoning more capital out in profits, debt payments, and illicit money laundering than it contributes in investment and aid. As decades pass, Northern countries will either rapidly automate most functions for which they once imported Southern laborers, or they'll selectively recruit South American and African migrants for functions not already filled by Asians. The likely outcome is some combination of all of these scenarios.

## South America: Forever the "lost continent"?

South America has the largest freshwater reserves in the world, but that doesn't mean much in São Paulo, the continent's largest city, where the taps have run dry. For the Amazon River and its tributaries to reach the continent's overwhelmingly coastal populations, they must be allowed to flow freely—something the pernicious cycles of deforestation and drought have prevented. Brazil continues its swings between left-wing socialism and right-wing populism, the latter currently accelerating the devastation of the Amazon. Brazil could well leverage the Amazon to promote biomedical and pharmaceutical innovations, but as it torches its own future, more and more Brazilians are taking their families and money and moving away.

Hardly any Latin American country (save for small-size Costa Rica and Uruguay) appears free of rebel groups and sinister gangs; the region has the world's worst homicide rates. Latin youth cherish the digital tools that give them a medium for self-expression, but the Internet also shows them a better life if they can escape the plight of poverty, violence, and corruption.

None of South America's other largest countries give reason for optimism about the continent. In the nineteenth century, Argentina was so certain of its economic ascendancy that it became popular to display upside-down world maps in which the southern hemisphere was on top. But many decades of ideological seesaws made it an economic basket case, saddled with debt and unable to make essential investments without raising taxes on its already strapped population. No wonder desperate citizens have turned to Bitcoin to evade capital controls and get their money out of the country. Even worse, the capital, Buenos Aires, home to one-third of the population, has to worry about rising seas. Meanwhile, much of the rest of Argentina is receiving torrential rain—one year's worth in two weeks—causing flooding so extreme that cattle must learn to swim. Glacier melt will bulge rivers even further, until they disappear entirely—after which severe droughts may follow. Argentina produces enough food for 100 million people, but it will have to master agricultural engineering for its lush Patagonia region to remain a grocery store for the world—as well as to absorb climate migrants from the rest of the continent.

In the 2000s, Venezuela under Hugo Chavez fancied itself the successor power to both Argentina and Brazil. Instead, today it embodies one of the world's most acute refugee crises as malnourished Venezuelans flee to Colombia and other Andean nations. The mighty Orinoco River has suffered from a 50 percent decline in annual rainfall in the past decade, resulting in both water shortages and power cuts from its hydroelectric dams. The country also once had five glaciers in its western mountains, all of which have melted. It's conceivable that Venezuelans could one day return under new leadership to harness their country's enormous energy reserves, but nobody has any idea when that will be.

Even more promising Andean nations, such as Colombia, are headed for water shortages due to drought and excessive mining that have depleted their water basins. Peru's glaciers are all melting fast—resulting in floods at first, then nothing, especially for the country's 10 million rural poor. The populations of Ecuador, Peru, and Colombia may have to move inland toward their tri-border region to benefit from what remains of the rain forests—but only if they can control the fires there first.

The Andean nation of Chile exhibits a misalignment of resources and demographics that will have to be corrected for its people to adapt to climate change. Perpetual droughts in the country's arid north have forced farmers to migrate their livestock south toward more fertile terrain. The capital, Santiago, has gained more than a million people in just the past decade, and now has half of Chile's entire population of 18 million. Yet the city is running out of water, with ever more frequent droughts because of its high elevation. The government will have to channel Andean glacier melt and ramp up desalination on the Pacific coast, but still much of the country's population may have to migrate southward, where the majestic fjords in Antarctica-facing Magellan Province (named for the sixteenth-century Portuguese explorer who first circumnavigated the world) make it the southern hemisphere's answer to Norway. Snow-less seasons have already forced skiers to the southern Andes, and while summers in southern Chile are getting warmer, mountains and sea mitigate the heat (making it far more tolerable than scorching Australia across the

South Pacific). It was German immigrants who primarily settled southern Chile, starting in the nineteenth century, and Chileans will need their inherited engineering prowess to expand the currently two-lane north-south *Ruta 5*, Chile's 3,400-kilometer section of the Pan-American Highway.

## Can you live in Antarctica?

Antarctica has just witnessed its hottest year on record (crossing 18 degrees Celsius in February 2020), accelerating ice melt, increasing precipitation, and growing patches of vegetation. Antarctica has no permanent inhabitants yet, though during the summer months its various research stations host about five thousand scientists and staff, and New Zealand has begun expansion of Scott Base to make it a year-round livable facility. The lack of direct sunlight for half the year, however, makes self-sustaining agriculture difficult, though hydroponic production with indoor light is feasible. Antarctica may nonetheless help southern hemispheric countries cope with freshwater shortages: South Africa has made attempts to tow icebergs from there to its shores. The ice continent is most attractive to China for its mining potential, though the 1959 Antarctic Treaty bans mining activity. China may push to revise that rule when it's due for reconsideration in 2048—if not sooner.

## Australia: Too hot down under

For decades, two large nations on opposite sides of the planet have had remarkably similar trajectories. Both resource-rich continental expanses, Canada and Australia's commodities booms have delivered decades of uninterrupted economic growth for their small populations. But now their paths are diverging: Canada will be as close to a winner as there can be from climate change, while Australia will be a loser.

In the mid-twentieth century, Australian scholars raised concerns that global overpopulation and food shortages would prompt international agencies to seek to take possession of its agricultural bounty. This is no longer a scenario Australians need to fear. On the contrary, unlike Canada, whose vast interior is rich in forests and arable land, most of Australia consists of desert that is rapidly encroaching on coastal life. So too are wildfires and rising sea levels. Could Australia's climate misfortune scare away its long-standing immigrant surge—and even the descendants of its original settlers?

Climate change is ravaging the lucky country. Australia's outback rivers and reservoirs have dried up; no new crops are being planted, animals are dying, and people are leaving. The 2019 bushfires that ravaged Victoria Province scorched an area larger than Switzerland, killing hundreds of thousands of animals and dozens of people, reducing thousands of homes to ash, and requiring the country's largest ever peacetime evacuation. The fires were so large that they generated "pyro cumulonimbus" clouds that caused their own storms and lightning that caused new fires. In the words of one academic, the Anthropocene is more like the "Pyrocene."[6] Across New South Wales, Australia's most populous province, bushfires cut off major roads in and out of Sydney—after which it suffered cyclone-induced flooding in early 2020. Most of the year, however, its reservoirs are at low capacity and residents face significant water restrictions, even as industrial activity sucks up the water supply while generating a terrible carbon footprint.

Australia is a rich country. It has few people but generates enormous revenues from mineral and gas exports. Both its money and its energy could be used for water desalination to rehabilitate its agriculture. But Australia also has climate-skeptic politicians, as well as powerful industrial lobbies, that interfere in forward-looking regulation. As a result, strategic hydro-engineering projects like a north-south water canal linking

Queensland and New South Wales (NSW) have been left unattended even though they'll take many years to deploy. Who knows if either the migrants or the Australians will stick around that long.

Australia has long been a favorite destination for middle-aged Brits, Mediterranean and Arab migrants, and ambitious Asians, absorbing Chinese, Japanese, and South Koreans ditching social hierarchies, rigid educational systems, or suffocating politics (or all three). Australia already has the highest foreign-born share of its population among OECD (Organisation for Economic Co-operation and Development) countries, and takes in about two hundred thousand new migrants each year. The country is becoming more Asian than white: Currently just over half the population has two native-born parents, but China, India, Malaysia, and the Philippines are the fastest-rising origin countries for the parents of new Australians. Key city centers give a far better glimpse into the future demographics than homogenous rural areas: Immigrant youth flock straight to downtown Sydney, while older white families have moved out to the suburbs. As former foreign minister Gareth Evans wisely puts it, "Australia's future will depend much more on its geography than its history."

Australia's tech sector wouldn't exist without immigrants drawn to its comfortable cities such as Perth, Adelaide, Brisbane, and Melbourne, cities whose investments in walkability, education, and public services have made them attractive and productive hubs for both Australian and foreign talent. Given Australia's dependence on foreign brain power, the fringe One Nation Party does the country no favors with its xenophobia. Nor did the coronavirus, which did not kill many Australians but certainly dented the appetite of foreign students and property investors—two constituencies on which the economy depends. If and when Australia's lucky economic streak ends, geopolitics gets tense, or climate change drives migrants away—or all three—many might take their Australian passports and resettle elsewhere.

Don't be surprised if even proud Aussies do the same. Australia has a long tradition of restless youth wandering abroad, with many never re-turning. Now the government is actively subsidizing Australian students to study abroad and learn Asian languages so that they can be more use-ful overseas employees of Australian mining companies, universities, and hospitals—all of which are waking up to the need to expand abroad. The students are happy to oblige, since it takes them on average nearly three years after graduation to find a full-time job. No wonder so many Aussie youth go walkabout in the first place.

# CHAPTER 9
# THE ASIANS ARE COMING

## *The future is brown(ish)*

On the eve of the late-eighteenth-century Industrial Revolution, Asia—especially China and India—accounted for nearly 60 percent of the world economy. Two hundred and fifty years later, it does again. Western mastery of technology, rapid industrialization, population growth, and imperial ambition propelled Europe and then America to global dominance for the nineteenth and twentieth centuries. But as Asia's resurrection illustrates, in the long run societies with larger populations tend to become wealthier, as they aggregate and spread innovations that make their citizens more prosperous. Collecting people equals collecting power. Asia's population is now *five times larger* than the US and the European Union combined—and Asian powers command the latest technologies as well. Western societies, then, will continue losing their economic advantage to Asia unless they replenish their populations—most likely with Asians.

The colonial legacy has already woven Indians into the fabric of countries around the world. The Indian diaspora is the world's second largest (behind China) but the most geographically diverse, with a large presence on every continent (except South America). India already has the largest number of migrants living abroad who remain citizens of their home country (more than 17 million), far ahead of Mexicans (under 12 million) and Chinese (under 11 million). Indians are so settled in the UAE that the embassy there collects an expatriate tax that it pools to support nationals who run into trouble or need repatriation. The former president of Guyana, the former prime minister of Ireland, and the current prime minister of Portugal are of Indian descent.

The war for talent in medical, technology, and other fields has pulled ever more millions of South Asian families to the UK and North America, where English has given them an advantage over other nationalities in assimilation. I remember learning English the hard way, but I was young enough that being a non-native-speaker had ceased to matter by the time I was about eight. And precisely because there were relatively few Indian families in Westchester County (outside of New York City) in the mid-1980s, assimilation was the only option. Across Europe and America you find "Chinatowns" but no equivalent "India towns."

The next wave of global Indian migrants may be much larger than what the world has experienced so far. With a much younger median age than China, India has 600 million youth under the age of twenty-five. Already 3.1 million of the highly skilled foreign workers in OECD countries were born in India, far higher than China's 2.2 million. Given the post-Covid economic crash and the country's sinister levels of pollution, Indians are more motivated to leave the country than ever before. As India expands its universities, even more Indians will qualify for graduate degrees in the US, Europe, Australia, Japan, and Singapore. Chinese students presently outnumber Indians on Western campuses, but the runway for India to catch up is long. Furthermore, Indians do not face the suspicions Chinese do. With their combination of English language, technical education, and strategically nonthreatening identity, Indians are welcome everywhere, especially where Chinese no longer are. The CEOs of IBM, Google, Microsoft, Mastercard, Nokia, and Novartis are all Indian, as are the founders and executives of hundreds of other companies from Boston to Silicon Valley; it's highly unlikely they could ever be Chinese.

The flow of Indian talent to America and American capital into India is a formula that catapults ever more Indians everywhere. The vast majority of US H1-B visas have gone to Indians who boost America's software production and exports. The Brookings Institution estimates that President Trump's June 2020 executive order restricting nonimmigrant work visas cost the US economy $100 billion.[1] It also gave American tech giants an excuse to expand their already massive offshore footprint: Silicon Valley's investments in India are surging, from telecoms to e-commerce to AI. India wants to convince one hundred major universities to open campuses in India itself.

But remember: The combined effect of all this upskilling *in* India will be to make Indians even more qualified to apply for work visas for more livable places. Western multinational companies gush about the 3-billion-strong Asian middle class into which they want to sell, but Asia's billions are just as keen to save and move as they are to stay and spend. Indian men are suffering from a dearth of available women (due to decades of female infanticide), while Indian women want to escape a culture that tolerates gang rape. Both despise arranged marriages, and would rather go abroad—where they most often find other Indians socially or via dating apps.

The entire South Asian region contains educated and hardworking millennials and Gen-Z youth ready to go abroad and send home remittances that their families use to upgrade homes—or save up to follow their loved ones abroad. This is precisely how Pakistanis, Bangladeshis, and Sri Lankans have also rooted themselves across the Gulf, the UK, and North America—and how Urdu came to be the fastest growing language spoken at home in the US. There are another 130 million Pakistanis under the age of thirty, and the flagging economy can't find jobs for most of them. One way or the other, many will find a way out.

The next wave of mobile Indians couldn't be better timed. Whereas Mexicans are emigrating less and the Russian and Chinese populations are aging, India remains young and its men and women eager to flee their culturally and ecologically stifling country for North America, Europe, the Gulf countries, Russia, Japan, Australia, or Southeast Asia. In other words: anywhere.

## Asia's Dominant Diasporas

| | Chinese | | South Asian | |
|---|---|---|---|---|
| Australia | | 1,200,000 | | 962,000 |
| Canada | | 1,800,000 | | 2,000,000 |
| USA | | 5,100,000 | | 5,400,000 |
| South America | | 1,100,000 | | 553,000 |
| Africa | | 1,000,000 | | 3,500,000 |
| MENA | | 550,000 | | 19,000,000 |
| Europe | | 2,300,000 | | 5,000,000 |
| Russia | | 200,000 | | 42,000 |
| Southeast Asia | | 23,000,000 | | 7,400,000 |
| Japan | | 1,000,000 | | 75,000 |

= 1 million

The Chinese diaspora is the world's largest, but South Asian populations (particularly Indian) are growing worldwide. The Indian population in Europe, the Gulf, and Africa is already significantly larger than the Chinese. In North America, South Asian populations are growing far more quickly than Chinese.

## *The young and the restless*

Across Asia, technological shifts are propelling new waves of migration. In China, automation has devoured the jobs of millions of prime-age workers, from factory workers to fitness trainers, sending them off across the country and beyond, looking for new jobs. Low-wage industrial workers in Thailand and Vietnam face redundancy as electronics and car manufacturers deploy legions of industrial robots. In IT-powered India algorithms and chatbots are eviscerating call center jobs, pricing bright yuppies out of Bangalore not long after they arrived. Millions of Asians can no longer afford to stay where they live, and why stay anyway if there are no jobs? So they move.

Economic migrants beget ever more migration. In the twentieth century it was believed that temporary workers would eventually return home after some years: Sending money home was also supposed to discourage "them" from coming in ever larger numbers to "us." But instead, migrants settled and saved enough money to arrange for their families to join them in the West. Economic migration became chain migration. Because remittances can be unreliable, immigration policies can change, and currency values fluctuate, families would rather uproot themselves and become migrants as well. In these family diasporas, individual members often go in different directions and share money with one another using borderless financial apps such as Remitly.

Asia's middle-class billions may want to move either because they've become wealthy enough to do so or because jobs have disappeared at home. Meanwhile, the skills they acquire in IT, construction, and healthcare are *portable*, making them more qualified to get visas for higher-wage jobs abroad. According to the *International Handbook on Migration*, emigration increases substantially as per capita income rises from roughly $2,000 toward $10,000, exactly the curve on which most countries find themselves today as populations rapidly urbanize and economies become more service oriented. From some countries, emigration has tapered once incomes cross $10,000 per capita—but automation is preventing many people from reaching that middle income status. So they move to places where there is work.[2]

Asians already represent the majority of the 150 million semipermanent guest workers who crisscross the world's farmlands, con-struction sites, and other infrastructure projects. Beyond Indians and Pakistanis, underutilized Indonesian men would also benefit from basic training in carpentry and metalworking, and be more produc-tively employed in other countries than at home. There are also nearly 1 million mostly Asian sailors in commercial fleets and merchant na-vies plying the oceans on giant cargo ships (four hundred thousand of whom were stranded at sea during the Covid lockdown), their routes meandering as new ports are built and populations shift. Soon we might find battalions of Asian farmers and handymen building towns in the Arctic. The world needs these restless young Asians to stay on the move.

### Multinational maids

Reasonable people can debate how many total immigrants should be allowed into a country, from where they should be allowed, and how to maintain a common national ethos. But to qualify as a civilized society, a country should at least have a decent healthcare system—and that requires an adequate supply of doctors and nurses. In the 1970s, the US responded to a shortage of medical practitioners by bringing in large numbers of Indian doctors and pharmacists. But as the Covid pandemic bluntly revealed, neither the US nor the UK have adequately recruited for their sprawling medical commitments. One-third of all Covid-19 deaths in the US were in nursing homes, a reality that will perhaps lead today's baby boomers (and their children) to demand far better care when their turn comes. America's 3 million nurses are already the larg-est segment of its healthcare workforce, and America needs a lot more of them.

So does China. Like America and Japan, China is no longer the best place to open a kindergarten—but elderly homes are a thriving business. In addition to childless Chinese migrants, an estimated five hundred thousand to 1 million Filipinos work in the elder-care industry today. Given that half the world's cigarettes are sold in China, it seems relatively certain that even more nurses will be needed to care for those suffering from cancer and other chronic diseases.

The Philippines, already the largest supplier of nurses for the world's hospitals, can't train nurses fast enough to meet global demand—an expected 100 million new jobs over the next two decades. Meanwhile, as Filipino families get wealthier, they want to keep nurses and nannies at home rather than export them. Hence the intense international recruitment campaigns underway in Manila, where billboards advertise German lessons and fast-track visas to Europe. Germany is not only recruiting from Asia but siphoning hearty sixty-year-old women from Poland and Bulgaria who work 24-7 caring for Germany's half million homebound octogenarians and nonagenarians.

Nurses and household workers are an ideal lens for viewing the role of young women from poor countries in the global war for talent. Yale scholar Anju Paul more appropriately labels them "multinational maids" for the way in which they leverage diaspora networks and placement brokers to shift across Asia, the Middle East, and North America in search of higher wages. Experienced caregivers and maids are so in demand that they have bargaining power; Paul has even created an index they can use that ranks countries by the quality of treatment they can expect. It's sure to prove very useful to the next waves of outbound nurses from India and Indonesia, countries with far larger equally young female populations than the Philippines.[3] Tracking maids' movements around the world reveals how effective migrants (like the traders of the ancient world) can be at peer-to-peer intelligence sharing. Once they establish themselves somewhere, their presence is a bellwether for others looking for places worth going to. Whether in Japan, Australia, Saudi Arabia, or Canada, no professional better embodies the quantum worker of today and tomorrow than the Asian maid.

# MOVE

## *Mongrel humanity*

The relentless outward Asian migrations that lie ahead will change the complexion of the planet. Mass migrations have not only altered where people are but also *who* we are. Each year brings new archaeological, anthropological, and genetic research showing how truly mingled the world's many tribes have been over the millennia, and the genetic diversity that permeates almost all of us. My own DNA test reveals Baltic and Mediterranean lineage, which at first seems bizarre yet is quite sensible in light of India's history of invasions. So much of humanity has migration in its blood. This is a reminder that mobility—not tribalism—is our original instinct, more deeply hard-wired into who we are as humans than any contrived racial or ethnic allegiance. Indeed, recent paleontology research suggests that one reason Neanderthals became extinct is that they lacked the genetic diversity of our more mobile *Homo sapien* ancestors. Mobility refreshed and broadened our gene pool.

As in prehistoric times, today's intensifying mobility accelerates humanity's genetic collisions. The past eight decades of mass migrations have already forged an increasingly blended global society and undermined the very idea of the ethnically homogeneous "nation-state." While countries such as China and Bangladesh remain dominated by a single ethnic group, all major Anglophone states—America, Canada, England, and Australia—have more than 20 percent foreign-born populations in addition to their existing minorities. They're well on their way to becoming "majority-minority" countries in which minorities collectively represent the majority of the population. Already they're packed with hyphenated "Indian-Canadians," "Chinese-Americans," and so forth. A century ago, the white supremacist Ku Klux Klan insisted on such hyphenation to clearly demarcate immigrants from the majority. But when most people are hyphenated, then it is the hyphenated "nation-state" that has literally become passé.

Like climate change, racial dilution is a gradual process that has crossed a tipping point. North America has become a European, Native American, Latino, and Asian mélange. As of 2015, 17 percent of American marriages are mixed-race, with Caucasian-Asian mixed-race couples mushrooming. Today some young Asian-American women get harassed for marrying white men, and yet the next generation is unlikely to face the same challenges precisely because it has become so mixed-race. European societies are also melding with North African, Turkish, Slavic, and Arab peoples. In London, more than 10 percent of children are now born to couples mixing African or South Asian with Anglo-European. Mohammed has become the most popular name for newborn boys there. A 2020 survey shows that nine out of ten Britons would be comfortable with a mixed-race marriage in their society.[4] In Germany and France, inter-marriage with Arab, African, and Turkish populations has also become mainstream. Our demographic future will look ever more like a brown, yellow, black, and white milieu.

Asian people are increasingly mingling in the Far East as well. The 50-million-strong Chinese diaspora has become inextricably woven into the fabric of countries whose names suggest ethnic specificity, such as Thailand and Malaysia, but who in reality are much more a blend of indigenous, Chinese, and Indian people. Intermarriage among Chinese, Indian, and other races is growing. In China itself, zero interracial marriages were registered until the 1980s, but they have been on the rise, with other Asian nationalities, Europeans, and Africans.

Nobody is forced to marry outside their ethnic group; we do so voluntarily and in ever growing numbers. The delusion of racial purity has become a political choice racists inflict on the rest. But reality has irreversibly overtaken such regressive visions. Xenophobia in some countries can't unwind genetic mingling worldwide. We should therefore also be very cynical about the notion that "culture is destiny," as if there is a fixed national culture passed down from generation to generation without modification or adaptation. Just as there are few pure nation-states, there is no immutable culture. Assimilation may seem like a vicious contest, but fusion prevails in the end. Our destiny is to be a global mongrel civilization.

## Diaspora geopolitics

More Asian migration means ever larger Asian diasporas, the widely dispersed ethnic communities that keep one foot in each country—and wield influence *both* in their homelands *and* on their own behalf in their new homes.* The mass migrations of the nineteenth and twentieth centuries set the stage for diasporas to play a key role in American politics throughout the postwar decades. Notable examples are Jews with respect to Israel, Irish on the Northern Ireland dispute, and Eastern Europeans who lobbied extensively for the expansion of the NATO alliance in the late 1990s.

All the major Asian diasporas—Chinese, Indian, Bangladeshi, Pakistani, and Filipino—are digging deeper roots around the world. In Southeast Asia, large ethnic Chinese populations are increasingly considered a potential fifth column. Within one generation, Chinese migrants to Canada, Australia, Singapore, and the US have gone from working-class mercy cases to suspects in sophisticated foreign influence operations. By and large, however, assimilated Chinese immigrants in America have tended to be defensive about preserving their new way of life rather than importing oppression. That's why protests have broken out *between* Chinese-Americans and pro-Chinese nationalist camps over Hong Kong and human rights. Today's young Chinese students arriving in the US speak better English than their predecessors, but not necessarily to better fit in. Rather, they're more confident in China's

---

* For millennia, the Jewish people existed more as diaspora than nation, enduring expulsions from ancient Assyria to Nazi Germany—hence the saying that while trees have roots, Jews have legs. The Jewish diaspora was instrumental in the creation of Israel after World War II, but to this day the Jewish diaspora numbers an estimated 8 million people, still larger than Israel's 6 million population.

rise, egged on by the "College Daily" WeChat group that blasts out slanderous news about the US itself to maintain nationalism and urge them to return home. It seems to be working. The vast majority of Chinese students in America do return after graduation, or move on to other more hospitable countries. Where mobility and technology intersect, assimilation can no longer be assumed. Identities multiply and exist in tension.

But now that many Chinese immigrants have taken local citizenship (or maintained dual citizenship), their activities can't be treated purely as a foreign policy matter. Especially in Canada and Australia, "they" have become part of "we," and governments are struggling to determine who is loyal to which country. Australia recently banned foreign financial support for political parties, while Canada debates whether to extradite Chinese who have become Canadian residents.

As Indians' wealth and clout in the US have risen, so too has their funding of both Indian and American political parties. The diaspora has been instrumental in branding India as America's democratic ally in Asia. The "Howdy Modi" gathering in September 2019 packed fifty thousand diaspora members into Houston's NRG Stadium for a joint rally with Prime Minister Narendra Modi and Donald Trump. The generational divide is worth noting: While most in the rally were middle-aged, young Indian-Americans outside protested Modi with placards calling him (and Trump) a fascist.

Enough Indians have gained their most coveted UK citizenship over the past three generations that they now manipulate British politics. The Overseas Friends of BJP (Bharatiya Janata Party, or Indian People's Party), or OFBJP, is nowhere more active than the UK, where it rallied 1.4 million British Indians to vote for Boris Johnson's Tories against Jeremy Corbyn's Labour Party after the latter vocally called for international intervention in Kashmir. The Labour Party used to be able to count on almost all minority and immigrant voters, but no longer. (Corbyn's pro-Palestinian stance turned the Jewish diaspora against him as well.) But as in the US, younger British Indians are distinctly cooler toward their ancestral land.

The growing numbers of Indians in America and Britain embody how, over time, some pairs of countries have developed ritualized accords for managing the millions of families and students regularly flowing between them. Whether diplomatic ties stand at a high or low point, the penetration has crossed the point of no return.

# CHAPTER 10
# RETREAT AND RENEWAL IN PACIFIC ASIA

## Metropole China

The world's most populous country needs more people—fast.

The mass migration of hundreds of millions of Chinese from rural to urban areas has uprooted thousands of years of tradition by which extended families lived together under one roof. Younger Chinese are no longer home to take care of two aging parents just as the elderly population crests: By 2030, about a quarter of China's nearly 1.5 billion people will be over sixty-five, meaning China will have as many elderly people as America has people. By that time (and beyond), a young Chinese person will face the "4-2-1" problem: being alone but financially responsible for two parents and four grandparents.

But elder care is no more a job for hardworking, urban, and mobile Chinese as it is for Americans and Germans, hence China has begun a major binge of importing women. Already many thousands of Korean, Vietnamese, and Burmese women have been brought to China as brides for the surplus male population. Whether or not they have children, their main job will be to care for their husbands' parents.

And what will the men do? China's breakneck urbanization, rapid automation, and massive gender imbalance have created an enormous rump of underemployed men, many of whom lack high school degrees.

They make up the bulk of the 300 million migrants lacking registration (*hukou*) in the places they live, restricting their access to social benefits. The government recently began to eliminate *hukou* requirements so Chinese could be more freely mobile—but they also introduced the social credit system, which allows the government to determine anyone's right to travel anywhere.

Does China have a grand plan to sort out its massive demographic mismatches? Millions will continue to be drafted into the military and police, millions more will work on massive hydro-engineering projects across the country, yet more millions will be sent to resuscitate farmlands, and millions more will labor on energy and construction projects across Asia, Africa, and as far as South America in the service of China's Belt and Road Initiative. All of this should keep them off the streets.

Western and Asian powers have built coalitions to ensure China doesn't dominate them, but can foreigners adapt to a China that is a world unto itself? Only 1 million foreigners live in China; even five times more would scarcely register. More important than the number are the trends among them. At university campuses across China, one finds large numbers of European, African, Arab, and other Asian students—a total of nearly five hundred thousand in 2019 (only twelve thousand of which were American). On top of this there are growing numbers of young professionals from Nigeria to Pakistan who undertake vocational training in China. As one Peking University scholar put it to me, "Even if the number of students from the USA is down, the students from BRI is way up," referring to the nearly one hundred countries participating in the Belt and Road Initiative.

China is also, surprisingly, home to growing numbers of Japanese scientists who can't find jobs in Japan despite their advanced degrees. At least eight thousand of them are currently spread throughout Chinese universities and institutes advancing China's research into everything from astronomy to zoology, and most importantly climate science and engineering. China is acting more nationalist on the world stage, but

Beijing is also branding itself as a cosmopolitan metropole as London and Paris were to their colonial populations in centuries past.

Many view US-China trade and technological frictions as indications that American firms—and thus their expat employees—will retrench and return home. But companies follow supply chains, not government diktats. There are many reasons for foreign firms to reduce their exposure to China, such as rising local wages, intense competition from national champions, a crackdown on English teachers without advanced degrees, and more. But none of this suggests they'll come home. Indeed, the total number of Americans in China rose to seventy-five thousand in 2019 on the back of the country's consumer growth. From Apple to Nike to Tesla, American companies have adopted (or been forced to adopt) an "in China, for China" strategy, making locally what they sell locally. Europeans are in the same boat, for their companies depend even more on Asian revenue than American companies do. Expats who want to be employed as managers in these companies' operations will very much still need to learn Chinese.

## In search of the "Asian Dream"

These days, the phrase "family values" applies to stably married and loyal East Asians as much as or more than it applies to family units in Western societies. But as with Western youth, it's ever more difficult to pinpoint an age at which young Asians "settle down." Nearly 1 million Chinese have already moved to Japan, where they work across professions, from cashier to financial analyst, and a quarter of a million have moved to South Korea. The older generation of all three countries harbors deep mutual suspicions, but youth couldn't care less. As one thirty-year-old Chinese tech millennial in Singapore told me, "I don't want to get married and have kids. I'd like to retire by forty-five and spend some time in Japan on a farm, then travel more. I'll shift my assets into crypto and move around."

Asian tourists and business travelers are already unmissable in every corner of the globe—but the intensity of their cross-border movements is twice as high in their own region as outside of it. For thousands of years, Asia has featured multiple unique and deep civilizations; now it has the makings of a common one as well.

While South and Southeast Asian societies are still lower-middle-income compared to their neighbors to the northeast, their youth are in a similar boat. Millennials are already more than half of India's workforce, competing against one another as well as algorithms. India's annual job creation in manufacturing and tech is falling way below promises and expectations, and unemployment for India's university graduates is painfully high. For the millions of new labor force entrants each year—and those laid off due to automation—the jobs won't come to them. They'll move to the West or to Southeast Asia's dynamic economies.

Southeast Asia, the world's third most populous region after China and India, is also one of the youngest, with more than half of its 700 million people under the age of thirty. They too have two things on their minds: moving to cities and gaining relevant skills. With free labor mobility across the region, it's not uncommon to find upwardly mobile millennials in Singapore and Bangkok who have already lived in three or four countries. Southeast Asian millennials have rising rates of inter-marriage and share an optimistic outlook and progressive ethos. Despite their already giant populations, Asian countries have also thrown open their doors to foreign investment and talent. Starting in the 1960s, newly independent Singapore invited in multinational companies and workers, the two forces in tandem propelling the country's economic growth and diversification. Fifty years later, one-third of its population is foreigners and it ranks as one of the world's most innovative economies. Countries such as Indonesia, Vietnam, and the Philippines are now privatizing utilities, banks, farms, airlines, and other large state-controlled companies, bringing in fresh capital and management teams from around the world to guide more productive investments.

The number of expats populating Southeast Asia is growing every year as these countries roll out the red carpet with easy visas, good schools, quality healthcare, and fast connectivity. After witnessing how the US and much of Europe mishandled the coronavirus, Western expats in Asia have no plans to voluntarily return to their low-growth and populist homelands. During the pandemic, some Western expats lost their jobs and had to return home against their will, but at the same time, American and Australian applications for Thailand's "Elite Residence" program surged because of the country's low infection rate and affordable medical tourism offerings.

Asia today features ever more people who never thought they'd be there: not just Western expats but Asians themselves who left decades ago for the West but have returned as executives and entrepreneurs—and with their families. So many such "re-pats" are part of the great global migration story that we need to reverse familiar formulations: I use the term "American-Asians" to describe myself and many thousands of Asian-Americans who have returned to Asia even though our parents and siblings remain in the West. The going is good for the foreseeable future, but should things change, we can always move again.

## Asia's swirl of climate migrants

While much of the world gets hotter and drier, Asia's high altitude and tropical wetlands are getting wetter. Two hundred and forty million people live in the Hindu Kush and Himalayan region—across Pakistan, India, Nepal, China, and Bhutan—but about 1.6 *billion* depend on the ten river systems originating there. At a time when droughts have parched China, India, and Pakistan, the melting of fifteen thousand glaciers in the Himalayan Mountains and Tibetan Plateau might be seen as a welcome development. But torrid glacier runoff and extreme rainfall have caused dams to burst, resulting in treacherous flooding and landslides across India's northeast. If two-thirds of the Himalayan glaciers melt in the coming decade, hundreds of millions of lives will be imperiled. Melting glaciers are already contributing to the permanent flooding of the Ganges delta across India and Bangladesh. But eventually, the rivers will dry up, with floods giving way to droughts. Over the coming decades, hundreds of millions of people will have to move due to rising seas, flooding rivers, and droughts—both within and across Asia's many borders.

The headwaters of the Ganges, Brahmaputra, and Mekong Rivers all lie in Tibet, whose importance to China rests not in its tiny population but its environmental geography: China wants to ensure uncontested control over the Earth's "third pole." China has built or planned hundreds of dam projects to direct flows into its gargantuan South-to-North Water Diversion Project, a system of canals transferring water from the Yangtze and Yellow Rivers to those supplying the water-stressed northeast, where hundreds of millions of Chinese drink contaminated water every day. China is the only country that can spend the eventual price tag of $100 billion and force more than a dozen provinces to coordinate their infrastructure investments while displacing millions of people (as it did to build the Three Gorges Dam, the world's largest hydroelectric power plant). And it has to, since it can't get its citizens or companies to better conserve water, nor can it count on buying bottled water plants in countries such as New Zealand, where protests have forced a halt on siphoning the country's pristine lakes. Meanwhile, China has been less than transparent with its downstream neighbors about its plans: It has no formal water sharing agreements with India, Bangladesh, or other countries. Even if it did, water levels have begun to fluctuate so unpredictably that on some tributaries dams have been built for water that may never arrive.

India possesses even less freshwater than China for its 1.4 billion people who inhabit dozens of the world's most polluted and freshwater-deficient cities. That's why India has launched enormous efforts to channel Himalayan water to farms and urban reservoirs. In the western Himalayan territory of Ladakh, ingenious solutions have been tried such as piping glacial runoff into stupa-shaped formations (appropriate for the Buddhist faith prevalent in the region) that melt slowly and can be used to irrigate high-altitude farming. The Modi administration has also planned a Chinese-style National River Linking Project (NRLP) to ensure India's continued role as a global breadbasket.

India's tumultuous internal migration has not only been from villages to cities but also from north to south in search of jobs and better climate. Forty percent of those surveyed in New Delhi in 2019 about their likely response to the city's worsening air quality said they were considering moving farther south to cities with cleaner air. Large southern states such as Andhra Pradesh and Karnataka have witnessed millions of north Indians moving in over just the past ten years, and the beachfront paradise of Goa has been overrun by north Indians (and European tourists) as well. Bangalore has gone from India's "garden city" to its "garbage city." Meanwhile, Chennai's 2019 water shortage required the government to dispatch several fifty-carriage locomotives each day carrying millions of liters of water from more than three hundred kilometers away.

Maybe the many Indians that have moved south will recirculate back north toward the Himalayas again. In 2019, the Indian government administratively separated Buddhist-populated Ladakh from Muslim-majority Jammu and Kashmir, revoking their semi-autonomous special status and converting them into "union territories" directly governed from New Delhi. This political maneuver made it possible for any Indian—not just Muslim Kashmiris—to buy land in Kashmir, something many Indians would no doubt be eager to do given its moderate, seasonal climate and breathtaking Himalayan scenery. Equally importantly, Kashmir is home to the headwaters of the Indus River and all of its tributaries. India is expediting major dam projects on the upper Indus to boost irrigation for Kashmir and Punjab, which produces more than 10 percent of India's wheat and cereals.

For more than seventy years, Kashmir has been part of India but not quite. Like Han Chinese moving into Muslim Uighur homeland

Xinjiang, Hindu Indians will colonize Kashmir, showing how domestic population shifts can be just as strategically significant as international ones. Such demographically motivated decisions can also alter the regional power balance, for India can now cut off water flows to Pakistan, as it threatened to do in February 2019 after a terrorist attack in Kashmir.

With no hope to settle Kashmir in its favor or control its crucial water supplies, Pakistan will also have to become more strategic about its demographics and geography. Currently, the country's two most potentially livable provinces are its most sparsely populated. Stunning and mountainous Gilgit-Baltistan has for the past two decades been in the news more for harboring Islamist terrorist groups than as home to more than one hundred 7,000-meter plus peaks (such as K2). But with accelerating glacial melt causing torrential flooding, Pakistan's government has to invest large sums into disaster management and channeling river run-off. Prime Minister Imran Khan has also pledged to reforest neighboring and rugged Khyber-Pakhtunkhwa Province with ten billion trees. With the country's teeming megacity of Karachi on the Arabian Sea baking in early summer heat waves and drowning in late summer monsoons, and droughts ravaging Pakistan's populous breadbaskets of Punjab and Sindh, many more Pakistanis may soon head north as well.

More than four hundred dams and two hundred hydropower projects are planned across the Himalayan region, making even small kingdoms such as Nepal and Bhutan key players in the region's resource maneuvers. Nepal has the potential to produce eighty times more hydropower than it currently does, which it desperately needs to avoid its own regular power cuts, fuel basic industries, and sell electricity to India. Just as significant will be hydro infrastructure to pipe irrigation water to India's Gangetic plain states such as destitute yet fertile Bihar. As the government finally invests in better roads and water management, Bihar could go from basket case to fruit and vegetable powerhouse.[1] If Nepal expands its own agriculture, it could wind up with millions of Indians filing northward toward—or across—their eighteen-hundred-kilometer open border.

Bhutan too allows Indians to visit without visas—but certainly not to reside. The kingdom most associated with mystical Shangri-La lore has only eight hundred thousand people and allows fewer than thirty thousand tourists each year. Extensive tree planting has even made it a negative emissions carbon sink. Given its rudimentary infrastructure, Bhutan is viewed more as a source of hydropower for India and Bangladesh than a permanent destination—but soon enough it will be geopolitically coveted as a high-elevation climate oasis. China has been chipping away at its territory from the north, while more Indians may flow in from the south. Even across the world's highest frontiers, people will be on the move.

China's Himalayan strategy of directing water and power from the upper Yangtze River to industrious Sichuan (population: 90 million) and verdant Yunnan (population: 50 million) Provinces will reinforce their status as scenic and low-cost alternatives to China's overpriced and polluted coastal provinces. Chinese youth have been flocking to Sichuan's capital, Chengdu, and Yunnan's capital, Kunming, where new railway lines into Laos and Thailand have made those cities the de facto capitals of the southern silk roads.

Yunnan is also a magnet for displaced Southeast Asian farmers and other poor laborers—downstream victims of China's upstream water and energy policies. For low-lying Southeast Asian nations, too much water is as much a problem as too little. The region's coastal megacities, such as Bangkok and Ho Chi Minh City, may all be sunk by 2050. Vietnam's Mekong River delta lies barely one meter above sea level, meaning tens of millions of rural Vietnamese may need to retreat upland within a decade or two. Yet even as sea-level rise nudges coastal Vietnamese inland, they face more frequent droughts in the lower Mekong plains due to China's hoarding of the watershed, pushing them northward toward China itself. Today there are tens of thousands of Laotians and Vietnamese who have crossed into Yunnan in search of work; soon it could be millions.

Devastating cyclones are already driving the coastal populations of India, Indonesia, and the Philippines inward. Mumbai needs to replicate itself on sturdier ground rather than the exposed peninsula on which it currently sits. Indonesia is planning to relocate its entire capital, Jakarta, from coastal Java (the world's most populous island, with nearly 150 million people) to the far larger island of Borneo. Whether or not that ever happens, Indonesia needs a sustainable strategy for its largest island, Sumatra, which is home to 50 million people and lush tropical jungle. Given its much vaster terrain and higher elevation, Indonesia would be wise to conserve Sumatra for future habitation rather than recklessly slashing its precious rain forests.

Oceania's low-lying island nations don't have the luxury of relocating citizens across Indonesia's sprawling archipelago. Instead, they're planning for their own evacuation. The 2.3 million citizens of Pacific island states such as the Marshall Islands, Tuvalu, Kiribati, and the Solomon Islands have been the first to take up New Zealand's "climate visa" program. Eventually all will have to relocate there, to Australia, or other countries with which they have strong demographic or political associations. Some have asked China to help finance raising their roads so they can withstand rising seas awhile longer, but China surely prefers the islands vacated so China can mine the phosphate deposits and seabed minerals without local protest.

Perhaps the worst fate has been dealt to those who are both political and climate refugees at the same time, such as the Muslim Rohingya of Myanmar. More than 1 million persecuted Rohingya have fled to Bangladesh—where their main refugee camp (known as Cox's Bazaar) gets flooded during monsoon rains. Since Bangladesh is hardly a climate haven, soon there will be millions of Bangladeshis fleeing in the opposite direction toward the temperate highlands of northern Myanmar (and the hills of northeast India) near the Chinese border, from which the Irrawaddy River flows southward and nourishes the country's farms and fisheries. If Myanmar gets its act together, it could go from military-run basket case to climate oasis within a generation.

Climate refugees from Bangladesh and Muslim political refugees from Myanmar may well wind up farther south, in fellow Muslim Malaysia, the regional nation least vulnerable to adverse climate effects with its dense forests and hydrating monsoon rains. Conveniently, all these countries are undergoing a strong improvement in their overall ties. As part of its "Act East" policy, India is investing in robust road connections through Bangladesh and Myanmar to Malaysia, seeking to boost cross-border trade in energy, raw materials, and textiles. Such connectivity isn't designed to smooth the path for mass migrations, but that's likely what will happen anyway.

## Japan: High-tech melting pot?

Throughout the late twentieth century, Tokyo held the title of world's largest megacity. Today, of the world's two-dozen megacities, Tokyo is the only one registering a noticeable population *decline*—much like Japan as a whole. Nationwide, Japan has the world's largest vacant housing stock: One out of every seven homes is abandoned, a share expected to rise to one-third in the coming decade. Entire towns are emptying as the elderly pass away and the young move to cities.

To convince people to occupy the country's charming towns, Japan is literally giving away homes to young couples on the promise that they'll have children and contribute to the revival of civic life. At least they're doing something, which is more than one can say for the more than six hundred unemployed middle-age (mostly) men known as *hikikomori*, who live in total seclusion, unable or unwilling to find jobs. With more women working (and more elderly staying in the workforce), Japan's birth rate has collapsed.

Perversely, this is why longtime Japan watcher Jesper Koll argues that now would be the ideal time to be reincarnated as a twenty-three-year-old Japanese millennial. Your parents would be the world's richest baby boomers, with full ownership of their homes and low debt, world-class medical care, and protected pensions. You could live off their savings in multigenerational homes and have cheap immigrant maids or robots (or both) taking care of their and your needs. Out in the professional world, university students get jobs within a week of graduation, part-time workers are moving into full-time employee status, and the corporate old boys' club is cracking open as firms restructure and divisions are spun off into new ventures. Japanese corporations are also getting serious about investing in blockchain and IoT sensors, with SoftBank and other VCs (both domestic and foreign) making big investments in startups. Writing off Japan has become passé. What if the country is headed for a renaissance? The scenario is not only plausible but likely—if Japan reverses its demographic freefall.

Even countries with high automation need migrants. Japan is famous for having robotic seals as companions for the elderly; robots handle check-in at hotels, and there's even an android Buddhist priest who delivers sermons at a temple in Kyoto. But still there are worker shortages in farming, healthcare, education, and other essential services. However, other than the periodic waves of Koreans who have been brought to Japan as laborers or artisans, Japan has historically been averse to immigration—until now.

Indeed, Japan has never been as open to migrants from all over the world as today—and they have come in record numbers. In fact, Japan ranks in the top tier for the number of migrants entering the country each year, about four hundred thousand. The foreign population in Japan is touching 3 million, a record that gets reset each year as the number of students, vocational trainees, and skilled professionals continues to expand. Another surprise: At least 1 million are Chinese. When Japan began to open to increased migration a decade ago, it hoped for almost anyone but Chinese to come and settle. Yet today, Chinese constitute the largest share of foreigners, and the largest number of annual tourists as well. Chinese are followed in share of the population by seven hundred thousand South Koreans and three hundred thousand Vietnamese, with all three nationalities continuously increasing their presence in Japan. The number of Indians has also risen by one-third every five years and stands at more than fifty thousand. Indians and Nepalis are visible at construction sites and convenience store checkouts across the country. But with continuous aging combined with labor shortages, Indian doctors and nurses could be next.

For rank-and-file foreign workers, Japan's regimented ways persist: Migrants are classified based on their education level and sector, such as construction or shipbuilding, and are usually restricted from bringing family members. That is a telltale sign that Japan is primarily interested in plugging labor shortages, not in becoming like America, Australia, or Canada. But as one finds in North America, once migrants arrive, few want to leave—especially if rights groups succeed in advocating for higher pay for migrant workers, making Japan (inadvertently) even more attractive. This has already led to novel culture clashes: Long-term Muslim immigrants from Indonesia and Pakistan seek to bury their dead, but in a land of cremation, space for cemeteries is heavily restricted, leading to petitions and negotiations to establish special graveyards.[2]

Higher up the value chain, Japan's evolving immigration policy represents a new era of radical openness. Taxes are being slashed to attract finance and tech talent. Blue-collar workers are offered five-year renewable visas, and high-earning professionals are granted permanent residency, including for their families. Servicing these new long-term arrivals requires legions of cooks, cleaners, and nannies from Thailand, the Philippines, Indonesia, and Myanmar. Not surprisingly, Japan has long been a favorite expat destination, the utter antithesis of a hardship post. From chic Tokyo developments to ski resort towns, the foreign population is rising in all of more than forty prefectures. Japan is becoming not just a posh expat contract, but home.

The Japanese government has favored locals with incentives to buy abandoned properties, but there aren't nearly enough takers. So-called *akiya* banks dedicated to financing the purchase of vacant homes will soon expand their offerings to foreigners. Expats are already snapping up land for as little as $20,000 and fixing up traditional homes or building new condo-style compounds with a dozen or more units. They're taking to the local customs of neighborhood sharing of everything from bamboo to beer. Japan, like China, is not going to become demographically diluted or evolve into a multiethnic melting pot, but its doors are open to more "new Japanese" than ever.

Given Japan's insular history, there is a generic notion that foreigners could never "fit in" with Japan's old-world customs. But as with many things in Japan, reality is more counterintuitive. It's the *older* Japanese who went out into the world in pursuit of commercial conquest on behalf of "Japan Inc.," learning English and adopting cosmopolitan mannerisms, while *younger* Japanese have grown up complacently enjoying the fruits of their parents' labor, speaking only Japanese and barely traveling abroad. It's perhaps also to compensate for the reclusiveness of its youth that Japan hosts more than three hundred thousand foreign students at a time, with universities actively recruiting and offering entire degrees in English. New international schools are allowed to mix foreign and local students, and Japan's leading gaming company, Rakuten, has adopted English as its office language. Densely packed with colleges and language schools, Tokyo's Shinjuku ward is fully 50 percent populated by foreigners—not just from China and South Korea but from places as far-flung as Africa and Brazil.

All of this is before climate change wrecks Australia, India, and China, prompting even more people from Asia and beyond to decamp to Japan, which is in many ways the ultimate island fortress. Its ultramodern infrastructure and massive healthcare spending have made it a blue zone par excellence, with the highest life expectancy in the world and lowest Covid deaths per capita of any large country.

No doubt Japan is vulnerable to severe typhoons that lead to intense flooding and strong earthquakes, such as the 2011 earthquake-tsunami combo that devastated the coastal city of Sendai (on the main island of

Honshu) and flooded the Fukushima nuclear reactor. In the north, tiny islands off Hokkaido have already sunk into the Sea of Okhotsk, while in the south, Typhoon Jebi in 2018 flooded the runway of Osaka's Kansai Airport. Record rainfall on Kyushu in 2019 led to the forced evacuation of more than 1 million people. The Siberian air stream has made Honshu one of the world's snowiest places, while summer heat waves led to events such as the Tokyo Marathon being shifted north to Sapporo on Hokkaido island.

But Japan also has the political will, financial firepower, and technical prowess to fortify itself. On Honshu, engineers are busily deploying alternative energy systems, structurally reinforcing buildings against earthquakes, designing high-throughput floodwater control and irrigation systems, and protecting towns and roads against landslides and other damage resulting from super-typhoons. In the foothills of Mount Fuji, Toyota is breaking ground on a new city where only renewable and driverless cars will ply the streets. Honshu's 100 million residents today—and perhaps double that in the coming decades—are better off than people in almost any other geography on Earth.

Just steps from the famously crowded Shibuya crossing is an eight-story wonderland of high-tech tinkering called EDGEof. A sleek creative space that brings to mind the MIT Media Lab—but with a tropical-themed rooftop lounge—EDGEof is home to Silicon Valley and Japanese VC-funded startups in areas such as neuro-wellness, with one company making meditation-inducing chairs. There is also a zen tea garden in the basement where the bamboo ceiling slides open to reveal a large flat-panel TV screen for 4K video conferencing. Funded by tech companies, development institutes, and research centers, EDGEof hosts incubators from Canada, France, Sweden, and Israel, who alternate in putting on product demos, game nights, and art exhibitions. One hundred meters away and connected via elevated gardens, EDGEof is opening a co-living (three or more biologically unrelated tenants) property, a pay-as-you-go-style residence for startup hipsters, making the heart of Tokyo affordable. EDGEof and its partners are also working with mayors in various prefectures to turn their idyllic but depopulated towns into "Prosperity Villages" that will feature the yin and yang of urban and rural life that millennials want, as well as multigenerational housing, blended education, and other lifestyle offerings. EDGEof's ventures thus embody the future of Japan: Full of young people from just about everywhere, a multiracial civilization is displacing an older Japanese one.

Of all the countries opening to mass migration, only Japan is also a living experiment in the coexistence of humans and all manner of technologies. Everywhere you look in Japan you see vacant buildings in immaculate condition, minimal traffic on roads, ferryboats sitting idle, and bridges connecting sparsely inhabited districts over calm waters. Today we fumble through communicating with the Japanese taxi driver who wears a suit and tie, white gloves, and a germ-protecting white mask, but soon there will be language translation devices on every mobile phone, and the cars will be driverless. Where all signs are digital, the language can also be changed.

# CHAPTER 11
# QUANTUM PEOPLE

## Welcome to Expatistan

For all intents and purposes, an MBA is a passport. The world's eight hundred business schools spread across fifty countries are perhaps the leading agents in stirring the pot in the global war for talent. They recruit worldwide for students and compete fiercely to feed their graduates into multinationals, which then circulate them around the world. Each new cadre of MBAs joins the growing ranks of effectively stateless tech and consulting firms, often feeling a greater sense of belonging to their professional circuit than to any one country.

The same goes for a wide range of nomadic tribes that migration expert Malte Zeeck categorizes as "go getters" (for example, IT technicians or international schoolteachers who chase higher salaries), "optimizers" (those seeking better lifestyle or medical care), "romantics" (who follow a spouse to his or her home country), and "re-pats" (who take advantage of economic growth in their country of origin, such as the millions of "sea turtles" who have returned to China or the millennial Jews of Europe who are buying up Tel Aviv's real estate).

The coronavirus pandemic has done nothing to change expats' motivations. In a time of economic stagnation, everyone is seeking to stretch their savings by cutting their expenses. It's much easier to live somewhere three times cheaper than San Francisco than to magically earn three times more in San Francisco, and with tech jobs going perma-

221

nently remote, that could mean moving anywhere you've ever wanted to live. Renting or buying a house is much cheaper in Mexico or thriving Southeast Asian countries such as Thailand. As one real estate executive confided to me during the pandemic paranoia, "My job is to sell homes in America to foreigners, but maybe I should be selling homes abroad to Americans instead."

Talent doesn't identify itself by nationality; it identifies itself as talent. It is geographically mercenary. With the right skills, today's young talent can move practically anywhere they want based on lower taxes; better public services; more affordable housing, education, and healthcare; more predictable politics; or other preferences. Ample websites such as Nomad List, Expatica, and Expatistan have cost-of-living calculators to help current and aspiring nomads arbitrage across hundreds of cities—and keep moving among them.* Those who are sedentary find such a lifestyle unbearably complicated, but movement is easier when you are already in motion.

Where talent meets opportunity, migration will occur. The combination of global education and identity, remote work, and shifting growth markets will add considerably to the number of so-called "perma-pats" for whom home is wherever they are, for however long they're there. Like riding a bicycle, the first move may be the hardest, both logistically and emotionally. But after that, moving becomes routine. Each year, more countries, cities, and companies join the global war for talent—and more people too.

## Permanent until it's time to go

Few fields on an online form annoy a young professional more than "Address." Does it mean they'll have to wait for a letter and physically sign a

---

* Expatistan uses the city of Prague as the base price city, and gives percentages above and below living there. Living in New York, the Bay Area, Switzerland, or London costs nearly triple the cost of Prague, while you could live comfortably in Hanoi or Buenos Aires for just over half the Prague budget.

form? What if they no longer live there in a few months? Will they have to get the mail forwarded? Why does anyone still use paper anyway?

Their frustration is warranted. After all, you can be found in far more places in the digital world than the physical one. Rather than an office address, young people's business cards list a slew of digital contacts: multiple email addresses and handles for Facebook, Twitter, LinkedIn, Instagram, WhatsApp, Telegram, and others. In China, it's just a QR code for WeChat, the mobile portal through which about 1 billion people organize most of their lives—real and virtual. In the age of the mobile entrepreneur, files are not stored in cabinets but in the cloud, payments are not made by check but through apps, management isn't done around tables but on Slack, documents aren't signed with ink but on DocuSign, and Webex and BlueJeans are the conference rooms. You don't go to an office; you are the office—and you have one in a VR world as well. New Zealand's fabled animation studio Weta Digital (which brought you *Avengers: Endgame, Justice League,* and other international hits) has partnered with California-based Magic Leap to create immersive AR environments and 3D telepresence systems for lifelike interaction and perpetual live streaming. Entire virtual cities have sprung up in cyberspace in which showrooms, embassies, pavilions, conferences, and other gatherings convene thousands of participants at a time. For many youth, the purpose of the real world is to enable maximum convenience for their online lives, which are increasingly spent inside this immersive "spatial web."

But just because you *can* live anywhere (so long as the Internet speed is adequate), it doesn't mean you *will* settle for just anywhere. Youth are attuned to the gap between where they are and where they want to be, so they keep moving. According to the International Data Corporation (IDC), there are about 1.5 billion mobile workers who can do their jobs remotely, which amounts to nearly 40 percent of the global workforce. In the cat-and-mouse game of global taxation, the number of mice is rising substantially.

Hustling is life—and it's not done standing still. The cardinal virtues for talented youth today are connectivity and mobility: the skills to work from anywhere and the willingness to go anywhere. The word "hub" is defined as a place where people or businesses converge; now it's also a verb: Young people "hub" out of cities and move around between them. This new "cloud lifestyle" entails "living on demand" in various membership communities as well, depending on where you need to be or simply want to be, or where the best offer presents itself.

A pair of Estonian startups has paved the way for the growing caste of digital nomads who spend an estimated $2 billion per year just on visa processing. Jobbatical, which arranges positions for young professionals based on skills and geographic interests, now also provides relocation services. Its motto is: "Your skills matter more than your passport." Similarly, Teleport created a marketplace for tech talent seeking short-term positions around the world, along the way building an enormous dataset of their preferences and advising cities on how to attract them.[1] Its motto: "Free People Move." The easier mobility becomes, the more youth will take advantage of it, treating each location as, in the words of Jobbatical founder Karoli Hindriks, "permanent until it's time to go."

From Canada to Singapore, highly skilled migrant programs are proliferating as countries seek to recruit skilled workers.* Some already have the legal infrastructure to make it as easy as possible to be a nomadic global citizen. Estonia's e-residency program offers business registration with EU access, and comes with a glossy ID card and sleek black USB key that decrypts your entry to the country's online services—which is *all* services. So far the offering has attracted mostly other Europeans, but also entrepreneurs from as far as Brazil, who are using Estonia as a base to raise European capital for online learning platforms targeting Asia. In

---

* Numerous countries, such as the UK, have a four-step immigration policy involving basic due diligence done by World-Check (a firm owned by Thomson Reuters), which searches public databases for criminal history, followed by a deeper investigation of residency and employment records, verification that a person is not under sanction by international bodies such as the Financial Action Task Force (FATF), and lastly approval from the foreign ministry. Almost all of this could be done much more efficiently if more records were stored on blockchains.

2020, the country adopted a "digital nomad visa" allowing visitors to stay and work remotely for foreign companies, and it is developing a cloud-based pension system that mobile workers can pay into and collect anywhere. In a world of e-wallets and cryptocurrencies, today's youth need not be tied to a single national financial system.

Across the world, debt is saddling public finances and higher taxes are stifling citizen spending. Logically, enterprising youth will decamp to places where today's oceans of financial capital actually translate into tangible opportunities for them, whether through crowdfunding or rebates for software and equipment. In Sweden and Singapore, governments actively distribute grants to startups as well. Youth also want to live in countries with guaranteed wages and benefits, as well as four-day workweeks (or shorter workdays). Finland and New Zealand have become the pioneers of such policies, which have resulted in higher productivity, lower incidence of mental illness, and for women better work-life balance.

It's revealing that the countries ranking high in *both* competitiveness and resilience to disruptions are all *small* countries.[2] With little land or margin for error, they treat people as their most precious resource, regularly retraining workers for higher-skilled jobs. Singapore is relentless in preparing youth for careers as fintech investors, digital healthcare specialists, data scientists, and cybersecurity experts.[3] Many countries, such as Portugal and Canada, are retooling themselves to attract those who are digitally global but want the best of life that is physically local. Lifestyle-conscious Europeans have come to favor small cities in small countries, motivated by articles in *Lonely Planet* and *Monocle* that put Lausanne, Bergen, Innsbruck, Porto, Reykjavik, and Eindhoven on their radar.

Not everyone has the ability to move to such bucolic settings and work remotely, but with digital mobility, jobs can come to you even if you are not (yet) geographically mobile. Technology has dematerialized goods, services, and money, turning them into bits instantaneously warped around the world. It was inevitable that this would happen to human minds too. As Harvard economist Ricardo Hausmann explains, in the knowledge economy, each of us is a "person-byte" in the ecosystem that produces software and apps. We make code, do translations, upload photos, edit text, and other functions. Richard Baldwin of the University of Geneva similarly points to how people's brains "migrate" when they become "tele-migrants."[4] The very phrase "knowledge society" better describes this transnational digital milieu than it does any single country.

America's biggest tech companies are headquartered in California, but in reality they're everywhere in the cloud. Their AI-powered recruitment platforms evaluate millions of job applications from every corner of the planet, and they manage globally distributed virtual teams. The Trump administration unwisely suspended the H1-B visa program to prevent Indian software engineers from coming to America, but Silicon Valley smartly responded by outsourcing more work to Hyderabad and Hanoi. Whether on Amazon Mechanical Turk or GitHub, tens of millions of people have already achieved economic mobility through digital mobility—mobility without moving. But as with step migration from rural to urban to international, economic mobility is followed by physical mobility: moving to a better home or city, or abroad for a better job with a higher salary. The more people get educated and employed online, the more we can expect this chain reaction to catapult people away from home.

Cloud companies and their workers are prepared for a mobile world in ways their countries of origin are not. A handful of sovereign governments have awoken to the opportunity to offer digital services to citizens of anywhere. Indeed, what a number of these new "residency" schemes have in common is that they do *not* actually require you to be a resident. Estonia is just as interested in global nomads using its banks and doing business across the EU as it is in them physically living in Estonia. (Appropriately, in the event of another Russian occupation, Estonia has all of its data and functions backed up onto servers distributed around the world, so it could become a diaspora cloud nation if need be.) Similarly, Dubai's Virtual Commercial City (VCC) license provides a portal for foreign businesses to have an *onshore* presence in a tax-free country, a modification of the UAE's recent history of providing *offshore* "freezones." There are an estimated 35 million companies in the world that are location independent and could register anywhere. Dubai wants to get a bigger slice.

As a next phase, chief futurist of the Dubai government Noah Raford wants city-states to look beyond onshore-versus-offshore distinctions toward a "no shore" model in which countries actively lease space to innovators seeking test beds for their new technologies, regulations, and communities. They are not selling their sovereignty but rather upgrading into hybrid physical and digital republics that provide financial, medical, and educational certifications. In this emerging marketplace of governance services, the physical-digital sequence is inverted: You build a digital relationship with a government service provider (not necessarily your own), use its services wherever you are, and leverage its credibility to gain physical access to that country or associated ones.

What comes next as our world becomes ever more a hybrid reality? Imagine a corporate or civic platform established in an allied state that hosts its servers. Using blockchain protocols, it operates like a cross between Tor (encrypted browser), GitHub (coding collaboration), Bitcoin (cryptocurrency), and TransferWise (cross-border finance), enabling digital work with masked IPs and global access to cash. Millions of remote workers join this cloud republic, voting on its internal policies and building bargaining power over the governments where they each physically reside. Countries will then have two choices: either extort the cloud-based workforce within your country—which may prompt many to leave—or join with other host states in forming a digital version of the medieval Hanseatic League that grants access to more members of this nomadic class and benefits from its innovations.

Remember that most countries are small—both geographically and demographically. They resemble atoms in which most of the population and economic mass is located in the capital city and the rest is hinterland. As their populations age or depart, they may have little choice but to sell off land or islands to startup nations shopping for the right jurisdiction. This may be geopolitics in a quantum age.

## Aging but not slowing down

Fifty is not the new twenty. But fifty-somethings now have to play the same mobility arbitrage game as their children. In 2008, many dreams of beachfront retirement went up in smoke. Comfy pensions evaporated as workers were shoved into early redundancy in their prime. The pandemic has done the same—but with even longer-lasting consequences when compounded by automation and an anemic economic recovery. Many laid off during the financial crisis never recovered; they moved to cheaper towns, where they string together various gigs, such as driving for Uber, to cover their bills or care for their spouse. They'll have to keep working: On average, today's retirees have only half of what they need given their longer lifespans. And as the debt soars, the retirement age will rise, as will income taxes. Now it's happening all over again to an even younger cohort—except it's way too early for today's mid-career victims of the pandemic depression to retire—not that they could afford to. The nicest euphemism for what lies ahead is "life transition."

For Americans who only have the energy or cash for one last move, Canada has become the sensible choice. The number of American retirees collecting their Social Security abroad is highest in Canada, followed by Mexico and Japan.* Many websites already advertise the best places to retire in Canada—and the list just keeps getting longer. But now that Mexico, Costa Rica, and Panama have launched retirement visas and physical communities explicitly to attract Americans, they'll also attract ever more aging Americans. These Central American coun-

---

* This data might not represent the real number of American retirees abroad, since some might be receiving their Social Security in the US despite residing overseas, or not receiving Social Security at all.

tries rank far higher in happiness surveys than they do in wealth, indicating a low cost of living with general societal stability. Canadian "snowbirds" (retirees who used to flock to Florida for the winter) may well migrate to Central America too as Florida's climate worsens. Or, as Canada warms, they might as well stay in Canada during the milder winters as well.

For those with chronic conditions or concerns about healthcare costs, medical tourism abroad will become medical residency. Already more than 1.4 million mostly middle-aged and elderly Americans travel abroad annually for operations ranging from knee replacements to fertility treatments to plastic surgery. Even millennials have reported traveling as far as Egypt and Colombia for skin treatments and dental work. While the most popular destinations for American medical tourists have been India, Israel, Malaysia, Thailand, and South Korea, Canada could easily take top spot if it brands itself as an affordable climate and health oasis for American retirees. They can be forgiven for taking their savings elsewhere after witnessing their medical system triage away elderly lives during the coronavirus pandemic.

Europeans have a higher life expectancy than Americans as well as greater pension portability, making international retirement even more seamless. As EU countries cut benefits and raise the retirement age, ever more elderly will shift to cheaper "Club Med" southern Europe—Spain, Italy, and Greece (while those countries send youth northward). Asian destinations will also continue to rise in the ranks of havens for cash-strapped Western retirees. In 2018, Thailand issued its highest ever number of retirement visas to Brits, followed by Americans and Germans. Even after a lifetime living in one country, such as America, their destiny is global.

Rich retirees have already opted for mobility as a lifestyle choice. Some reside 250 days or more per year on cruise ships such as the *Viking Sun*, perpetually sailing around the world, docking in more than one hundred ports across fifty countries. One ship known as *The World* is owned by the 130 families who permanently reside on it, making it something of a micro mobile sovereign. Healthy retirees with more modest means cleverly see the world by changing cruise ships every few months, paying less per month than they would in assisted living facilities. Before the pandemic, half of the 25 million annual cruise ship passengers worldwide were retirees or baby boomers. While the lockdown stranded many cruise ships at sea, a growing number, such as *Oceania* and *Utopia*, have been retrofitted with residences and full-time medical care to accommodate permanently mobile retirees. And the more cruise ships there are, the greater the demand for hundreds of thousands of cooks, cleaners, singers, card dealers, doctors, and nurses, especially from India, Indonesia, and the Philippines. In the future, they may well be safer than those staying on land.

## Why it's time for a global "passport"

For centuries before World War I, people traveled the world without passports. European settlers arrived in North America as pilgrims fleeing monarchy or migrants fleeing famine, with neither money nor documents to their name. The fluidity of imperial zones such as the British empire nurtured generations of subjects moving across colonies from East Africa to Southeast Asia. The origin of the passport is much less as a restrictive certificate denoting exclusive identity than a *laissez passer*, a request for safe passage. While serving as ambassador to France in 1780, Benjamin Franklin made his own American passport to request entry into the Netherlands. But after World War I, migration became so bureaucratized that passports are now one of the chief barriers to a more sensible human geography.

How can we return to a world where passports don't stand for who you are, but simply identify you on your way to where you're going? The first step would be a technological platform at the intersection of blockchain and biometrics. Embassies and consulates today are overwhelmed with visa applications, each with marginally different requirements that could easily be streamlined. Global databases could also iron out the discrepancies between physical and digital IDs, and border checkpoints could be better connected to them. This data could be stored on the blockchain, updated and verified for ongoing usage. For several years, the International Air Travel Association (IATA), customs agencies, and booking websites have been working to digitize these pain points. They advocate an opt-in repository of traveler data to be shared as needed for speedy approval. Remember that almost all countries and their businesses *want* these tourists and businesspeople, but their movement is stifled in pre-technological bureaucratic purgatory. It should matter less that you are Bolivian, Nigerian, or Vietnamese, and more that you *as an individual* have provided sufficient accurate information to gain entry, such as your recent whereabouts, criminal history, employment records, and health status. Many Americans can surely appreciate the desire to be differentiated from their countrymen: Having failed to sufficiently lock down, Americans were collectively punished, barred from travel to Canada, Europe, and most other desirable destinations where the coronavirus was more effectively contained.

This same system could eventually liberate billions of working-class individuals from the friction associated with their national identity, whether Asians from China, India, and Southeast Asian nations, or Arabs, Turks, and South Americans. As economist Branko Milanovic argues, their citizenship is a tax arbitrarily assigned based on their location of birth. Yet these regions are home to the labor pool dozens of countries need, whether farmers or construction workers or nurses. The most important passports of the future are skills and health rather than nationality. We should judge individuals not by the accident of birth, but on their potential to contribute to society. By divorcing mobility from nationality, we circumvent biases people face for coming from countries that are poor or at war. The mobile workers of the world don't have collective bargaining power, but everyone would benefit from certifying their mobility.

The global education sector also desperately needs such a system, both to maintain the large number of foreign students on which Western universities depend and to ensure a steady supply for their international branches that deliver classes on-site in developing countries. The same goes for global companies moving employees around along their supply chains. Universities and companies should team up and push for a large-scale *laissez passer* to overcome the redundancies they face in moving students and professionals around the world.

A parallel digital identification that circumvents unnecessary bureaucracy is not a competitor or threat to national citizenship and passports. Citizenship confers rights to land ownership, voting, and legal protections, and denotes significant obligations ranging from military service to taxation. What is needed is a supplemental protocol and clearinghouse that crowds in data: national ID cards, passport photos, fingerprints, mobile phone accounts, bank statements, criminal history, employment records, travel logs, health status, and so forth. Once verified, this information could be visible only temporarily, as needed, to relevant authorities. Indeed, it would be just as useful for domestic priorities such as digital voting as for international mobility.

A globally trusted ID database would help countries know whom they can safely let in based on their good standing, and it can also help them more easily decide whom to keep *out*—including some of their own citizens. Four of the eight terrorists in the November 2015 attacks in Paris were French citizens. Thousands of Western passport holders from America to Australia have pledged allegiance to Al Qaeda or ISIS and fought on their behalf in Iraq and Syria. Whether racially Caucasian, Arab, or African, their passports have allowed them to easily return home and wreak havoc. Anti-immigrant European politicians have cited terrorism as an excuse to restrict refugee inflows, but migration restrictions won't diminish the pool of homegrown radicals. Requiring individuals to rigorously demonstrate where they have been and then verifying that information is a better way to stay ahead of nimble terrorists of all complexions.

Now is a unique opportunity to bring about a system that empowers rather than restrains the billions of individuals whose freer mobility could benefit world society. It's also a chance to digitally prepare for an era of mass migrations resulting from political collapse and climate change, in which hundreds of millions of people may circulate in a constant flux of unpredictable multidirectional movements. Mankind is capable of a better approach to managing cross-border movements, whether on the blockchain or eventually chips embedded under our skin. Mobility is our best insurance against volatility. When the next crisis comes, we'll be glad we have it.

## The global citizenship arbitrage

At the height of the global coronavirus lockdown, the Covid-free island of Fiji sought to lure the ultra-rich for an open-ended sojourn, inviting them to arrive in their private jets or yachts and ride out the pandemic in tropical comfort. Barbados and Bermuda did the same—no visa required. These tourism-depending nations would surely let you stay as long as you could afford to, no questions asked.

Our idea of citizenship originates in the ancient city-states of the Mediterranean and Tigris-Euphrates River Valley, which competed to expand territory and absorb people into their empires but established hierarchies favoring the dominant tribe. The idea that one tribe defines the right to (and the rights of) citizenship for the rest has held across the world for millennia since. But these antiquated practices are giving way to a vast global marketplace in which people choose their nationality based on which country offers the most benefits to *them*. In a world of demographic deflation, countries are competing to attract talented and wealthy people to settle within their borders. Countries don't dictate to them but bend over backwards to lure them.

The rise of a citizenship marketplace represents an important turning of the tables in the relationship between individuals and states. American legal scholar David Franck speaks of individuals becoming more "autonomous, empowered actors."[5] Passports are becoming like mileage programs, flags of convenience, not the embodiment of one's identity. The French Revolution's ideals were "liberty, equality, fraternity." Today's opportunistic jet set lives by the motto "mobility, liquidity, optionality."

The passport one carries therefore tells others ever less about *who* one is. When it comes to citizenship arbitrage, one country's loss is another's gain, and each crisis in one place is an opportunity for more stable countries to poach talent. At least 1 billion people live in an almost post-citizenship world where nationality matters less than their bank balance or skills. They think of citizenship as a service and a passport as a membership card that can be upgraded for greater freedoms, protections, mobility, and other privileges. Tens of millions of people have changed their nationality in the past five decades. As the number of high-net-worth individuals in developing countries expands, it should come as no surprise that many consider their nationality to be a liability and have been mercenary with their citizenship. Indeed, the strong majority of applicants for second passports are Asian. The state is not a mother: You are born in it but can disown it. One expert claims that only five thousand people purchased "golden visas" (citizenship by investment) in 2017, but in the first six months of 2020 alone, that figure rose to twenty-five thousand.[6]

Historically, citizenship has been granted by birth (*ius solis*) or descent (*ius sanguinis*), with naturalization by residency rising during recent generations of migration waves. To this we now add *ius doni*, meaning citizenship via investment. The idea is fiscally sensible. For poor Caribbean nations, like St. Kitts, St. Lucia, or Antigua, that have a small tax base and face high borrowing costs, attracting "sovereign equity"—selling a piece of themselves such as land—is preferable to taking on more debt.

Ideally, they'll use this investment from new migrants to finance better infrastructure and economic diversification, eventually building a more robust welfare system.

London-based Henley & Partners pioneered the *ius doni* concept and advises dozens of the more than *one hundred* countries that have such citizenship-by-investment programs. To consider this a fringe phenomenon perpetrated only by shady tax havens would be to miss the forest for the trees. Ironically, European countries that have long had strict nationality laws have run the most brisk business in selling citizenships to Indians, Nigerians, Russians, Chinese, and others. They are, after all, the most desirable for these migrants: Europe sweeps the top twenty spots in Henley's Quality of Nationality Index (based on political stability, human development, public services, and passport access), while the US ranks only twenty-seventh and Australia thirty-second. Cyprus and Austria are particularly popular with Russians.* Spain's golden visa program grants residency to investors and their families upon investing 500,000 euros in real estate. Portugal has sold more than two thousand golden visas to wealthy Britons and Chinese, generating more than $2 billion in investment. Given the country's climate resilience, it's a good bet. In the neighboring enclave of Andorra in the Pyrenees, an investor visa is 400,000 euros and comes with three hundred days of sunshine.

Each time a country joins the EU, it becomes attractive for foreign investor migrants. During the Soviet era, Russia dominated Baltic countries such as Latvia. Now that Latvia is an EU member, Russian citizens are buying Latvian passports. Montenegro saw a surge of applicants for its passport during the coronavirus lockdown—especially as it's on the cusp of joining the EU. As Swiss legal scholar Christian Joppke points out, EU citizenship is the embodiment of a post-national "instrumental" citizen-

---

* Monaco is not an EU member but has a customs agreement with it. Most of its thirty-eight thousand residents are ultra-wealthy tax citizens of other European countries.

ship because it doesn't presuppose or demand any common European identity.

Recruiting more investor migrants could help Europe stave off its demographic deflation. As Chinese and Indians pour into Europe's university towns, Asian private equity firms and sovereign wealth funds follow, buying up and retrofitting student dorms, making investments Germany has neglected for more than a decade. And now that America is blocking Chinese students and birth tourist mothers, these two groups may well spend more on investment residency and citizenship in European countries, and the mothers may have their children there instead.

Some European conservatives argue that citizenship should only be conferred on those with a "genuine" link to the country. This usage of "genuine" is specious, effectively reducing citizenship back to the arbitrary happenstance of birth, hardly a measure of genuine volition. The actual intent of criticizing citizenship-for-sale programs, of course, is to avoid losing tax revenue. The "Paradise Papers" (a trove of 13 million documents disclosing offshore financial holdings of elites from around the world) revealed the extent to which wealthy individuals, like stateless global companies, will go to hide their assets in offshore jurisdictions— with a strong number of them being British nationals. Try to untangle the ironies: Britain has sovereignty over tax havens such as Jersey and the British Virgin Islands through which British people (and countless others) launder their investments. But after Brexit, its own passport has weakened in global access, leading to a surge of Brits taking citizenship in Ireland, Germany, or Portugal. Then there are the 5.5 million British expats who have lived overseas for so long that they have formally lost the right to vote, giving them even less incentive to maintain their UK citizenship. There should be little doubt that the UK government itself is most responsible for turning many of its own citizens into citizens of somewhere else. Is it any wonder that British finances are so dire? And that Britain itself sells investor visas for $2.6 million?

The EU is certainly pushing back, demanding that companies registered in low-tax countries to prove that their "economic substance" involves actual people living there. In other words, there must be employees, not just shell companies. Governments are counting the number of days people spend within their borders to tax them based on the location at which they work; soon they will check not just your passport dates and stamps, but the IP address from which you did the work you claimed to do, and for whom you did it. The likely result, though, is that people will vote with their wallets, moving themselves or their staff to more tax-efficient places. Companies certainly are, whether Dyson shifting its headquarters from London to Singapore or SoftBank's Vision Fund relocating from London to Abu Dhabi.

Ireland is already a tax haven for global tech companies and also takes in tens of thousands of new skilled residents each year—many living in "Googleville" in central Dublin. After just one year and paying 1 million euros, residents are eligible to apply for citizenship, enabling them to move at will to other EU countries competing to attract migrant investors. (In mid-2020, Hong Kong tycoon Ivan Ho proposed building a new city in Ireland called Nextpolis to which to relocate fifty thousand Hong Kong citizens.)

If countries don't do a better job moving their passports up the rankings of global access, their citizens will just move and change citizenship. While Asian passports from Japan, South Korea, and Singapore now sit atop the ranking of most powerful passports, China ranks seventy-fourth, and India far lower still. Each year, about one hundred thousand mostly Chinese and Indians have come into New Zealand either to stay or use it as a back door to enter Australia. After alarm bells sounded, New Zealand backtracked on allowing any foreigners (save for those from a handful of friendly countries, or selected billionaires) to buy property at all. Now those would-be Kiwis will likely become Canucks instead. A Chinese proverb advises that a wise rabbit always has three holes to burrow in. Chinese should know: They're buying up properties and passports from Canada to Portugal to Singapore.

So too are Americans. Historically, Americans only expatriate after many years of frustration at US tax filings. The ultra-rich 1 percent of American expats can easily afford either to renounce or to keep US citizenship, but it's the 2 percent, 5 percent, 10 percent, and everyone else that struggles to save money while paying taxes in two countries at the same time.* Punitive tax policy, political populism, and Covid mismanagement all drove a growing number of Americans to the exits throughout the 2010s. In the first half of 2020 alone, American expatriation reached nearly six thousand worldwide, a 1,200 percent jump over the entire total of 2019—and would have been even higher if not for the backlog of applicants at various embassies. Departing elites have their pick of justifications: authoritarian populist Republicans or woke socialist Democrats. Ironically, Italy and Ireland, which provided so many grateful migrants to America in the nineteenth century, are top destinations for Americans using their lineage to obtain European passports for themselves—and for their children too. Who knows where America's growing diaspora will go next?

Even those for whom an American passport or green card has been a hedge against turbulence at home no longer consider America a safe haven. An estimated 6 million American citizens also hold other passports—they're "American" on paper, but America for them is more a backup plan than a pledge of allegiance. Now *both* Americans and these secondary US passport holders are having second thoughts. In fact, even more foreigners give up their green cards each year than Americans give up passports. Much as America has lost its dominant grip on the best and brightest students, it's also losing appeal as a nationality just as other countries are vigorously competing in a war for global wealth and talent—including Americans.

---

* The IRS clearly lacks the discipline it imposes on US citizens abroad, piling on more paperwork each year such as FATCA regulations, which are meant to target onshore Americans with offshore accounts, but wind up penalizing millions of Americans already making an honest living abroad.

# CHAPTER 12
# *PAX URBANICA*

### Green zone networks

There are some coffee table books that most coffee tables just aren't sturdy enough to support. One is the magnificent *Architekturtheorie im deutschsprachigen Kulturraum (1486–1648)*, a 750-page tome of such girth it might itself be used as a coffee table were it not so precious. Compiled by Switzerland's leading ETH Zurich University, it captures how Renaissance dukes and princes commissioned the leading architects of the day to redesign Europe's medieval cities to accommodate the rising number of merchants shuttling between its bustling trading hubs. Trade routes became part of the city's essence. Connectivity and mobility transformed the meaning of space.

It's commonly thought that diplomacy was born during this period when European nation-states took shape, but in fact, diplomacy's origins lie in the nascent trade relations between the ancient city-states of Mesopotamia. (Diplomacy truly is the second oldest profession.) Baghdad, Damascus, and Beirut are far older cities than any particular empire or nation that has appeared—and disappeared—since. Across the ages, the diplomacy among cities—what I call "diplomacity"—has been a continuous feature of human civilization. Its future patterns may well mimic those of the past.

The Middle Ages may be particularly instructive. During the fourteenth to sixteenth centuries, the northern European Hanseatic League, comprising cities spanning the North and Baltic Seas, formed a tacit alliance to defend their trading rights and political autonomy against the encroachments of the Holy Roman Empire, England, and other foes. Their trade in fabrics, armor, engraved woods, and metals also accelerated the arrival of Renaissance ideas to northern Europe. The balance Hanseatic cities struck between internal security and external connectedness is fundamental to imagining how the next era of "diplomacity" could unfold, with leading cities engaged in a healthy competitive cooperation with each other. The future could be defined by a progressive new peace among small states and cities: a *Pax Urbanica*.

During the pandemic spring of 2020, our Mesopotamian and Hanseatic instincts refreshed as naturally as riding a bicycle. Australia and New Zealand, Switzerland and Austria, Finland and Estonia—pairs of like-minded neighbors with small populations reopened borders exclusively to each other. "Green lanes" and "immunity bubbles" kicked in, signifying how trust in each other's health systems mattered more than centuries of inter-state diplomatic conventions. The US passport was suddenly welcome in just 30 countries instead of the usual 150.

Nobody wants a trade-off between health and wealth. Our vague loyalty to the nation pales in comparison to our visceral desire to be ensconced inside a green zone. Well-governed territories would rather connect to one another than be chained to weak links next door. Indeed, most striking was the behavior of states and provinces *within* countries that had no formal right to close internal borders. Hawaii sought to reopen tourism for Australians and Japanese—but not fellow Americans. Police in Rhode Island searched neighborhoods for New York license plates; even fellow New Yorkers in the Hamptons suspected wealthy refugees from New York City of unfairly plundering their grocery stores. As Scotland brought Covid under control, it had no interest in letting in undisciplined compatriots from England.

Anyone who can afford to is on the move *away* from red zones and *into* green zones, places with robust virus testing and vaccination programs. Within the US, that means ditching states where armed militias occupy capitol buildings to prevent lockdowns while anti-vaxxers and other "Covidiots" run amok. More broadly, green zones tend to be countries where politics doesn't interfere with science, and where technology is aggressively being applied to public health, such as South Korea. Canada's BlueDot system integrates medical records, geolocated web search metadata, and mobile phone patterns to warn of virus outbreaks. Swedes have begun having RFID-tagged chips inserted under their skin that can affirm their health status. In China, Singapore, and elsewhere, AI now scans health records, and free screenings anticipate the potential onset of cancer and other conditions. Next we might see governments proactively offer treatments using genomics and synthetic biology.

No doubt public health will become a major priority in countries that failed the Covid test—much as after the Black Death European societies introduced sewers and paved roads. But why gamble with your life when life is no longer short? Indeed, today's mobile class are looking for "blue zones" that combine preventive measures and pro-longevity interventions. Places such as Sardinia in Italy and Okinawa in Japan have earned the blue zone moniker for their combination of fresh environment, organic diet, regular exercise, and strong community bonds that have propelled locals to the longest lifespans of any place on Earth. Most of humanity would be better off with the blue zone diet of vegetables, grains, seeds, fruits, nuts, beans, and fish. Longer biological lifespans could elevate people's desire to live in places free of arbitrary violence. Since America is the only rich country with frequent mass shootings, talented people with a healthy sense of self-preservation will either continue to raise their security walls or move to more trustworthy communities. In 2019, San Francisco labeled the NRA a "domestic terrorist organization," but now that guns can be 3D-printed, sensible locales will have to monitor those technologies as well. At the intersection of green zones and blue zones one finds societies that have affordable housing and wage protections, as well as female leaders and community policing.*

---

* According to the Healthcare Access and Quality (HAQ) Index, the three best healthcare systems are in Iceland, Norway, and the Netherlands. Universal healthcare is offered in eighteen countries: Australia, Canada, Finland, France, Germany, Hungary, Iceland, Ireland, Israel, the Netherlands, New Zealand, Norway, Portugal, the Slovak Republic, Slovenia, Sweden, Switzerland, and the United Kingdom. In addition, Austria, Belgium, Japan, and Spain have near universal health coverage.

This is a reminder that people don't plan their next moves searching for high GDP growth. GDP as a measure of welfare is the statistical equivalent of gold: It's only valuable if people believe in it. Instead, today's youth are more inclined to put their faith in sustainable economies, diverse and inclusive societies, and a culture of rights and wellness. There is an arms race underway to rank countries according to their balance of socioeconomic inclusion and environmental sustainability. Comparing countries by their GDP versus their rank in the recently launched Social Progress Index (SPI) is startling. The US, for example, is wealthier per capita than all but a few small European tax havens. But given its poor healthcare, violence, and inequality, it ranks only twenty-sixth in the SPI. The top tier of SPI countries is made up not only of the usual suspects in northern Europe as well as Switzerland, Ireland, Australia, and New Zealand, but also large countries such as Germany, Japan, Canada, and France. Even amid Europe's low-growth trajectory, wealth tempered by fairness suggests greater social stability.

## The Most Progressive Societies

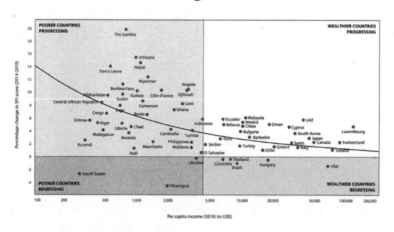

The Social Progress Index measures countries by their performance in meeting basic needs (such as nutrition, water, shelter, and safety), providing the foundations for well-being (education, healthcare, access to information, and clean environment), and enabling opportunity (political rights, personal freedoms, and inclusive economies). Many poor countries in Africa and Asia have been making steady improvements over the past five years. In wealthier countries, gains have been slower, while several advanced countries have been backsliding.

Many countries ranking high in social progress (such as the Scandinavians), however, fare horribly in the Sustainable Development Index (SDI) due to their carbon consumption from mining, construction, transport, and aviation. By contrast, the countries that come closest to meeting their people's needs with low resource consumption are Costa Rica, Sri Lanka, Albania, and Georgia. In these countries, most people have sufficient income and education, life expectancy and happiness are high, but per capita greenhouse gas emissions are low.[1] Countries in this economic tier are often described as being caught in a "middle-income trap" in which productivity stalls while rising prices make them uncompetitive. But they're also using land reform, education, and technology to diversify their economies and upskill youth. In a world no longer obsessed with GDP, they may be role models for societies that can't afford growth for its own sake— which is all societies.

## Truly Sustainable Societies

| SDI Rank | | Country rank in SPI | SPI Rank | | Country rank in SDI |
|---|---|---|---|---|---|
| 1 | Costa Rica | 28 | 1 | Norway | 158 |
| 2 | Sri Lanka | 88 | 2 | Sweden | 144 |
| 3 | Albania | 52 | 3 | Switzerland | 151 |
| 4 | Panama | 41 | 4 | Iceland | 155 |
| 5 | Algeria | 85 | 5 | New Zealand | 128 |
| 6 | Georgia | 60 | 6 | Canada | 159 |
| 7 | Armenia | 61 | 7 | Finland | 156 |
| 8 | Cuba | 84 | 8 | Denmark | 139 |
| 9 | Azerbaijan | 76 | 9 | Netherlands | 147 |
| 10 | Peru | 55 | 10 | Australia | 161 |

The Sustainable Development Index (SDI) ranks countries according to their ability to meet their population's needs while also maintaining a low carbon footprint. In contrast to the Social Progress Index (SPI), which is led by European countries or other Western nations with small populations, the SDI is led by small countries known for prudent resource management.

## *Fed, fueled, and circular*

The coronavirus hit at a time of steady harvests and food reserves, but sudden processing breakdowns threw the global food supply system into disarray. Thousands of tons of Montana potatoes went to waste, as did millions of eggs normally exported from poor countries. As border closures kept out migrant workers, the French economy minister called on his countrymen to take up their patriotic duty to become farmers. Belgians were urged to eat fries twice a week to absorb the huge potato harvest. The Covid lockdown also forced countries to invoke "food nationalism," with Russia banning the export of wheat, Vietnam of rice, and Serbia of vegetables and food oils. Would we all be better off growing more of our own food, or living in places that do?

The pandemic forced every country to rethink its preparedness for apocalyptic scenarios. Island fortresses such as New Zealand had the good fortune and foresight to have engineered their agricultural independence from the rest of the world. China, which imported almost as much food as America, sped up the demolition of rural villages to increase its acreage of farmland. Then there were countries such as Japan and South Korea that not only raise cattle and grow crops, but also ramped up hydroponic food production and urban farming. Rather than waste food, South Korea composted food waste into fertilizer used in urban farms.

Our city-based civilization has lulled us into thinking anything is available anytime, but cities *consume* vastly more energy, water, and food than they produce. Though cities are our most formidable infrastructural constructs, they're vulnerable in their immobility. In the tenth century, droughts forced the Mayan people to abandon their mighty fortress cities such as Chichen Itza on the Yucatán Peninsula. One millennium later, Mexico City has so badly drained its aquifers that it's sinking due to subsidence. Mexico City could be the next Chichen Itza: Its people can move, but the city can't.

Long before the Mayans, droughts dealt fatal blows to the Egyptian and Roman empires as well. Today's largest food producers face a potential crisis as industrial farming has disrupted the natural symbiosis between seeds and soil, and water shortages deplete the ground's nutrients. Instead, we should expand regenerative agriculture techniques such as crop rotation, and nitrogen-fixing bacteria instead of chemical fertilizers.

We must modify the narrative that we have evolved from agriculture to towns to cities—with the former serving the latter without regard to environmental cost. Instead, we should rethink how and where we produce food and energy, how and where we consume it, and the distance between the two. In the framing of World Future Council president Herbert Girardet, we must unwind the far-flung energy and food supply chains of the "Petropolis" era and turn each of our major settlements into a self-sustaining "Ecopolis" of localized food production, renewable energy, and material recycling.

Water-stressed and densely populated places will have to use the latest technologies to ride out more frequent drought periods. A single one-acre building can generate almost two tons of produce daily using eighteen times less water than conventional agriculture and with a cooling system that recycles freshwater back to plant roots. In bustling cities, shipping containers are being repurposed into "food generators" with hydroponic equipment inside. China has broken ground on an entire city that aims to be both pandemic-proof and self-sufficient in food and energy. Mallorca is one of Spain's highest-grossing tourist hubs and gentrifying rapidly, yet it's running out of water. But Spain is also the home of companies such as Arpa and Genaq, which have developed some of the most advanced atmospheric water generators, already sold to dozens of militaries around the world. Mallorca could become a circular island.

A circular diet is an important complement to circular energy. Plant-based diets further reduce our carbon-and-water footprint, as well as the need to live near grocery stores that chill our meat supplies. Americans increasingly identify as "flexitarians" (who only occasionally eat meat), while the UK has recognized veganism as a philosophical belief and tantamount to a religion. One viral joke during Covid-19 suggested that the solution to combating the ills of pandemics, climate change, and social unrest was to act more Hindu: greet with joining one's own hands and saying "Namaste" rather than shaking hands, wash your feet before entering homes, practice yoga and meditation, follow a vegetarian diet, use water for cleansing rather than toilet paper, and burn the dead. Hinduism is nothing if not a circular religion.

Canadian, European, and Australian cities have made the greatest strides in shifting toward alternative and renewable energy such as solar, wind, and nuclear power. No country is decarbonizing faster than France, which has invited a multinational consortium to construct the world's most powerful fusion reactor. Cold fusion technology has the support of Google and Japan's Mitsubishi, as well as Bill Gates, who also backs Heliogen, a concentrated solar technology that could provide enough power even for industrial cement making. (Companies such as Carbon Cure also inject carbon captured from cement making back into the cement.) Hydrogen power can already replace coal and gas for steel making and energy extraction (two other emissions-intensive sectors). Japan is building two dozen new coal-fired power plants to compensate for its closing of nuclear plants after the Fukushima disaster, but it's also importing compressed liquid hydrogen from Australia in a bid to become the world's clean energy leader. South Korea is well on its way to having multiple cities fueled by hydrogen for heating, cooling, and electricity. Fusion, hydrogen, solar, and wind power can also be used to cool our data centers, the fastest growing source of emissions. A city of any size should be able to power itself.

This also means that our mobility within and between cities should have a far smaller environmental footprint. Thanks to Tesla in the US, BYD in China, and the many European and Japanese carmakers ramping up electric vehicle production, the EV share of total car sales is rising steadily worldwide. But even though Germany and Sweden have roads that charge electric vehicles that drive on them, the global supply chain for lithium-ion batteries is (like oil) both dirty and vulnerable. That's why China's CATL is developing (for Tesla) cobalt-free batteries that don't require mining in Africa and South America. Hydrogen-powered public transport and cars are taking off in Japan, South Korea, and China. Organic waste can be turned into synthetic gas to power garbage trucks, as Sierra Energy is doing in Canada. And Toyota's solar panel–covered car provides a day's worth of urban driving with no charging required.

A self-sufficient city should also have sustainably powered homes and offices. Rooftop solar power alone can already provide about half the energy most buildings use, while white paint reflects solar heat, and trees and shrubs planted into buildings provide natural shading and cooling. Dozens of other features are being integrated into new building designs to make them more circular: rooftops that absorb and channel storm water into reservoirs, air pump systems that perform both heating and cooling functions, and integrated ventilation and insulation systems. Solid-state thermoelectric cooling and heating devices use far less power and emit fewer vapors than traditional refrigeration. But we can also rely less on air-conditioning if we build homes using traditional building methods and materials such as terra-cotta plaster in honeycomb designs that wick away moisture and naturally cool air. From Canada to Norway, mass timber wood buildings are built as dorms and offices, and they continue to absorb carbon for decades. Technologies that have been conceived but not yet deployed could further allow us to square the circle: trees that generate electricity as they sway and liquid nitrogen refrigeration, for example. This is how we should retrofit our current cities—and power our next ones.

The most expensive investment many countries have yet to make is in desalination plants, which already provide half or more of the water supply of Israel and the Gulf countries; 90 percent of the UAE's water consumption is desalinated ocean water. India, Japan, and Kazakhstan also have nuclear-powered desalination plants, which massively reduce the energy input costs (and emissions) associated with producing water safe for agriculture and public consumption. Water pipelines from these large water filtration plants could be piped inland to farms in America, India, Australia, China, and other countries threatened by mega droughts. If water is the new oil, countries should invest accordingly in water pipelines—otherwise people will move to where there is more water.

## Air-conditioned nations

Humans can change their geography; cities can't. They can only be adapted to the needs of the times, whether erecting coastal barriers to ward off rising seas or adding bicycle lanes to reduce automobile congestion. Especially for coastal cities near the equator, the to do list of adaptations is quite long.

Singapore and Dubai stand out as crucial experiments in what many cities in similar circumstances may need to do to survive the decades ahead. Both are home to highly diverse global populations above 4 million people comprising a mixture of the global elite, upwardly mobile youth, and legions of guest workers busily building future infrastructure. The climates of Singapore and Dubai of course differ considerably: Dubai lies at the fringe of an arid desert, while Singapore is in a tropical jungle. Dubai's rains are infrequent; Singapore's are constant. But both cities have made aggressive use of land reclamation: More than one-quarter of the entire island nation of Singapore is built on reclaimed land (making it one of the most voracious consumers in the global market for sand), while Dubai (as well as the UAE federal capital Abu Dhabi) has undertaken ambitious artificial island projects. Both can afford the significant costs of raising roads, expanding seawater canals, and powering water desalination. And both are investing in hydroponic food production (indoors and underground), offshore fish farms, and plant-based meat companies. But can they beat the heat?

## UAE: A Domed Country?

Nearly forty years ago, as a kindergartener in the UAE, I remember my father coming home from the office for a late lunch and relaxing with the family before returning to the office for a few hours in the late afternoon. Just in from frolicking in the playground under the hot sun, I was in daily need of cold towels to thwart my throbbing headaches. At least we had air-conditioning.

For hundreds of thousands of Western expats living in the Gulf region, the routine hasn't changed for decades: enjoy balmy weather during the school year, spend the summers back home in Europe while the Gulf bakes in dry desert heat for three months, then return once the air cools down and schools reopen. But now things are different. With wealthy Gulf cities such as Doha, Riyadh, Dubai, and Abu Dhabi fully outfitted with full-blast air-conditioning—while less than 10 percent of Western Europeans have air-conditioning despite their intense heat waves—many Europeans are now avoiding returning home during the summer and opting to stay cool in the Gulf instead. (And amid Europe's Covid-induced winter lockdowns in late 2020, Dubai's seaside hotels were suddenly sold out for several straight months.)

Air-conditioning is ubiquitous in Dubai's offices, malls, apartments, and residential developments, but the city's future plan features bringing all of these under one roof—literally. The city's latest mega-project, Dubai Square, will be a city within a city with all environments from schools to sports parks spread across broad indoor boulevards covered with glass domes. While this climate-controlled environment will only be necessary during the hottest months or times of day, it will be available year-round. Air-conditioning is a big electricity drain and $CO_2$ emitter, but at least Dubai Square residents won't have to drive cars anywhere.

Since most Dubai residents still prefer single-family accommodation, their neighborhoods might come to resemble the new zero-emission "Sustainable City" district that has solar panels atop every home and parking space. Dubai has also inaugurated a photovoltaic solar park generating enough power for more than 1 million homes. Just outside the UAE's capital of Abu Dhabi lies Masdar City, which was originally conceived as a stand-alone pedestrian and electric golf cart community, but is also joining this air-conditioned archipelago of Emirati cities. Farther north from Dubai, the emirate of Ras-al-Khaimah has branded itself as an affordable expat hub where every day is a pool party. One can imagine numerous Gulf states building such air-conditioned cities in the years ahead, as well as Hyperloop trains between them.

Far larger Saudi Arabia has 40 percent of its population made up of migrant expatriates—more than 11 million people, with Indians representing 4 million, Egyptians 3 million, and Pakistanis 2 million. But the post-2014 slump in oil prices combined with the country's efforts to get Saudis to take on more domestic jobs led to an *outflow* of 1.5 million migrants back to their home countries. Saudis are indeed taking blue-collar jobs in manual industries like operating machinery—about fifty thousand of them. Count on the Indians to be back—building new air-conditioned domes and other infrastructures to keep the country livable amid the searing heat.

Saudi Arabia and India have a constructive complementarity of the Saudis exporting oil to India and India exporting laborers and software to the Kingdom. As Saudi Arabia attempts to diversify and upgrade its economy, it will need IT workers, vocational institutes, and other white-collar technicians to operate its various smart city projects. Indeed, the country's post-Covid vision involves turning Riyadh into a climate oasis and cultural hub with tens of millions of new trees planted. Who will do the gardening, drive the taxis, and operate the data centers? This is why Saudi Arabia has just scrapped its long-standing *kafala* system of sponsorship and supervision of foreign workers. As of 2021, migrants can travel freely in and out of the country and change jobs based on opportunities in the market. Eventually, driverless cars and robots may eliminate the need for Indian and Pakistani laborers, but Saudi Arabia will also want to build more cars and drones inside its borders, leading to more jobs for skilled workers. The Kingdom has even taken the step of offering full citizenship to foreign entrepreneurs. A country seeking to redefine itself can't do so alone.

Despite warnings that the UAE and other Gulf countries will be unlivable by 2075 or sooner, people keep moving there—and Gulf states keep building to absorb them. The Gulf Cooperation Council (GCC) was founded in 1981, and though there are bitter rivalries among its members (such as the ongoing blockade of Qatar that began in 2017), they are also fusing through pipelines, railways, and new regulations that allow any approved resident of Saudi Arabia to buy property in the UAE and go live there instead. They know that their countries are neither the first nor the last place people move to or from, but at least they have the strongest air-conditioning.

## Singapore: Cooling the Heat-Island

On weekend mornings at MacRitchie Reservoir, a jungle in the heart of Singapore, healthy residents from all corners of the world mingle on jogging trails while discussing real estate deals, clean tech investments, and brunch plans—always keeping an eye out for playful monkeys and sneaky monitor lizards. Unlike the Gulf countries, which still have seasons, Singapore lies directly on the equator: It's hot and humid almost every day. Locals have grown accustomed to a routine of early morning exercise, staying indoors much of the day, from 9 a.m. to 6 p.m., and then coming out to enjoy breezy evenings by the beach, in public parks, and on rooftops. With plenty of outdoor shaded areas and ceiling fans, sitting outside during the day can be refreshing if a bit sticky, especially during the powerful thunderstorms.

Reflecting on his success in turning Singapore into an iconic first world city-state, Singapore's founding father Lee Kuan Yew listed a number of the young nation's well-known virtues, such as corruption-free politics and multiethnic harmony. But then he got really philosophical: "Air-conditioning was a most important invention for us, perhaps one of the signal inventions of history. It changed the nature of civilization by making development possible in the tropics."[2]

There is an irony to some of the hottest countries in the world attracting more residents amid global warming, but it also reveals which places have the capacity and willpower to invest in adaptation. Another irony, of course, is maintaining livability through installing millions more air-conditioning units whose emissions exacerbate greenhouse effects. Even though we share a global climate, regional and even local microclimates matter a great deal, especially as urban industrial activities elevate temperatures. Singapore and other dense cities have such a "heat island effect" in which transport congestion traps heat and raises the temperature as much as seven degrees above what it would naturally be. Furthermore, pumping imported oil and gas into power stations generates massive amounts of heat (more than half of it wasted in production) that wafts into the city itself. All of this leads to people cranking up their air conditioners even further. This is how air-conditioning, our solution to heat, makes the heat even worse.

But the future of air-conditioning may be much more sustainable than its present. The National University of Singapore has developed an air conditioner that uses solar thermal energy both to generate power and to wick water from the air, using the former to chill the latter, meaning less than half the electricity and none of the chemical CFCs. Each district of the island is getting integrated centers that enclose in a single solar panel–covered and air-conditioned area amenities like shopping, libraries, swimming pools, childcare, restaurants, and medical clinics. Using the scorching sun to cool us is the wave of the future.

Singapore is also a leading example of how natural canopies of tree-covered walkways and spacious parks remain the best strategy for preserving urban biodiversity. The new Oasis Terrace is a breezy indoor-outdoor mixed-use complex of tree-covered slanted walkways with rooftop gardens, and public fountains for cooling.

Even cities dependent on food and water imports can become more circular. Singapore already has extensive rainwater collection and a sophisticated water treatment system that produces "New Water" piped across the island. It could, and perhaps should, ban private bottled water imports. The Swiss university ETH Zurich's "Cooling Singapore" project brings together climate specialists from MIT, Berkeley, Princeton, and other universities to identify these and other ways to reduce the urban heat island effect. Capturing heat from power plants and directing it toward industry is one obvious step. Thanks to high taxes on car ownership and dense public transport, Singapore has only 460,000 cars for 5.8 million people. Converting all those vehicles as well as public buses into EVs would lower the temperature by at least one degree, which would reduce the air-conditioning load by 20 percent and reduce natural gas imports as well. The same electricity saved in less air-con usage could power the whole EV fleet.

For decades, Singapore has been dependent on importing water from Malaysia to its north. But today, Singapore's reservoir network feeds "New Water" treatment plants that pipe potable water across the country. As part of its "30 by 30" initiative to generate 30 percent of nutritional needs from domestic sources by 2030, it has also started large-scale hydroponic food production and is ramping up fish farming and plant-based proteins. After Covid-19, Singapore decided to bring the time line forward to 2023. If an urban city-state that's almost 100 percent dependent on imported food can generate more of its domestic food supply, then so can almost any place.

At the lotus flower–shaped ArtScience Museum, artist Alvin Pang's arresting exhibit titled *2219: Futures Imagined* depicts urban life in coastal cities such as Singapore under the deluge scenario: Streets have been replaced with broad Venetian-style canals, cars have given way to boats, and buildings are connected by sky bridges and hanging gardens with dripping vines. Every home is stuffed with hydroponic units growing vegetables, and boxes of worms for composting. It's a dystopian picture from today's standpoint, but an adaptive one.

## From "toxic tourism" to the war for tourists

During 2019, over-tourism or "toxic tourism" was a hotly debated nuisance—not so a few months later. Today most governments are begging tourists to come and spend in their economies. In parallel with the global war for talent is a global war for *tourists*.

Two decades ago, I used to wait an eternity (and pay hundreds of dollars) for each entry into countries such as Uzbekistan and Vietnam. Now they and dozens of other fast-growing economies grant visas on arrival with a stamp and a smile. At almost any Chinese consulate in the world, visas can be obtained within twenty-four hours. China has gone from five hundred thousand foreign visitors in 1980 to 63 million in 2018. India has finally implemented an online visa-on-arrival authorization for most nationalities. The United States has spent $2.8 billion on border-smoothing technologies such as Global Entry. Clearly, it's as focused on luring visitors as putting up walls.

It's a cruel irony that more countries than ever depend on tourism given the grave risks the industry faces. Tourism and hospitality represent almost 10 percent of global GDP *and* employment (330 million people). Tropical and island nations—such as the Seychelles and the Maldives in the Indian Ocean, and St. Kitts and Grenada in the Caribbean—not only saw tourism shattered by Covid-19 but are also at risk from rising sea levels.

Spain is accustomed to receiving the second most tourists each year of any country in the world (more than 80 million), and tourism is the second most important sector of the economy (behind industry but ahead of finance). But Spain's prime tourist destination is its southern coast, from the Costa del Sol to Catalunya, a region already so parched that it has to ship in water tankers from France. Brits represent the largest number of tourists in Spain, but as the UK's climate becomes more like Spain's, and Spain's more like Africa's, will so many northern Europeans keep heading south? Rather than sizzling on Spain's Mediterranean beaches, more Europeans will opt to head north to Scandinavia. The Spanish may well abandon their own country and head north too. Winter tourism—currently Spain's low season—will instead become more popular, both for the balmy beaches and hiking in the Sierra Nevada Mountains. The Scandinavians who have been buying up Mediterranean real estate to enjoy during their dark winters may still hold on to those condos.

We have little choice but to discover new destinations for sojourns since thousands of immovable monuments such as the Great Pyramids are located in rapidly warming geographies. Even with a new high-speed railway connecting Mecca, Medina, and Jeddah, it's already becoming too hot for many Muslims to perform the obligatory *hajj* to Saudi Arabia. The European heat wave of 2019 compelled Athens to close the Acropolis during peak hours, a loss in revenue that the ailing Greek economy could scarcely afford. Some of history's most durable cities also won't survive climate change. The Nile River is a swamp by the time it reaches Alexandria on the Mediterranean Sea, which is gradually rising to drown it. Venice's long relied upon sea barriers are already no match for the rising Adriatic floods. Eventually, nearby Padua and Treviso will become more visited bases from which to set off by car and then boat to explore the great submerged medieval republic.

The solution to over-tourism isn't to ban tourists but to sustainably develop new places for tourists to go. You may never have heard of Denmark's Faroe Islands (located between Norway and Iceland), but even they were closed to tourists briefly in 2019 for a "TLC" operation during which islanders and selected "voluntourists" undertook conservation projects.

## *Communal cities*

Today's cities were built for a previous era's industries and lifestyles. Commercial real estate and shopping malls were struggling even before the pandemic and remote work. Self-storage units represent the hoarding culture of boomers and older Gen-Xers; their kids don't want their stuff. Cities need to be physically and politically regenerated to suit youth preferences: affordable housing, cheap transportation, green space, and liberal lifestyle. The cities that attract mobile youth will be those that offer shorter workweeks, wage insurance, skills training programs, and childcare—for the few children that exist.

Here is an obvious but logical point often overlooked when discussing the relatively childless future: Those millennials and Gen-Zers that do have kids will gravitate toward child-friendly communities with enough space to accommodate their sprightly Gen-X parents who'll babysit while they work. According to an index ranking thirty countries as the "best places to raise children" based on safety, cost, health, education, and benefits, almost all of the top twenty-five are in Europe, except for New Zealand, Japan, and Canada, while the US ranks with Mexico at the bottom of the list.[3] Sweden and Finland not only have among the world's most generous parental benefit policies, but cafes and community centers run programs for young parents to bring their children so that neither parenting nor only childhood are such a lonely experience.

In the 1970s, futurist Alvin Toffler predicted that families would convene in multi-family communes and raise children together. Today, couples increasingly buy or rent homes together in groups, sharing the costs and tasks of owning and maintaining property. Co-living creates a sense of community even in higher-priced neighborhoods of big cities such as Chicago and Boston.[4] From Oakland to Detroit, community land trusts give cooperatives discounted access to build affordable family housing. In New York, the Tishman Speyer co-living property called "Kin" is a set of multi-family buildings for young parents where they share common

256

spaces and childcare services. Such retrofitted properties allow professionals to afford New York City life while still raising a family.

During its brief heyday, WeWork sought to deploy its communitarian kibbutz model across all spheres of social life. Beyond co-working, it dabbled in schools (WeGrow), healthcare (Rise by We), and co-living (WeLive). Such urban kibbutz facilities are now popping up everywhere. Some (like PodShare in San Francisco) are month-by-month dorms that resemble a panopticon of micro-rooms. Any sacrifice of privacy is worth it compared to being a super-commuter traveling two or more hours each way to work. StarCity is also building affordable co-living properties across California to keep rank-and-file youth in the state. Tribe in Brooklyn provides physical community space for transient, rootless millennials who struggle to make friends. In New Jersey, vacant office parks are being converted into apartments and co-working spaces; their parking lots are now the sites of small homes, pop-up retail, urban farms, and public events. The digital environment could also promote positive social relations. MIT's Media Lab is testing wearable devices that help people discover common interests with strangers. Welcome to the new digital communitarianism.

With the majority of the world's population and youth, Asia is ground zero for co-living. Hundreds of millions of mobile millennials, whether students or workers, are spending indeterminate periods in multiple cities as they either telecommute or gig their way around the region. For a young Asian or Western expat, what's not to love about spending a few months or a year in Bali while saving most of a good salary? Multinationals even rent out entire co-living and co-working spaces on the island to reduce the costs of part-time or contract workers. With Covid-19 slashing inbound tourism from Australia and China, Bali launched a new campaign to attract digital nomads to buy villas and make the island their permanent home.

Europe is another region where the combination of longevity and financial stress are yielding novel solutions. Most of Milan's two hundred thousand students come from outside the city, and many can't afford to live alone. Under the "Meglio Milano" scheme, elderly couples or widows "adopt" a student to live in their homes, where the student pays reduced rent in exchange for doing chores and providing companionship. The old get to age in place while the young remain untethered. Such home sharing is the new "household" in a world where multiple generations coexist under one roof but not always from the same family.

Europe also leads in offering citizens "mobility as a service" to discourage car ownership. During the Covid lockdown, people began to pay closer attention to whether their immediate five-block radius contained green space, medical care, and food. Paris's mayor, Anne Hidalgo, plans to make all essential services available to anyone within a fifteen-minute walk from their home. From Milan to Toronto to Seattle, downtown centers are being closed to vehicles in favor of pedestrians and cyclists. Dedicated bicycle and scooter lanes cater to the growing share of youth who don't own cars or even have a driver's license. Mobility plans are becoming like data plans: a single app that suggests and coordinates your journey via rent-a-bike, e-scooter, train, bus, or rideshare, and divides your single payment up as needed across the various providers. Helsinki's Whim app covers taxis, buses, bicycles, scooters, and even rental cars. Eventually there will be driverless shuttles, drone taxi copters (piloted by Voom, an Airbus subsidiary), buzzing around above cities and connecting people out to suburbs as well.

Such services could be a game-changer for American cities with their wider geographic sprawl and lower population density. SolarCity's off-grid housing and charging could mean huge new suburbs that would be connected via smooth roads that take people in driverless cars to meetings. Those autonomous vehicle fleets could become so popular that they eclipse public trains and buses, perhaps in the end justifying why America spends so little on public transport. America has the money, technology, and talent to re-sort itself into a collection of future-ready cities, but political will and economic resources are not evenly distributed—thus neither is the future.

## The future of smart living

For youth, the term "user experience" applies as much to cities as it does to companies. They demand that local governance leapfrog from decrepit infrastructure and shoddy services to sensors managing traffic and digital referenda gathering their views in real time. Small and wealthy countries tend to offer the best combination of security and lifestyle that youth seek, but within large countries such as the US, cities will compete to be "smarter" than their peers.*

"Smart city" now denotes everything from tele-medicine to pervasive surveillance. The technological dimension of smart city life is a mix of alluring and discomforting. Apartments are becoming configurable spaces where furniture folds itself up to fit the space depending on whether you need a couch, bed, kitchen, or office. IoT, 5G, and AR/VR will deliver fully immersive streets and buildings. Mobile delivery by drone or robot means instant convenience but potentially clogged sidewalks and skies. Trucks outfitted with 3D printers can mobile-manufacture repair parts. Pizza Hut is piloting vans with ovens inside that make fresh pizzas while en route to deliver them. (There's nothing not to love about that last one.)

Youth want to live in places where technology serves the people rather than the reverse. Right now, tech and payment companies from Google to Mastercard are digitizing local government services (software) while e-commerce, real estate, and automotive companies from Amazon

---

* The most recent joint report by IMD of Switzerland and the Singapore University of Technology and Design (SUTD) ranks cities based on their deployment of technology to improve citizen experience. The top ten smartest cities for 2019 were (in order) Singapore, Zurich, Oslo, Geneva, Copenhagen, Auckland, Taipei, Helsinki, Bilbao, and Dusseldorf. *Smart City Index*, IMD, 2019.

to Waymo have been retrofitting the built environment (hardware). Data analytics units are popping up in mayors' offices from coast to coast. But because digital natives have taken on a heightened awareness of data privacy, the future is likely to be more pragmatic than extreme.

The first incarnation of smart city rhetoric gave off the whiff of corporatized digital smothering. With greater civic guidance, the emerging smart cities will be places where the Internet of things seamlessly blends into the background and affords residents a hassle-free lifestyle—a place where technology allows you to be you. The resurrection of Siemensstadt (an old factory town of the industrial giant's) into a futuristic residential hub outside of Berlin includes clear guidelines that the data will belong first and foremost to public trusts.

Next we can expect that more states will adopt "Digital Bill of Rights" statutes or offer a "data dividend" (paying users for their data) as California has proposed, and ban the use of facial recognition by corporations and law enforcement. There is also a strong push for digital authentication to prevent deep fakes and block cyber-clones, and to suppress hate speech and fact-check viral conspiracy theories. If there are going to be security cameras everywhere, then at least they could be used to stop the "porch pirates" who steal tens of millions of packages annually.

In the developing world, smart cities represent a seemingly necessary departure from the unfixable landscape of decrepit infrastructure, overcrowded tenements, snarling traffic, and rampant corruption. That's why Egypt has broken ground on a "New Cairo" city, for example. It remains to be seen if such projects will ever be completed, however. Amaravati in India was hailed as a cleantech capital for southern India's Andhra Pradesh state, but the government suddenly scrapped it in 2019 though construction was already underway. From Honduras to Madagascar, what Nobel laureate economist Paul Romer calls "charter cities" have also been attempted, but thus far more have failed than succeeded. Just because you can build something doesn't mean you should. Making existing cities more sustainable and investing in their residents' mobility would be money better spent.

This is a reminder that in countries rich and poor, "smart city" may be code for promoting a neo-medieval stratification: the privileged class building new cities or districts to isolate themselves from the unruly outside world. The medieval walls now located in the pedestrian areas of Edinburgh or Barcelona's Barri Gòtic remind us that such formations are the historical norm. Indeed, Plato wrote in *The Republic* that, "any city, however small, is in fact divided into two, one the city of the poor, the other of the rich." We may be heading toward an enlightened feudalism in which progressive cities profess to be open to all, but the cost of promoting order is entrenching a new kind of hierarchy. Even in cities without internal fortifications, such as New York, episodes such as Hurricane Sandy in 2012 and the coronavirus in 2020 laid bare the extent to which zip codes correlated to suffering. A quality-of-life map of America best resembles an airplane with separate entrances, cabins, seating areas, and bathrooms.

So much of the urban world is already stratified in this way, but with a different cast of characters. At the moment, cities like Dubai, Singapore, and Hong Kong are most associated with a bulging temporary foreign worker population living in effectively quarantined conditions separate from society at large. But as large states bring in more people without guaranteeing residency or living standards, stratification will inevitably take root among domestic and foreign, skilled and unskilled, rich and poor.

Smart cities won't truly be smart until we get smarter. Walling ourselves off from the insecurity outside hasn't brought us more security. Instead, it has stoked inequality and fear, while weakening our economy as more and more people have fallen out of it. Inclusive systems—whether cities or nations—empower everyone such that the whole becomes greater than the sum of its parts. Over the past decade, many of those who have become homeless for the first time have been retirees over the age of fifty with insufficient savings. Yet we have apps to help the homeless, released prisoners, and struggling students find affordable places to live. Shouldn't the hundreds of hotels going out of business due to Covid-19, from New York to Nairobi, be converted into residences for this underclass? The test of how "smart" we are isn't very difficult.

# CHAPTER 13
# CIVILIZATION 3.0

### Making the most of mobility

It's common today to hear pronouncements about the "death of glo-balization." Generations past have presumed the same about their times. Yet much like Europe after World War I, each period of retrenchment is followed by an even wider and deeper globalization wave. So it shall be again. Oil trade may decrease, but digital exchange is exploding. Trade in manufactured goods has ebbed, but capital flows and cryptocurrencies are thriving. Populism and the pandemic have tightened some borders, but climate change will drive ever more people across them. Remember the most fundamental truth about humanity through the ages: We keep building connectivity across the planet—and we keep using it. Mobility is destiny.

A map of the world population distribution in 2020 shows large concentrations along the coasts of North America and the Pacific Rim, as well as the dense urban clusters of Europe, Africa, and South Asia. But as we animate that map toward 2050, the coastlines of North America and Asia will submerge and their people will retreat inland. South Americans and Africans will surge northward as their farmland desertifies and their economies crumble. South Asia—India, Pakistan, and Bangladesh—will be the origin of an even greater exodus as sea levels rise and rivers dry up, while automation makes human labor redundant and governments fail to provide stability and welfare. As the decades unfold, dozens of new cities will pop up in previously uninhabited regions, from the Canadian Arctic and Greenland to Russian Siberia and the Central Asian steppe. Some towns will move with their inhabitants.

Will there ever be a stable harmony of our political, economic, environmental, and human geographies again? We would be very lucky to thread that needle. The complex chain reactions we have unleashed among industry, ecology, demographics, technology, and other factors spell continuous turbulence. It's more likely that over the course of one's lifetime, many more people will move multiple times for multiple reasons in multiple directions: in search of work, fleeing climate change, seeking a better political system, or acting from some other motivation. The decades ahead will witness constant circulation as we attempt to rectify the grave mismatch among resources, borders, industries, and people.

This sounds like chaos. But what if it's evolution? Our Paleolithic ancestors evolved biologically, socially, and technologically as they adapted to new environments. Bison, birds, and butterflies all shift their migratory behavior in order to survive. Today we possess the technology to make any part of the planet sustainably habitable, from equatorial rain forests to high Arctic latitudes.

History is not the best guide to this moment in which humanity has to collectively and proactively make big transformations. But perhaps the *present* is. As haphazard as the global response to the Covid-19 pandemic was, it prevented today's much larger population from suffering the scale of casualties experienced during the Black Death (100 million), Spanish Flu (50 million), or AIDS (40 million) epidemics. Rather than accept our fate against the unknown, mankind organized itself more rapidly than ever before.

If we could coordinate the Great Lockdown, can we not also *pre-design* the next Great Migration?

Civilizations of the past collapsed because they failed to adapt to the complexity they themselves created. This suggests that the great mission for mankind is to untangle that complexity, to re-localize while remaining globally connected. A world of more compact, even mobile communes could be less risky than one where huge populations are concentrated in coastal megacities vulnerable to sea-level rise and disease.

Much more than a shift from one place to another, we must evolve from one model of civilization to another. Civilization 1.0 was nomadic and agricultural: The world population was small and localized; the environment dictated where we could survive. Then came Civilization 2.0, in which we became sedentary and industrial. We settled in ever larger cities and commoditized nature through global supply chains. The negative feedback loop between man and nature is killing us both. Now we must adapt again. Civilization 3.0 will need to be mobile and sustainable: We will move inland toward higher elevation and into our vast northern expanses. Our carbon footprint will decrease through renewable energy, but we may migrate more frequently due to socioeconomic and environmental volatility. More people will be nomadic; settlements may be temporary. We will disperse, but we will remain connected.

The legendary British historian Arnold Toynbee spoke of "Civilization with a big 'C,'" asking what political or scientific practices advance our progress as a species, even across (small "c") civilizational divides. The journey of our big "C" Civilization, he wrote, "is a movement and not a condition, a voyage and not a harbour."[1] This is what Civilization 3.0 can be if we allow it.

This Civilization 3.0 scenario is one in which we constantly optimize our human geography. We create medium-size, low-rise settlements across Canada and northern Europe for the summer, and migrate south toward Mexico or the Mediterranean depending on climate conditions. Asians retreat from their coastal megacities and spread out farther toward the Himalayas, Central Asia, and Russia's vast eastern region. We spend less on pointless skyscrapers and more on carbon-fiber- and hydrogen-powered aircraft, Hyperloops, and hovercraft; invest more in water desalination and renewable energy than in coal-fired power plants; and grow more food through localized hydroponic agriculture rather than clearing forests to raise cattle. More societies continue on the path toward open immigration, and those that haven't will wither economically and be bought by migrants anyway. These and other steps will bring humanity closer to the new geography it needs to survive the complex twenty-first century. The only way to get there is to move.

There is a violent path to a similarly fragmented outcome: conflict among major powers with no winner, a war that makes everyone weaker. After the collapse of the Roman empire, Europe reverted to small and localized markets; people made what they could sell and bartered for what they needed. America's decline and China's retreat could plunge the world into such a hyper-fragmented, neo-medieval scenario. Rather than one civilization of many mutually recognized countries, well-armed bands of roaming groups—whether ISIS spin-offs, refugees, or prepper militias—will assert their "mobile sovereignty," ruling wherever they take root. This image of a postmodern feudalism appeals to some who call themselves anarcho-communists, anarcho-primitivists, or survivalist preppers: Let populations naturally decline, rewild nature, and return to our hunter-gatherer ways. But visions of Walden Pond don't explain where our smartphones, 3D printers, prefab houses, and solar panels come from. It's tempting to believe that we don't need connectivity, trade, and migration, but we do.

Our present reality is somewhere in between: geopolitical suspicions and climate volatility in a toxic brew. Without coordination over our common resources, we get land grabs and resource wars. In places with weak property rights, governments and their corporate allies can seize land by fiat. The number of Israelis living in West Bank settlements has grown from under two hundred thousand in 1995 to more than six hundred thousand today; China has stripped Xinjiang and Inner Mongolia of any autonomy and ramped up extraction of their energy and mineral reserves; and India has begun pushing Hindus into Muslim-majority Kashmir to access its glacier waters and build real estate in its scenic valleys. Russia and Vietnam are other countries where the government has total writ and property disputes can be resolved with a tank. Canada's indigenous people successfully fought for decades to gain self-governance over vast swaths of the country's northern territories; those gains can be reversed overnight by a conservative government and its oil company allies. We are moving, but bringing our politics with us.

## From sovereignty to stewardship

The Covid lockdown crushed the economy but (temporarily) cleared the skies. Millions of Indians living in the foothills of the Himalayas had never seen its peaks until March 2020 when decades of oppressive smog temporarily cleared. Can we maintain economic vibrancy while also eliminating noxious greenhouse gas emissions?

The Paris climate agreement has been held up as a road map for the world, but no collective action has backed it up. American presidents can make promises that their successors reject and Congress fails to legislate, and that would take decades to implement. Canada is a signatory to the Paris Agreement but has just approved development of a massive new tar sands oil field. Europe is reducing its emissions, but its efforts are more than outweighed by their growth everywhere else. China is cleaning up at home but exporting dirty coal abroad. India and Brazil decry climate colonialism while India remains reliant on coal power and Brazil logs the Amazon. Carbon taxes are gaining ground, but these are at best half measures. Markets, many critics argue, are what got us into this mess in the first place.

Our many arbitrary colonial-era borders hinder cooperation on today's existential demographic and environmental challenges. For example, India and Pakistan dispute the Sir Creek estuary that forms the Feni River's delta into the Arabian Sea. Here and elsewhere, countries can't agree whether a river border should be defined at the midpoint or the banks. Yet as University of Maryland professor Saleem Ali argues, such fragile ecosystems should have long ago been turned into wetland conservation areas rather than being militarized. Some sub-Saharan African nations, such as Botswana and Zambia, as well as Mozambique and South Africa, have managed to establish cross-border ecological preserves. The same should be done in the precarious but ecologically precious Demilitarized Zone between North and South Korea. Such thinking is needed across the world. Though the notorious 1885 Congress of Berlin is where Africa got many of its straight-line borders, Europeans also utilized the legal concept of *do ut des*, meaning "giving to receive," or simply tit-for-tat. Today countries can do better than that: They can also share sovereignty.

Sovereignty today serves to demarcate zones of political control, but it also shields governments from complying with transnational responsibilities. Yet climate change raises new questions about what obligations countries have to conserve habitats, reduce greenhouse gas emissions, and accept migrants. At the heart of these queries lies a stark choice. What matters more: nationality or sustainability? Should states be permitted to have leaders who ruin the Earth for all of us? Is the territory of Canada or Russia too important to the world to be left to Canadians and Russians alone to govern? Can we evolve from sovereignty to stewardship?

Repurposing entire swaths of the planet for large-scale resettlement requires re-coding territory away from strict sovereignty into administrative protectorates designated for agriculture, forestry, marine life, or habitation. In this spirit, countries could lease critical habitats to international cooperatives for their sustainable cultivation. When spaces are so important that no one country should control them exclusively, we can design mechanisms that balance sustainability with fair access. The International Union for Conservation of Nature (IUCN) helps countries designate nature reserves, wilderness areas, national parks, and sustainable resource development areas and finds the right partners to assist them to protect, regenerate, or attract tourists to these eco zones. To date, such technical support by IUCN and the World Wildlife Fund has led to 15 percent of the Earth's land area being designated as protected areas. E. O. Wilson argued our target should be 50 percent—half the Earth. Linking biospheres would allow many currently endangered species and natural habitats to regenerate, from North American forests to the Amazon river basin to African grasslands.

The equally important oceanic sphere includes not just fisheries and seabeds but also its renewable power potential, from tidal generators to wind turbines. Seventy percent of the Earth's surface is water, more than half of which lies outside any state jurisdiction. The Law of the Sea is currently being amended to protect the biodiversity of these high seas. Next, the World Ocean Council could be empowered to convene governments, companies, and environmental groups to undertake maritime spatial planning.

All of this constitutes a sensible application of the precautionary principle that an ounce of prevention is worth a pound of cure—especially when there may be no cure. But what if we need to *enforce* environmental protection? Harvard professor Stephen Walt has asked whether international humanitarian law should be invoked to justify military interventions to protect ecosystems. Former Obama administration science advisor John Holdren called for a "planetary regime," a super-agency to regulate the global environment, managing all natural resources and even regulating global trade and setting regional population quotas.

Far more likely, however, is that countries such as Russia and Brazil will have to be economically coerced or bribed into protecting their habitats as dearly as they guard their sovereignty. In 2019, Brazil deployed nearly fifty thousand troops to control forest fires—perhaps not coincidentally because France and Ireland threatened to block its EU trade agreement until serious action was taken against deforestation. The Global Commission on Adaptation argued that $1.8 trillion spent on adaptation investments (such as protecting coastal mangroves, boosting dryland crop production, and more efficient irrigation) could generate $7.1 trillion in economic benefits. In the absence of stronger sticks, these are some of the carrots that will need to be deployed to compel pro-ecological action.

## Vacated states

Some countries aren't going to make it through to our next era. Their ecological decay, unstable politics, freefalling economies, and brain drain mean they'll be left only with citizens dispossessed by the rest of the world—or perhaps they'll be fully abandoned. But it's part of the definition of a state that it has a permanent resident population, so what happens to states that have been totally vacated? Will they merge with neighbors or become multilateral protectorates? Either way, their geography can still be useful. Wherever their populations go, Central and West African countries have rich deposits of cobalt, iron ore, and bauxite that will be mined until there is nothing left, while sub-Saharan African countries such as Namibia, South Africa, and Angola hold significant reserves of diamonds, gold, uranium, zinc, and other minerals. Bolivia and Afghanistan have giant pits of lithium essential for batteries. The 6 million people of Turkmenistan (who live in the region's equivalent of basket case North Korea) may have to migrate into western Kazakhstan or southern Russia, even as their gas reserves and solar power are harnessed for regional markets. There are other roles that vacated states will play in the global division of labor: as dumps for briny refuse from desalination plants and waste from nuclear reactors.* As we abandon geographies we can no longer inhabit, we are learning not to take any geography for granted.

---

* Especially countries rich in granite and not seismically active are crucial locations to bury nuclear waste. Currently, most of the world's nuclear waste is stored in non-seismic granite mountains in countries such as Finland, Sweden, France, Spain, and the Czech Republic, or on-site of existing reactors in the US (due to local opposition to burying it in places such as Yucca Mountain, Nevada, near Death Valley and Las Vegas). But as these countries gain population from global migration, nuclear waste is better stored (and relocated) to places such as Sierra del Medio in Argentina's Patagonia region, which is depopulated and drying out due to climate change.

# CIVILIZATION 3.0

## *The geo-engineering solution*

There is another way in which today's climate nationalism could entail a certain militarism: preserving one's own natural resources by denying them to others. Some nativists argue that allowing more immigration would raise poor migrants' living standards and thus their total emissions. But by the same logic, stabilizing the climate of poor and overpopulated regions could be the North's preferred strategy to keep the people of the South from needing to migrate in the first place.

When acting in their own interest, countries have not been shy at environmental engineering. The US has been using cloud seeding to combat drought since the 1970s, and more recently to precipitate snowfall to improve ski conditions. India and Arab countries from Morocco to the UAE have been seeding clouds since the 1980s to compensate for weak rainfall; the UAE now seeds clouds almost daily and captures rainwater in giant dams and reservoirs. In Indonesia and Malaysia cloud seeding has been essential to quell the polluting haze from brushfires. A global cloud seeding initiative could bring at least temporary relief for water-stressed farming regions.

Reforestation initiatives could also benefit entire regions and the atmosphere. Trees are active cooling agents that absorb $CO_2$ and capture water evaporation, especially in tropical countries, where they grow much faster. (Hence cutting down the Amazon is worse than logging in Canada, and replanting the Amazon is more important than planting more trees in Canada.) According to ETH Zurich, extensive tree planting, totaling 1 billion hectares (about the size of the continental US), across Russia, Canada, America, Australia, Brazil, and China would capture two-thirds of our carbon emissions. But despite a recent global campaign calling for the planting of 1 trillion trees, we are currently losing more than 10 million hectares of forest per year, and newly planted trees still take decades to reach their full carbon absorption capacity.

Progressive powers may take the lead in launching geo-engineering schemes such as carbon sequestration (fertilizing the ocean with nutrients to enhance $CO_2$ absorption), high atmosphere deployment of sulphur dioxide particles to deflect sunlight, or coating fresh ice with white sand that reflects more light, so the ice can strengthen rather than melt. One hopes the world's philanthropic billionaires (such as Bill Gates and Jeff Bezos), NASA, and other bodies are already working in secret to launch such schemes. Scholars have argued that reflecting solar radiation across a range of latitudes could buy the whole world time and reduce climate injustice. But solutions benefiting just one region could have adverse effects. If people find out what these geo-engineering plans are and which places will benefit, they'll go there. Unless we find a solution for everyone, both mass migration and mass suffering will continue.

## Mass migrations and morality

Twenty years ago we still feared rampant overpopulation. Yet today's most urgent task is almost the opposite: We need to nurture those alive and yet to be born to ensure the maximal survival of humanity through this century. This means people will have to move—but will we let them?

What justification is there for a system in which large and resource-rich but depopulating countries close their borders, while those countries least responsible for climate change are sinking or running out of water? To lock the world population into its present position amounts to ecocide—yet it won't make those who survive better off. Our economies will still face acute labor shortages, and the wealth created from global exchange will halt. Instead, we should sustainably cultivate the planet's habitable oases and move people there.

Moral philosophers have nonetheless put the nation ahead of mankind in their inquiries. Seventeenth-century English philosopher John Locke, for example, made a pragmatic case for naturalizing immigrants to enlarge the labor pool and expand production and trade. He was clear, however, that migration should not deprive locals of their property rights. The eighteenth-century Prussian philosopher Immanuel Kant went a step further in advocating a right to hospitality for all people, but this was understood more as a temporary sojourn rather than permanent residence, and as with Locke, it was conditioned on the visitor not causing harm to his hosts.*

Kant's ideas continued to animate twentieth-century debates about migrant rights. Living through the postwar decades of significant migrations between Britain and its former colonies, the late Oxford philosopher Michael Dummett echoed Kant in his view that a moral state should provide fundamental rights to both citizens and noncitizens alike. The right to migrate is itself such a right, as is the right of stateless people to become citizens of some state. Jacques Derrida similarly argued for strict national sovereignty to soften in favor of a more ethical hospitality toward foreigners. But even for famed philosophers such as John Rawls, migration played little role in his thought experiments about self-contained states. He supported people's right to move, but not any imposition on national sovereignty. Instead, a just global system would eliminate the root causes of poverty, corruption, or other motivations for migration.

But the time for mere thought experiments has passed—our global system is far from fair. Humanity shares one climate that the North's industry has cataclysmically devastated, with the South bearing the brunt of the consequences. We have desertified lands across the South and agri-

---

* Kant was, not incidentally, one of the first philosophers to treat geography as a discipline, outlining its subcategories, such as physical, economic, and moral. He wrote of a "philosophical topography" to explain how spaces and places shape human experience and knowledge. Malpas and Thiel, "Kant's Geography of Reason," *Reading Kant's Geography* (2011), in Robert B. Louden, "The Last Frontier: The Importance of Kant's Geography," *Environment and Planning D: Society and Space* 32, no. 3 (January 2014): 450–465.

culturally abundant terrain in the North. We have abandoned towns full of modern homes in the North and millions of displaced refugees in the South. We have huge labor shortages in the North and labor surpluses in the South. Bryan Caplan's wonderfully illustrated narrative *Open Borders* argues that most migrants are neither school age nor retirement age but rather working age Gen-Xers and millennials whose long-term fiscal benefit amounts to about $259,000 per migrant in just the US alone. Economist Michael Clemens of the Center for Global Development estimates that opening the world's borders to even temporary migrant workers could literally double world GDP.

Despite all ethical and economic arguments in favor of mass migrations, we have no global migration policy. Instead, we face a growing number of moral tests: Africans crossing the Mediterranean and Latinos crossing the Rio Grande, and other crises. Migration has become a political Rorschach test in almost every Western democracy, yet still not enough migrants are let in while too many die on the way. Nor is enough done to repair their homelands in light of the external pain inflicted on them (such as military interventions and ecological ruin) and their own internal failings (such as corruption and reckless population growth). Both Kant and Rawls would be very disappointed in us.

Few other living philosophers have thought harder about what our obligations are in light of our failures than Peter Singer, who argues that the logical conclusion of holding all people as equal (cosmopolitanism) as well as striving for maximum collective happiness (utilitarianism) is that the fortunate give as much as possible to those less fortunate, irrespective of their geography or nationality. The maximalist version of this thesis is open borders and mass wealth redistribution, while the minimalist case is far greater aid to poor countries.

We have ample evidence, however, that aid barely keeps people alive, while moving people gives them a chance to live. For most of the world population that lives in poor countries, 3D-printed homes won't magically materialize after a cyclone, nor will hydroponic food after a drought, nor will large sums of money appear in their mobile wallets during civil wars. The truest way to care is to let victims become neighbors. Western countries promote human rights abroad knowing that their pressure will yield few results, whereas the surest path to improving the human condition is migration. Migration is as much a human right as freedom of speech or due process—and indeed, for many, crossing a border is the only way to attain these rights. Mobility thus ought to be one of the paramount human rights of the twenty-first century.

If there is a term for my position, it's "cosmopolitan utilitarianism": We should realign our geographies to bring maximum welfare to current and future generations. It's also a cosmopolitan realism: States make their own decisions, but more migration is very much in the national interest. Indeed, smart governments don't talk about immigration as an all-or-nothing proposition. Instead, they forecast labor demand by sector and recruit foreigners to fill those gaps so that domestic unemployment remains low even as the population grows. Remember there is no zero-sum competition between local and foreign workers: A greater influx of labor itself stimulates the economy and creates greater demand for labor. At the same time, compromises can be made to maintain support for openness such as stronger curbs on illegal immigration and local preferences in hiring. Another way to sustain a pro-migration orientation: distribute the revenues from foreign investment to native citizens as a dividend. Such measures are a small price to pay to achieve a more productive and humane distribution of people around the world.

To achieve a more fair and sensible human geography will require arguments based on both rights and obligations—especially since politically, neither is sufficient. In 2018, governments agreed to a "Global Compact for Safe, Orderly, and Regular Migration" that recognized the rights of migrants to work and contribute rather than be a financial burden. But the US has rejected both the Migration

Compact and a parallel Global Compact for Refugees. During the 2016 wave of Arab migrants into Europe, German chancellor Angela Merkel initially advocated for the rights of asylum seekers, but later shifted toward stricter controls to avoid losing political ground to far right anti-immigrant parties. Perhaps then the dilemma is less about morality than the contrast between ethically sound and demographically necessary immigration and the self-defeating shortsightedness of democratic politics.

Almost no Western democracies are prepared for the new age of mass migrations. As the Indian-American novelist Suketu Mehta points out, "Never before has there been so much human movement. And never before has there been so much organized resistance to human movement."[2] Mehta argues for reparations as a form of North-South atonement, but also points out that the North needs migrants more than ever anyway. The brain drain may as well continue. But reparations arguments have long fallen flat among historically ignorant and fiscally constrained Western publics. Furthermore, the countries that may be absorbing the most migrants in the future, such as Canada and Russia, never colonized Africa and South Asia. Reliving past disputes won't bring us to our collective senses about the future.

We also can't pretend that population control will revert us to a less burdensome demography anytime soon. American Geographical Society chairman Chris Tucker argues that the ideal world population is 3 billion, roughly what it was in the mid twentieth century, a time when we benefited from industrialization but before the acceleration of global warming. But today we stand at nearly triple that number of people, making the question of how many people there *should* be somewhat moot. Whatever the human population settles at in the future, we still should move those we do have now.

The fact is that there has never been a status quo where mankind stood still, comfortably confined to predetermined national boundaries—and there never will be. Today we debate whether or not migrants should be allowed; tomorrow we will focus on our *absorptive capacity* for new migrants. Each country and regional group should proactively be formulating answers to questions such as: Where should migrants go? What work can they do? How can they be assimilated? How can we design expanded habitats in the most sustainable fashion? As anthropologist David Graeber wisely noted, "The ultimate, hidden truth of the world is that it is something that we make, and could just as easily make differently."[3]

Many large and wealthy countries across North America, Europe, and Asia already require mass immigration to maintain their standard of living, yet none are absorbing nearly as many migrants as they need. Demographic decline in rich countries sparks socioeconomic tension, while booming populations in poor countries retard equitable development. More migration could balance these out, preventing the world from collectively becoming poorer and more unequal at the same time. A large-scale re-sorting of the global population would therefore be in everyone's best interest. Our choice is either a progressive redeployment of especially the world's youth to geographies where they can be gainfully employed or a global underclass revolt. Recent years have given us a taste of what the latter looks like. Are we brave enough to take the other path?

## Repopulating the world

The world is running out of people and places to live at the same time. Moving resources to people has been environmentally catastrophic; now we must move people to resources, without destroying them in the process. The major states of the North—America and Canada, Britain and Germany, Russia and Japan—need more expansive immigration as well as substantial new investments in agriculture and infrastructure to prepare for what lies ahead. But the generosity of countries in accepting migrants must be weighed against the potential tragedy to the commons of having too many people arriving at once.

The constant movement of especially young people around the world combined with aging demographics and climate stress also mean we need to actively repurpose existing infrastructure and other facilities to serve humanity. Idle planes can airlift the poor and stranded, empty cruise ships and hotels can house refugees and the homeless, shopping malls can become warehouses and makerspaces, and golf courses can become farms. One wonders if we can spare land for all the cemeteries that will be necessary as today's baby boomers expire.

## Where to Now?

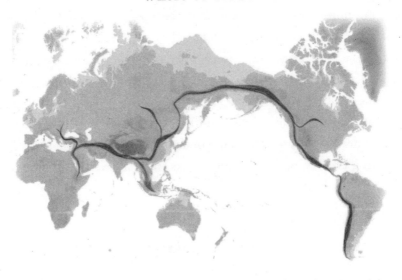

Mankind's migrations over the past 100,000 years brought us out of Africa and onto every other continent, where we have concentrated along coasts and rivers. Where will we move over the next 100 or 1,000 years?

There is something demographically poetic about populations organically dying off in our prime geographies yet being dynamically backfilled by youth from far and wide. If we allow ourselves to go with the flow—moving inland, upland, and northward, and taking advantage of the latest advances in sustainability and mobility—we will not only evolve toward a new model of human civilization, but may even regain the confidence to revitalize our population. As Mohsin Hamid poignantly writes in *National Geographic*, "A species of migrants at last comfortable being a species of migrants. That, for me, is a destination worth wandering to."[4]

"Map of the Modern World," that coveted undergraduate class at Georgetown, was pass/fail. Today we can either pass or fail the test of devising a new philosophy of geography. In 1946, American geographer John Kirtland Wright coined the term "geosophy" to signify the intimate and ever evolving relationship between geography and human nature.[5] Geosophy inspires us to overcome artificial authority: Borders can bend, infrastructure can shift, people can move. Satellite imagery of our changing climate fuses with billions of political, economic, and social data points to produce vivid scenarios for how humankind can relocate and thrive. No wonder geography is once again gaining popularity in high schools, and Earth Observation (EO) and Geographical Information Systems (GIS) are sought-after courses in universities, with their graduates getting jobs that have tangible positive impact. There is nothing more important for youth to study. These fields hold the key to how we survive the complex decades ahead. Geography evolves, and human society must evolve with it.

# ACKNOWLEDGMENTS

This book is dedicated to the memory of David Held, the celebrated political theorist who supervised my PhD thesis at LSE (London School of Economics and Political Science). David was the selfless mentor and friend, and his authentic but realistic cosmopolitanism remains a perpetual source of inspiration. It does not seem common to have warm memories of doctoral struggles, but it is a testament to David's character that I miss him every day.

As with my previous book, the faculty and students at Yale-NUS in Singapore have proven to be an invaluable intellectual resource. Conversations with my good friend Ravi Chidambaram again required my nonstop note-taking, and his masterful lecture on "the good company" and our joint article on redefining human capital were very useful in shaping this narrative. Anju Paul's deep scholarship on the realities of low-income migrants was equally impactful for her on-the-ground perspective. Both Ravi and Anju's brilliant cohorts of Yale-NUS students were a pleasure to engage with and learn from. I'd also like to thank my old friends Brian McAdoo and Paul Wilt for being consistent sounding boards intellectually, and directing me to the Yale-NUS undergraduates who made such a deep contribution to this book. Helena Auerswald, Raya Lyubenova, and Anmei Zeng have my deepest appreciation for their meticulous and insightful research as well as their cheery outlook. Xiao You Mok, Adity Ramachandran, and Sai Suhas Kopparapu were also once again unflappably diligent and creative in steering me down interesting cultural avenues.

My team at FutureMap, composed of colleagues and friends old and new, has been invaluable in professionalizing every aspect of this book. Kailash K. Prasad is an interdisciplinary thinker who found novel ways to combine qualitative insights with data. Jeff Blossom and April Zhu produced superb maps and visualizations to bring ideas to life, and Scott Malcomson once again provided substantive feedback, on almost every paragraph of the book. And without Jennifer Kwek, I don't know how I would even find time to write.

A wide range of organizations generously assembled next-generation leaders with rich perspectives which I found invaluable. For their generous support of this research, I'd like to thank Ngaire Woods of Oxford's Blavatnik School of Governance, Jonathan Bright of the Oxford Internet Institute, and the Oxford Urbanists. I also enjoyed discussions with well-informed and ambitious youth hosted by the Mercator Stiftung in Berlin, and the Doha Debates team of Amjad Attalah, Amy Selwyn, Caroline Scullin, and Nelufar Hedayat. Special thanks to Maya Hari of Twitter for convening an eclectic and multinational group of "Tweeps" from across Asia. I am also grateful to veteran global explorer Martin Gray, who found time during a brief respite from his spiritual wanderings to comment on the entire manuscript.

I also wish to thank numerous others with whom conversations (in person or virtual) have been helpful in formulating and testing ideas presented in this book (in alphabetical order): K. D. Adamson, David Adelman, Rukhsana Afzaals, Ellie Alchin, Nick Alchin, Tracey Alexander, Alisher Ali, Rafat Ali, Saleem Ali, Amit Anand, Simon Anholt, Yusuke Arai, Lorig Armenian, Maha Aziz, Richard Barkham, Umej Bhatia, Helena Robin Bordie, Fabio Brioschi, Chris Brooke, Mat Burrows,

# ACKNOWLEDGMENTS

Penny Burtt, Heng Wing Chan, Chris Chau, Andrea Chegut, Holly Cheung, Renato Chizzola, Neel Chowdhury, Michael Chui, Andy Clarke, Steve Clemons, Andy Cohen, James Crabtree, Louis Curran, Anna Dai, Hugues Delcourt, James Der Derian, James Dorsey, Steve Draper, Brooks Entwistle, Chris Eoyang, Reza Etedali, Hany Fam, Nick Fang, James Fazi, Michael Ferrari, Elie Finegold, Dennis Frenchman, Yoichi Funabashi, Miguel Gamino, David Giampaolo, Loretta Girardet, Bruno Giussani, Jan-Philipp Goertz, Lawrence Groo, Sandro Gruenenfelder, Amol Gupte, Nina Hachigian, Kyle Hagerty, Niels Hartog, Jason Hickel, David Hoffman, Paul Holthaus, David Horlock, John Howkins, Greg Hunt, Pico Iyer, Josef Janning, Namrata Jolly, Christian Kaelin, So-Young Kang, Prakash Kannan, Sagi Karni, Tarun Kataria, Gerry Keefe, Shane Kelly, Sanjay Khanna, Sid Khanna, Gaurang Khemka, Eje Kim, Brett King, Ryushiro Kodaira, Natasha Kohne, Daniel Korski, Sung Lee, Mark Leonard, Steve Leonard, David Leonhardt, Adam Levinson, Beibei Li, Yingying Li, Mike Lightman, Greg Lindsay, Christopher Logan, Pierre-Yves Lombard, Karen Makishima, Aaron Maniam, Ali Mansour, Greg Manuel, Chris Marlin, Rui Matsukawa, Sean McFate, Suketu Mehta, Pankaj Mishra, Afshin Molavi, Brent Morgans, Mazyar Mortazavi, Mary Mount, Cameron Najafi, Kimi Onoda, Thomas Pang, Charles Pirtle, Todd Porter, Kailash Prasad, Noah Raford, Adam Rahman, Julia Raiskin, Adi Ramachandran, Anne Richards, Oliver Rippel, Anthea Roberts, Undine Ruge, Alpo Rusi, Manny Rybach, Karim Sadjadpour, Rick Samans, Rana Sarkar, Gerhard Schmitt, Annette Schoemmel, Peter Schwartz, Zeynep Sen, Neeraj Seth, Reva Seth, Andres Sevtsuk, Ankur Shah, Lutfey Siddiqi, Graham Silverthorne, J. T. Singh, Jason Sosa, Balaji Srinivasan, Juerg Steffen, Seb Strassburg, Joe Teng, Jakob Terp-Hansen, Barbara Thole, Ryan Thomas, Chris Tucker, Jan Vapaavuori, Sriram Vasudevan, Ivan Vatchkov, Dominic Volek, Kirk Wagar, D. A. Wallach, Yukun Wang, Nellie Wartoft, Steve Weikal, Ernest Wilson, Shawn Wu, Sasha Young, Mosharraf Zaidi, Mikhail Zeldovich, Graham Zink, Michael Zink, and Taleh Ziyadov.

# ACKNOWLEDGMENTS

My family has been living the thesis of this book since before I was born, yet another reason to thank Mom and Dad for their tireless support, spontaneous anecdotes, and continued willingness to read my manuscripts start to finish. My wife, Ayesha, has also peppered me with a continuous stream of relevant material, and her intuitions about our own family travel destinations have tilted my thinking in very useful ways. Our global kids, Zara and Zubin, are no longer in the back of my mind as I write but front and center as they quiz us on facts about the world and weigh in with their observations and judgments about all the places they've been and want to go. My brother Gaurav and sister-in-law Anu also radiated insights about so many topics covered herein, and my niece Anisha and nephew Roshan are the finest incarnations of the next-gen digital natives shaping the future.

This book evolved considerably from its original formulation, and many of those improvements are thanks to my transatlantic editorial team of Rick Horgan at Scribner (Simon & Schuster) and Jenny Lord at Orion (Hachette). Thanks deeply to both for their confident guidance in this genuinely fruitful partnership. As ever, I am eternally indebted to Jenn Joel at ICM; the word "agent" does not even remotely capture the role her wise counsel and friendship plays in all aspects of my work. At Curtis Brown in London, the team of Jake Smith-Bosanquet, Richard Pike, and Savanna Wicks have been a thoroughly positive force in ensuring that my work receives a global audience. Deepest thanks to my entire dream team.

# BIBLIOGRAPHY

Abdelal, Rawi E., Alastair Iain Johnston, Yoshiko Margaret Herrera, and Rose McDermott. *Measuring Identity: A Guide for Social Scientists*. Cambridge: Cambridge University Press, 2009.

Agnew, John. *Human Geography: An Essential Anthology*. Oxford: Blackwell, 1996.

Alba, Richard. *The Great Demographic Illusion: Majority, Minority, and the Expanding American Mainstream*. Princeton: Princeton University Press, 2020.

Allen, John. *Lost Geographies of Power*. Oxford: Blackwell, 2003.

Alter, Charlotte. *The Ones We've Been Waiting For: How a New Generation of Leaders Will Transform America*. New York: Viking, 2020.

Anderson, Benedict. *Imagined Communities: Reflections on the Origin and Spread of Nationalism*. London: Verso, 1983.

Andres, Lesly, and Johanna Wyn. *The Making of a Generation: The Children of the 1970s in Adulthood*. Toronto: University of Toronto Press, 2010.

Anholt, Simon. *Competitive Identity*. London: Palgrave Macmillan, 2006.

# BIBLIOGRAPHY

Anholt, Simon. *The Good Country Equation*. New York: Penguin Random House, 2020.

Arendt, Hannah. *The Human Condition*. Chicago: University of Chicago Press, 1958.

Aziz, Maha Hosain. *Future World Order*. Independent, 2019.

Balarajan, Meera, Geoffrey Cameron, and Ian Goldin. *Exceptional People*. Princeton: Princeton University Press, 2012.

Baldwin, Richard E. *The Globotics Upheaval: Globalization, Robotics, and the Future of Work*. Oxford: Oxford University Press, 2019.

Bauwens, Michel, Vasilis Kostakis, and Alex Pazaitis. *Peer to Peer: The Commons Manifesto*. London: University of Westminster Press, 2019.

Bejan, Adrian. *Evolution and Freedom*. New York: Springer International Publishing, 2019.

Benhabib, Seyla. *The Law of Peoples, Distributive Justice, and Migrations*. Cambridge: Cambridge University Press, 2004.

Benjamin, Walter, and Rolf Tiedemann. *The Arcades Project*. Cambridge: Belknap Press, 1999.

Berggruen, Nicolas, and Nathan Gardels. *Renovating Democracy*. Berkeley: University of California Press, 2019.

Bostrom, Nick. *Superintelligence: Paths, Dangers, Strategies*. Oxford: Oxford University Press, 2014.

Brannen, Peter. *Ends of the World*. London: Oneworld Publications, 2018.

# BIBLIOGRAPHY

Bray, Mark. *Antifa: The Anti-Fascist Handbook*. London: Melville House Publishing, 2017.

Bregman, Rutger. *Utopia for Realists*. New York: Little Brown and Company, 2017.

Bremmer, Ian. *Us Versus Them: The Failure of Globalism*. New York: Portfolio, 2018.

Bricker, Darrell, and John Ibbitson. *Empty Planet: The Shock of Global Population Decline*. Toronto: McClelland & Stewart, 2019.

Bruder, Jessica. *Nomadland: Surviving America in the Twenty-First Century*. New York: W. W. Norton, 2017.

Caplan, Bryan. *Open Borders: The Science and Ethics of Immigration*. New York: St. Martin's Press, 2019.

Clausing, Kimberly. *Open: The Progressive Case for Free Trade, Immigration, and Global Capital*. Cambridge: Harvard University Press, 2019.

Colin, Nicholas. *Hedge: A Greater Safety Net for the Entrepreneurial Age*. CreateSpace Independent Publishing Platform, 2018.

Combi, Chloe. *Generation Z: Their Voices, Their Lives*. New York: Random House, 2015.

Coupland, Douglas. *Generation X*. New York: St. Martin's Griffin, 1991.

Dalby, Simon. *Anthropocene Geopolitics: Globalization, Security, Sustainability*. Ottawa: University of Ottawa Press, 2020.

Dartnall, Lewis. *Origins: How the Earth Shaped Human History*. London: Bodley Head, 2019.

Davis, Garry. *My Country Is the World: The Adventures of a World Citizen.* CreateSpace Independent Publishing Platform, 2010.

De Haas, Hein, Mark Castles, and Mark J. Miller. *The Age of Migration: International Population Movements in the Modern World.* London: Guilford Press, 2013.

Deparle, Jason. *A Good Provider Is One Who Leaves.* New York: Viking, 2019.

Dewey, John. *Art as Experience.* London: George Allen & Unwin Ltd, 1934.

Dewey, John. *Experience and Nature.* London: George Allen and Unwin, Ltd, 1929.

Dummett, Michael. *On Immigration and Refugees.* London: Routledge, 2001.

Edmunds, June, and Bryan Turner. *Generations, Culture & Society.* Philadelphia: Open University Press, 2005.

Eichengreen, Barry. *The Populist Temptation: Economic Grievance and Political Reaction in the Modern Era.* Oxford: Oxford University Press.

Elder, Glen H. *Children of the Great Depression.* Boulder: Westview Press, 1998.

Esty, Daniel C. *A Better Planet: Forty Big Ideas for a Sustainable Future.* London: Yale University Press, 2019.

Fallows, James, and Deborah Fallows. *Our Towns: A 100,000-Mile Journey into the Heart of America.* New York: Pantheon Books, 2018.

Farmer, Roger. *Prosperity for All: How to Prevent Financial Crises.* Oxford: Oxford University Press, 2016.

Fish, Eric. *China's Millennials: The Want Generation.* Lanham: Rowman & Littlefield Publishers, 2015.

# BIBLIOGRAPHY

Florida, Richard. *Who's Your City? How the Creative Economy Is Making Where You Live the Most Important Decision of Your Life.* Toronto: Random House of Canada, 2008.

Foroohar, Rana. *Don't Be Evil: How Big Tech Betrayed Its Founding Principles—and All of Us.* New York: Currency, 2019.

Fouberg, Erin H, Alexandra Murphy, and Harm J. de Blij. *Human Geography: People, Place and Culture.* Hoboken: Wiley, 2015.

Fraser, Evan D. G., and Andrew Rimas. *Empires of Food: Feast, Famine, and the Rise and Fall of Civilizations.* New York: Free Press, 2010.

Frazier, Mark, and Joseph McKinney. *Founding Startup Societies: A Step by Step Guide.* Salt Lake City: Startup Societies Foundation, 2019.

Gaul, Gilbert M. *The Geography of Risk: Epic Storms, Rising Seas, and the Cost of America's Coasts.* New York: Sarah Crichton Books, 2019.

Gertner, Jon. *Ice at the End of the World: An Epic Journey into Greenland's Buried Past and Our Perilous Future.* New York: Random House, 2019.

Ghosh, Amitav. *The Great Derangement: Climate Change and the Unthinkable.* Illinois: University of Chicago Press, 2017.

Goodell, Jeff. *How to Cool the Planet: Geoengineering and the Audacious Quest to Fix Earth's Climate.* Boston: Houghton Mifflin Harcourt, 2010.

Goodell, Jeff. *The Water Will Come: Rising Seas, Sinking Cities, and the Remaking of the Civilized World.* New York & Boston & London: Little, Brown and Company, 2017.

Goodhart, David. *Road to Somewhere: The Populist Revolt and the Future of Politics.* London: Hurst, 2017.

# BIBLIOGRAPHY

Graeber, David. *Bullshit Jobs: A Theory*. London: Allen Lane, 2018.

Greene, Robert Lane. *You Are What You Speak: Grammar Grouches, Language Laws, and the Politics of Identity*. New York: Delacorte Press, 2011.

Haidt, Jonathan. *The Righteous Mind: Why Good People Are Divided by Politics and Religion*. New York: Knopf Doubleday Publishing Group, 2012.

Hankins, James. *Virtue Politics: Soulcraft and Statecraft in Renaissance Italy*. Cambridge: Harvard University Press, 2018.

Hannant, Mark. *Midnight's Grandchildren: How Young Indians Are Disrupting the World's Largest Democracy*. London: Routledge, 2018.

Hardt, Michael, and Antonio Negri. *Assembly*. Oxford: Oxford University Press, 2017.

Harris, Malcom. *Kids These Days: Human Capital and the Making of Millennials*. New York & Boston & London: Little, Brown and Company, 2017.

Hayden, Patrick. "Political Evil, Cosmopolitan Realism, and the Normative Ambivalence of the International Criminal Court." In Steven C. Roach. *Governance, Order, and the International Criminal Court: Between Realpolitik and a Cosmopolitan Court*. Oxford: Oxford University Press, 2009.

Henig, Robin. *What Is It About Twenty-Somethings?* New York: *The New York Times*, 2010.

Herz, Marcus, and Thomas Johansson. *Youth Studies in Transition: Culture, Generation and New Learning Processes*. Basel: Springer Nature Switzerland AG, 2019.

Hertz, Noreena. *The Lonely Century: How Isolation Imperils Our Future*. London: Hodder and Stoughton, 2020.

Hickel, Jason. "Degrowth: A Theory of Radical Abundance." *Real-World Economics Review* 87 (2019): 54–68.

Hill, Alice C., and Leonardo Martinez-Diaz. *Building a Resilient Tomorrow*. Cambridge: Oxford University Press, 2019.

Hockfield, Susan. *Age of Living Machines: How Biology Will Build the Next Technology Revolution*. New York: W. W. Norton & Company, 2019.

Houlgate, Laurence. *John Locke on Naturalization and Natural Law: Community and Property in the State of Nature*. Cham: Springer International Publishing, 2016.

Inglehart, Ronald F. *Cultural Evolution: People's Motivations Are Changing, and Reshaping the World*. Cambridge: Cambridge University Press, 2018.

International Organization for Migration. *Migration, Environment and Climate Change: Assessing the Evidence*. Geneva, 2009.

International Organization for Migration. *World Migration Report 2020*. New York: UN, 2019.

Iyer, Pico. *This Could Be Home: Raffles Hotel and the City of Tomorrow*. Singapore: Epigram, 2019.

Janmohamed, Shelina. *Generation M: Young Muslims Changing the World*. London & New York: I. B. Tauris, 2016.

Kaiser, Shannon. *The Self-Love Experiment: Fifteen Principles for Becoming More Kind, Compassionate, and Accepting of Yourself*. New York: TarcherPerigee, 2017.

Kant, Immanuel. *Perpetual Peace*. Minneapolis: Classics, 2007.

Keane, John. *Global Civil Society?* Cambridge: Cambridge University Press, 2003.

# BIBLIOGRAPHY

Kerr, William. *The Gift of Global Talent: How Migration Shapes Business, Economy & Society*. Stanford: Stanford University Press, 2018.

Keynes, John Maynard. *The General Theory of Employment, Interest and Money*. London: Palgrave Macmillan, 1936.

Kissinger, Henry. *A World Restored: Metternich, Castlereagh and the Problems of Peace, 1812–22*. Boston: Houghton Mifflin Company, 1957.

Kotkin, Joel. *The Human City: Urbanism for the Rest of Us*. Chicago: Agate B2, 2016.

Kronin, Audrey Kurth. *Power to the People: How Open Technological Innovation Is Arming Tomorrow's Terrorists*. Cambridge: Oxford University Press, 2019.

Kunreuther, Howard, Erwann Michel-Kerjan, and Neil A. Doherty. *At War with the Weather: Managing Large-Scale Risks in a New Era of Catastrophes*. Cambridge: MIT Press, 2011.

Levine, Jonathan. *Zoned Out*. London: Routledge, 2005.

Lieven, Anatol. *Climate Change and the Nation State: The Case for Nationalism in a Warming World*. Oxford: Oxford University Press, 2020.

Lillis, Joanna. *Dark Shadows: Inside the Secret World of Kazakhstan*. London & New York: I. B. Tauris, 2018.

Lovelock, James. *Gaia: A New Look at Life on Earth*. London: Oxford University Press, 1979.

Lubin, David. *Dance of the Trillions: Developing Countries and Global Finance*. Washington DC: Brookings Institute Press, 2018.

Lucas, Robert E. B. *International Handbook on Migration and Economic Development*. Cheltenham: Edward Elgar Pub, 2015.

# BIBLIOGRAPHY

MacIntyre, Alasdair. *After Virtue: A Study in Moral Theory.* Third Edition. Indiana: University of Notre Dame Press, 2007.

Mann, Geoff, and Joel Wainwright. *Climate Leviathan: A Political Theory of Our Planetary Future.* New York: Verso, 2018.

Mazzucato, Mariana. *The Value of Everything: Making and Taking in the Global Economy.* London: Penguin Press, 2018.

McKibben, Bill. *Falter: Has the Human Game Begun to Play Itself Out?* New York: Henry Holt & Company, 2019.

McNeill, John Robert, and Peter Engelke. *The Great Acceleration: An Environmental History of the Anthropocene Since 1945.* Cambridge: Harvard University Press, 2015.

Mehta, Suketu. *This Land Is Our Land: An Immigrant's Manifesto.* New York: Farrar, Straus and Giroux, 2019.

Milanovic, Branko. *Capitalism Alone: The Future of the System That Rules the World.* Cambridge: Harvard University Press, 2019.

Morland, Paul. *Human Tide: How Population Shaped the Modern World.* New York: PublicAffairs, 2019.

Muenkler, Herfried. *Die neuen Deutschen: Ein Land vor seiner Zukunft.* Berlin: Rowohlt Taschenbuch, 2017.

Murphy, Alexander. *Progress in Human Geography.* Thousand Oaks, CA: Sage Publications, 1991.

Norris, Pippa, and Ronald Inglehart. *Cultural Backlash: Trump, Brexit, and Authoritarian Populism.* New York: Cambridge University Press, 2019.

Oreskes, Naomi, and Erik M. Conway. *The Collapse of Western Civilization: A View from the Future.* New York: Columbia University Press, 2014.

# BIBLIOGRAPHY

Ostrom, Elinor. *Governing the Commons: The Evolution of Institutions for Collective Action*. Cambridge: Cambridge University Press, 1990.

O'Sullivan, Michael. *The Levelling: What's Next After Globalization*. New York: PublicAffairs, 2019.

Paul, Anju Mary. *Multinational Maids: Stepwise Migration in a Global Labor Market*. Cambridge: Cambridge University Press, 2017.

Pearlstein, Steven. *Can American Capitalism Survive?: Why Greed Is Not Good, Opportunity Is Not Equal, and Fairness Won't Make Us Poor*. New York: St. Martin's Press, 2018.

Pentland, Alex, Alexander Lipton, and Thomas Hardjono. *Building the New Economy*. Cambridge: MIT Press, 2020.

Philippon, Thomas. *The Great Reversal: How America Gave Up on Free Markets*. Cambridge, Massachusetts: Harvard University Press, 2019.

Rajan, Raghuram. *The Third Pillar: How Markets and the State Leave the Community Behind*. London: Penguin Press, 2019.

Rawls, John. *Political Liberalism*. Columbia: Columbia University Press, 2005.

Rich, Nathaniel. *Losing Earth: A Recent History*. New York: MCD, 2019.

Rossant, John. *Hop, Skip, Go: How the Mobility Revolution Is Transforming Our Lives*. New York: Harper Business, 2019.

Rushkoff, Douglas. *Team Human*. New York: W. W. Norton & Company, 2019.

Sachs, Jeffrey. *The Ages of Globalization: Geography, Technology, and Institutions*. New York: Columbia University Press, 2020.

Samaranayake, Nilanthi, Satu P Limaye, and Joel Wuthnow. *Raging Waters:*

*China, India, Bangladesh, and Brahmaputra River Politics.* Virginia: Marine Corps University Press, 2018.

Scranton, Roy. *Learning to Die in the Anthropocene: Reflections on the End of a Civilization.* San Francisco: City Lights Publishers, 2015.

Scranton, Roy. *We're Dead. Now What?* New York: Soho Press, 2018.

Shah, Sonia. *The Next Great Migration: The Beauty and Terror of Life on the Move.* New York: Bloomsbury Publishing, 2020.

Skidelsky, Robert. *Money and Government: The Past and Future of Economics.* London: Yale University Press, 2018.

Slobodian, Quinn. *Globalists: The End of Empire and the Birth of Neoliberalism.* Cambridge: Harvard University Press, 2018.

Smil, Vaclav. *Growth: From Microorganisms to Megacities.* Cambridge: The MIT Press, 2019.

Smith, Laurence. *Rivers of Power: How a Natural Force Raised Kingdoms, Destroyed Civilizations, and Shapes Our World.* New York: Little, Brown Spark, 2020.

Smith, Laurence. *The World in 2050: Four Forces Shaping Civilization's Northern Future.* London: Penguin, 2010.

Snowden, Frank. *Epidemics and Society: From the Black Death to the Present.* New Haven: Yale University Press, 2019.

Steinem, Gloria. *My Life on the Road.* New York: Random House, 2016.

Stephenson, Neal. *Snow Crash.* London: Penguin, 2011.

Strauss, William, and Neil Howe. *Generations: The History of America's Future, 1584 to 2069.* New York: Quill, 1992.

Strauss, William, and Neil Howe. *The Fourth Turning: What the Cycles of History Tell Us About America's Next Rendezvous with Destiny*. New York: Three Rivers Press, 2009.

Taleb, Nassim Nicholas. *Antifragile: Things That Gain from Disorder*. New York: Random House, 2012.

Taylor, Charles. *The Ethics of Authenticity*. Cambridge: Harvard University Press, 1992.

Taylor, Paul. *Next America: Boomers, Millennials, and the Looming Generational Showdown*. New York: PublicAffairs, 2014.

Toffler, Alvin. *Future Shock*. New York: Bantam Books Inc., 1984.

Tucker, Christopher. *A Planet of 3 Billion*. Virginia: Atlas Observatory Press, 2019.

Tucker, Patrick. *The Naked Future: What Happens in a World That Anticipates Your Every Move*. New York: Current, 2015.

Unnikrishnan, Deepak. *Temporary People*. New York: Restless Books, 2017.

Victor, Peter. *Managing Without Growth: Slower by Design, Not Disaster*. Cheltenham: Edward Elgar Publishing, 2008.

Wagner, Gernot, and Martin L. Weitzman. *Climate Shock: The Economic Consequences of a Hotter Planet*. Princeton: Princeton University Press, 2015.

Wallace-Wells, David. *The Uninhabitable Earth: Life After Warming*. New York: Tim Duggan Books, 2019.

Walsh, Bryan. *End Times: A Brief Guide to the End of the World*. New York: Hachette Books, 2019.

# BIBLIOGRAPHY

Westlake, Stian. *Capitalism Without Capital: The Rise of the Intangible Economy*. Princeton: Princeton University Press, 2018.

Wester, Philippus, Arabinda Mishra, Aditi Mukherji, and Arun Bhakta Shrestha. *The Hindu Kush Himalaya Assessment: Mountains, Climate Change, Sustainability and People*. London: Springer Nature, 2019.

Wilson, E. O. *Half Earth: Our Planet's Fight for Life*. New York: Liveright, 2017.

Wohl, Robert. *The Generation of 1914*. Cambridge: Harvard University Press, 1979.

Wyatt, David. *Out of the Sixties: Storytelling and the Vietnam Generation*. Cambridge: Cambridge University Press, 1993.

Zuckerman, Ethan. *Rewire: Digital Cosmopolitans in the Age of Connection*. New York: W. W. Norton & Company, 2013.

# NOTES

## Chapter 1: Mobility Is Destiny

1   Ducker, Peter. *Managing in Turbulent Times* (New York: Harper & Row, 1980).

2   Marie McAuliffe and Martin Ruhs, *World Migration Report 2018* (Geneva: International Organization for Migration, 2017).

3   Jonathan Woetzel et al., "People on the Move: Global Migration's Impact and Opportunity," McKinsey Global Institute, December 2016.

4   Bill McKibben, "A Very Hot Year," *New York Review of Books*, March 12, 2020.

5   Chi Xu et al., "Future of the Human Climate Niche," *Proceedings of the National Academy of Sciences* 117, no. 21 (2020): 11350–11355.

6   "The Top 10 Categories for Small Businesses to Make Millions in 2020," *Business Insider*, December 16, 2019; "The 10 Best US States for Entrepreneurs to Start Businesses in 2020," *Business Insider*, January 3, 2020.

7   Paul Salopek, "A Twenty-Four-Thousand-Mile Walk Across Human History," *New Yorker*, June 17, 2019.

# NOTES

## Chapter 2: The War for Young Talent

1  "This Is the Impact of the 2008 Crisis You Might Not Have Expected," World Economic Forum, November 15, 2018.

2  Jeanna Smialek and Zolan Kanno-Youngs, "Why a Top Trump Aide Said 'We Are Desperate' for More Immigrants," *New York Times*, February 27, 2020.

3  Neil Irwin and Emily Badger, "Trump Says the U.S. Is 'Full.' Much of the Nation Has the Opposite Problem," *New York Times*, April 9, 2019.

4  Eduardo Porter, "The Danger from Low-Skilled Immigrants: Not Having Them," *New York Times*, August 8, 2017.

5  Lazaro Zamora and Theresa Cardinal Brown, "EB-5 Program: Successes, Challenges, and Opportunities for States and Localities," Bipartisan Policy Center, September 2015.

6  Mohsin Hamid, "In the 21st Century, We Are All Migrants," *National Geographic*, August 2019, p. 20.

7  Matthew Smith, "International Survey: Globalisation Is Still Seen as a Force for Good in the World," YouGov, November 17, 2016.

8  Yasmeen Serhan, "Are Italy's 'Sardines' the Antidote to Populism?," *Atlantic*, January 24, 2020.

9  David Hasemyer, "U.S. Military Precariously Unprepared for Climate Threats, War College & Retired Brass Warn," *InsideClimate News*, December 23, 2019.

# NOTES

## Chapter 3: Generation Move

1   Karl Mannheim, "The Sociological Problem of Generations," in *Essays on the Sociology of Knowledge* (Oxford University Press, 1952 [1929]).

2   Kim Parker et al., "Generation Z Looks a Lot Like Millennials on Key Social and Political Issues," Pew Research Center, January 17, 2019.

3   Christopher Kurz et al., "Are Millennials Different?," Finance and Economics Discussion Series (Washington, DC: Board of Governors of the Federal Reserve System, November 2018); Derek Thompson, "The Economy Killed Millennials, Not Vice Versa," *Atlantic*, December 6, 2018.

4   "The Deloitte Millennial Survey 2017," Deloitte, 2017.

5   Malcolm Harris, "Keynes Was Wrong. Gen Z Will Have It Worse," *MIT Technology Review*, December 16, 2019.

6   Kim Hong-Ji and Hayoung Choi Ju-min Park, "No Money, No Hope: S. Korea's 'Dirty Spoons' Turn Against Moon," The Wider Image, *Reuters*, November 30, 2019.

7   Jeanna Smialek, "How Millennials Can Make the Fed's Job Harder," *New York Times*, February 17, 2020.

8   The number of schools offering IB programs jumped by 40 percent between 2012 and 2017, and more than 10 percent since. One-third of IB schools are in the US, nearly 30 percent in Europe, and 20 percent in Asia, where the IB uptake is expanding at double the global rate.

# NOTES

9   Iyer, Pico. *This Could Be Home: Raffles Hotel and the City of Tomorrow*
    (Singapore: Epigram, 2019), 34.

10  Lisa O'Carroll, "Number of UK Citizens Emigrating to EU Has Risen
    by 30% since Brexit Vote," *Guardian*, August 4, 2020.

11  Suketu Mehta. *This Land Is Our Land: An Immigrant's Manifesto* (New
    York: Macmillan, 2019).

12  Allison Schrager, "The Looming $78 Trillion Pension Crisis," *Quartz*,
    February 27, 2019.

13  Len Kiefer et al., "Why Is Adulting Getting Harder? Young Adults and
    Household Formation," Freddie Mac, March 16, 2018.

14  One survey by a leading consultancy revealed that the top priorities
    for high-net-worth individuals under the age of forty seeking private
    wealth services were real estate, tax, and inheritance advisory. CapGem-
    ini, *World Wealth Report 2020*.

15  Jun Suzuki, "Asia's Millennials Finding Their Political Voice," *Nikkei
    Asian Review*, March 27, 2019.

16  Laurie S. Goodman and Christopher Mayer, "Home Ownership and
    the American Dream," *Journal of Economic Perspectives* 32, no. 1 (2018):
    31–58.

17  Hillary Hoffower, "The 25 Most Expensive Cities Around the
    World to Rent a Two-Bedroom Apartment," *Business Insider Singa-
    pore*, January 14, 2020.

18  "Younger Americans Much More Likely to Have Been Arrested Than

Previous Generations; Increase Is Largest Among Whites and Women,"
RAND Corporation, February 25, 2019.

19  Ben Schott, "Which Nations Are Democracies? Some Citizens Might
Disagree," *Bloomberg*, June 26, 2020.

20  Pico Iyer, "Where is Home?" TED Talk. 17 July 2013.

21  Brandon Busteed, "Americans Rank a Google Internship over a Harvard Degree," *Forbes*, January 6, 2020.

## Chapter 4: The Next American Dream

1  U.S. Census Bureau, "Housing Inventory Estimate: Vacant Housing Units for
the United States," FRED, Federal Reserve Bank of St. Louis, July 28, 2020.

2  William H. Frey, "For the First Time on Record, Fewer Than 10% of
Americans Moved in a Year," Brookings Institution, November 22,
2019; James Manyika et al., "The Social Contract in the 21st Century:
Outcomes So Far for Workers, Consumers, and Savers in Advanced
Economies," McKinsey Global Institute, February 2020.

3  Raj Chetty et al., "Where Is the Land of Opportunity? The Geography
of Intergenerational Mobility in the United States," *Quarterly Journal of
Economics* 129, no. 4 (November 2014): 1553–1623.

4  Kyle Nossaman, "A Year in a Skoolie: What We Love (and What We
Don't)," *Gear Junkie*, January 23, 2019.

5  Rilwan Balogun, "RV Sales Jump 170% During Coronavirus Pandemic, Says Association," WAFB Channel 9, May 25, 2020.

# NOTES

6   Sarah Baird, "Mobile Homeland," *Curbed*, September 13, 2017.

7   Of the 32 percent of millennials that own homes, two-thirds have regrets because of the additional costs such as insurance, property taxes, variable mortgages, and maintenance. Megan Leonhardt, "63% of Millennials Who Bought Homes Have Regrets," CNBC, March 1, 2019.

8   Helen Edwards and Dave Edwards, "It's Becoming Economically Desirable to Live in a Trailer Park," *Quartz*, January 16, 2018.

9   Caleb Robinson et al., "Modeling Migration Patterns in the USA Under Sea Level Rise," *PLoS ONE* 15, no. 1 (January 2020).

10  Christopher Flavelle, "U.S. Flood Strategy Shifts to 'Unavoidable' Relocation of Entire Neighborhoods," *New York Times*, August 26, 2020.

11  James S. Clark, C. Lane Scher, and Margaret Swift, "The Emergent Interactions That Govern Biodiversity Change," *Proceedings of the National Academy of Sciences* 117, no. 29 (2020): 17074–17083.

12  Nancy Gupton, "Boulder, Colorado: The Happiest City in the United States," *National Geographic*, October 27, 2017.

13  Kendra Pierre-Louis, "Want to Escape Global Warming? These Cities Promise Cool Relief," *New York Times*, April 15, 2019.

14  Mary Caperton Morton, "With Nowhere to Hide from Rising Seas, Boston Prepares for a Wetter Future," *Science News*, August 6, 2019.

15  Steven Luebke, "How to Help Employees Buy Homes—and Help Your Company's Bottom Line," *Milwaukee Business Journal*, March 28, 2017.

16  Auren Hoffman, "What Would Happen If All Job Offers Had to Be Quoted Post-Tax and in PPP-Adjusted Dollars? (Thought Experiment on Compensation)," Summation by Auren Hoffman (summation.net), March 27, 2019.

17  William H. Frey, "How Migration of Millennials and Seniors Has Shifted Since the Great Recession," The Brookings Institution, January 31, 2019.

18  "Why 18-Hour Cities Are Attracting Commercial Real Estate Interest," JLL, February 5, 2019.

19  Robert D. Atkinson et al., "The Case for Growth Centers: How to Spread Tech Innovation Across America," The Brookings Institution, December 9, 2019.

20  Mohamed Younis, "Americans Want More, Not Less, Immigration for First Time," Gallup, July 1, 2020.

21  Alex Nowrasteh and Andrew C. Forrester, "Immigrants Recognize American Greatness: Immigrants and Their Descendants Are Patriotic and Trust America's Governing Institutions," Cato Institute, February 4, 2019.

22  Anjali Enjeti, "Ghosts of White People Past: Witnessing White Flight from an Asian Ethnoburb," *Pacific Standard*, June 14, 2017.

## Chapter 5: The European Commonwealth

1  Paul Hockenos, "Europe's Future Looks Bleak If It Can't Make the Case for Itself," CNN, March 4, 2019; Bruce Stokes, "Who Are Europe's Millennials?," Pew Research Center, February 9, 2015.

2   Richard Wike et al., "European Public Opinion Three Decades After the Fall of Communism," Pew Research Center, October 14, 2019.

3   "Romania, Hungary Recruit in Asia to Fill Labour Shortage," *Channel News Asia*, October 28, 2019.

4   Dany Mitzman, "The Sikhs Who Saved Parmesan," *BBC News*, June 25, 2015.

5   Andrew Nash, "National Population Projections," Office for National Statistics, October 21, 2019.

## Chapter 6: Bridging Regions

1   Bruce Bower, "The Oldest Genetic Link Between Asians and Native Americans Was Found in Siberia," *Science News*, May 20, 2020.

## Chapter 7: Northism

1   Mary Beth Sheridan, "The Little-Noticed Surge Across the U.S.-Mexico Border: It's Americans, Heading South," *Washington Post*, May 19, 2019.

2   Abrahm Lustgarten, "The Great Climate Migration," *New York Times Magazine*, July 23, 2020.

3   Rahul Mehrotra, "The Architectural Wonder of Impermanent Cities," TED Talk, July 22, 2019.

# NOTES

## Chapter 8: Will "The South" Survive?

1  Sunil John et al., "Arab Youth Survey 2017," ASDA'A Burson-Marsteller, 2017; "Unemployment with Advanced Education (% of Total Labor Force with Advanced Education)," The World Bank, 2019.

2  "Young Adults Around the World Are Less Religious by Several Measures," in *The Age Gap in Religion Around the World*, Pew Research Center, June 13, 2018.

3  Kristofer Hamel and Constanza Di Nucci, "More Than 100 Million Young Adults Are Still Living in Extreme Poverty," The Brookings Institution, October 17, 2019.

4  Nicole Flatow, "The Social Responsibility of Wakanda's Golden City," *Bloomberg CityLab*, November 5, 2018.

5  "'Climate Apartheid' Between Rich and Poor Looms," *BBC News*, June 25, 2019.

6  Steve Pyne, "The Australian Fires Are a Harbinger of Things to Come. Don't Ignore Their Warning," *Guardian*, January 7, 2020.

## Chapter 9: The Asians Are Coming

1  Danny Bahar, Prithwiraj Choudhury, and Britta Glennon, "The Day That America Lost $100 Billion Because of an Immigration Visa Ban," Brookings Institution, October 20, 2020.

2  Michael Clemens, "Does Development Reduce Migration?," in *Inter-*

national *Handbook on Migration and Economic Development* (Cheltenham, UK: Edward Elgar Publishing, 2014).

3   Stefan Trines, "Mobile Nurses: Trends in International Labor Migration in the Nursing Field," *World Education News and Reviews*, March 6, 2018.

4   Kully Kaur-Ballagan, "Attitudes to Race and Inequality in Great Britain," Ipsos MORI, June 15, 2020.

## Chapter 10: Retreat and Renewal in Pacific Asia

1   Amarnath Tewary, "Bihar's Economy Registers Higher Growth Than Indian Economy in Last Three Years," *Hindu*, February 24, 2020.

2   Junya Hisanaga, "Muslims Struggle to Bury Their Dead in Japan, a Nation of Cremation," *Nikkei Asia*, November 29, 2020.

## Chapter 11: Quantum People

1   Teleport was sold to London-based MOVE. Guides, part of the Topia network of companies facilitating relocation for professionals.

2   "IMD World Competitiveness Ranking 2020," IMD World Competitiveness Centre, 2020; "The New Economy Drivers and Disruptors Report," Bloomberg, 2019.

3   "2020 Emerging Jobs Report Singapore," LinkedIn, 2020.

4   Ricardo Hausmann, "Economic Development and the Accumulation of Know-how," *World Economic Review* 24 (Spring 2016); Richard

Baldwin, *The Globotics Upheaval* (London: Oxford University Press, 2019).

5   Christian Joppke, "The Rise of Instrumental Citizenship," *Global Citizenship Review* (Fourth Quarter, 2018).

6   Kate Springer, "Passports for Purchase: How the Elite Get Through a Pandemic," CNN, August 7, 2020.

## Chapter 12: *Pax Urbanica*

1   See Jason Hickel, "Is It Possible to Achieve a Good Life for All Within Planetary Boundaries?" *Third World Quarterly*, 2018; "The Sustainable Development Index: Measuring the Ecological Efficiency of Human Development in the Anthropocene," *Ecological Economics* 167 (2020).

2   Lee Kuan Yew, "The East Asian Way—With Air Conditioning," *New Perspectives Quarterly* 26 (October 2009).

3   "The Best Countries to Raise a Family in 2020," Asher & Lyric, July 24, 2020.

4   Melanie Curtin, "Thousands of Millennials Are Opting Out of Renting Their Own Apartments and Going for This Instead," *Inc.*, September 28, 2017.

## Chapter 13: Civilization 3.0

1   Arnold J. Toynbee, quoted in *Reader's Digest*, October 1958.

2   Suketu Mehta, *This Land Is Our Land*.

# NOTES

3    David Graeber, *The Utopia of Rules* (London: Penguin Random House, 2015).

4    Mohsin Hamid, "In the 21st Century, We Are All Migrants," *National Geographic* (September 2019).

5    Innes M. Keighren, "Geosophy, Imagination, and Terrae Incognitae: Exploring the Intellectual History of John Kirtland Wright," *Journal of Historical Geography* 31, no. 3 (July 2005): 546–562.

# ILLUSTRATION CREDITS

# ILLUSTRATION CREDITS

# INDEX

race and racism (*cont.*)
    interracial marriage, 81,
        109–110, 201
    youth-government tension, 78
Raford, Noah, 227
RAND Corporation, 56
Ravenstein, Ernst Georg, 7
Rawls, John, 273
reforesting programs, 114, 145, 151,
    157, 271
refugees, climate vs. political, 20,
    141
Regional Fortress scenario, 25–28,
    *26*
religion. *See also* Islam
    communing events as spiritual-
        ity, 85–87
    migration and religious iden-
        tity, 54–55, 60–61
    population of Christians and
        Muslims, worldwide, 60
    population of Jews in US and
        Israel, 202n
*The Republic* (Plato), 261
Revolution, 105
*The Rights of Man* (Paine), 70
Roma, 135
Romania, 46, 119
Romer, Paul, 260
Royal Institute of Chartered Sur-
    veyors, 88
Russell, Bertrand, 55–56
Russia
    civilizational state concept, 53

forces shaping mobility, 3
former Soviet republics and,
    143–146, 152–158
Little Ice Age in, 162
Mongolia's proximity to,
    151–152
nationalism and conscription
    in, 57
need for immigrant labor by,
    146–151
Northism scenario and, 165,
    277
youth-government tension,
    75–76
RV Industry Association, 93

Salopek, Paul, 24
Salvini, Matteo, 45, 51
Sami people, 166
SAP, 131
Sarkissian, Armen, 145–146
Saudi Arabia, 45, 177, 178, 250–251,
    255
Sawiris, Naguib, 124
Scandinavia. *See individual countries*
Scotland, 138–139
Scranton, Roy, 18
Shafak, Elif, 80
Siberia, climate change in, 147–151
Sidewalk Labs, 260
Sierra Energy, 247
Singapore, 40, 81, 208–209, 225,
    248, 251–254

# INDEX

# INDEX

**Which lines on the map matter most?**

It's time to reimagine how life is organized on Earth. In *Connectography*, Parag Khanna guides us through the emerging global network civilization in which mega-cities compete over connectivity and borders are increasingly irrelevant. Travelling across the world, Khanna shows how twenty-first-century conflict is a tug-of-war over pipelines and Internet cables, advanced technologies and market access.

Yet *Connectography* also offers a hopeful vision of the future – beneath the chaos of a world that appears to be falling apart, a new foundation of connectivity is pulling it together.

'For those who fear that the world is becoming too inward-looking, *Connectography* is a refreshing, optimistic vision'
*The Economist*

'Incredible . . . With the world rapidly changing and urbanizing, [Khanna's] proposals might be the best way to confront a radically different future'
*Washington Post*

'Parag Khanna has vision'
NASSIM NICHOLAS TALEB

**CONNECTOGRAPHY**
Mapping the Global
Network Revolution

PARAG KHANNA